ECOCINEMA THEORY AND PRACTICE 2

This second volume builds on the initial groundwork laid by *Ecocinema Theory and Practice* by examining the ways in which ecocritical cinema studies have matured and proliferated over the last decade, opening whole new areas of study and research.

Featuring fourteen new essays organized into three sections around the themes of cinematic materialities, discourses, and communities, the volume explores a variety of topics within ecocinema studies from examining specific national and indigenous film contexts to discussing ecojustice, environmental production studies, film festivals, and political ecology. The breadth of the contributions exemplifies how ecocinema scholars worldwide have sought to overcome the historical legacy of binary thinking and intellectual norms and are working to champion new ecocritical, intersectional, decolonial, queer, feminist, Indigenous, vitalist, and other emergent theories and cinematic practices. The collection also demonstrates the unique ways that cinema studies scholarship is actively addressing environmental injustice and the climate crisis.

This book is an invaluable resource for students and scholars of ecocritical film and media studies, production studies, cultural studies, and environmental studies.

Stephen Rust is a Senior Instructor of English at the University of Oregon. He is co-editor of *Ecocinema Theory and Practice* (2013) and *Ecomedia: Key Issues* (2016) and an advisory board member of *Media+Environment* and the *Journal of Environmental Media*. He has published several articles in the field and is currently writing an ecocritical analysis of Merchant Ivory Productions.

Salma Monani is a Professor at Gettysburg College's Environmental Studies department. She has extensively published on explorations of Indigenous eco-media, film, and environmental justice, and is the co-editor of three ecocritical media anthologies. She is currently writing a monograph on *Indigenous Ecocinema*. As part of her college's Land Acknowledgment Committee, her scholarship also engages the practice of digital, public eco-humanities along with community research with Indigenous partners.

Seán Cubitt is a Professor of Screen Studies at the University of Melbourne. His publications include *The Cinema Effect* (2004), *Finite Media: Environmental Implications of Digital Technologies* (2016), and *Anecdotal Evidence: Ecocritique from Hollywood to the Mass Image* (2020). Co-editor of *Ecomedia: Key Issues* (2016), and series editor for Leonardo Books, he researches the history and philosophy of media, ecopolitical aesthetics, media arts and technologies, and media art history.

ECOCINEMA THEORY AND PRACTICE 2

Edited by
Stephen Rust, Salma Monani, and Seán Cubitt

Routledge
Taylor & Francis Group

NEW YORK AND LONDON

Designed cover image: Photo Courtesy of Gregg Mitman

First published 2023
by Routledge
605 Third Avenue, New York, NY 10158

and by Routledge
4 Park Square, Milton Park, Abingdon, Oxon, OX14 4RN

Routledge is an imprint of the Taylor & Francis Group, an informa business

ISBN: 978-1-032-15985-0 (hbk)
ISBN: 978-1-032-15413-8 (pbk)
ISBN: 978-1-003-24660-2 (ebk)

DOI: 10.4324/9781003246602

Typeset in Bembo
by codeMantra

Stephen: For Professor Jon Lewis, who has been instrumental in my career

Salma: For the old guard and the new, whose conversations animate my continued love for cinema as *eco*cinema

Seán: In memoriam Geoff Lealand and for all our students

CONTENTS

FIGURES

CONTRIBUTORS

Mariam Abazeri is a PhD candidate at the University of Miami's Abess Center for Interdisciplinary Ecosystem Science and Policy (United States), a visual artist and former SVA Lemelson Fellow. Her current research focuses on how participatory visual methods organize and facilitate adaptive strategies to social and climatic changes in Iran.

Seán Cubitt is a Professor of Screen Studies at the University of Melbourne (Australia). Co-editor of *Ecomedia: Key Issues* and series editor for Leonardo Books at MIT Press, his recent publications include *Finite Media: Environmental Implications of Digital Technology* and *Anecdotal Evidence: Ecocritique from Hollywood to the Mass Image*.

Jennifer Fay is the Gertrude Conaway Vanderbilt Chair of Cinema & Media Arts at Vanderbilt University (United States). Her recent publications include *Inhospitable World: Cinema in the Time of the Anthropocene* and the essay "Do I Know the Anthropocene When I See It?" in *Representations*.

Carolyn Fornoff is an Assistant Professor of Latin American Culture at Cornell University (United States). She examines extractivism and environmental crisis in contemporary Mexican and Central American media. She is co-editor of *Timescales: Thinking Across Ecological Temporalities* and *Pushing Past the Human in Latin American Cinema*.

Elio Garcia is an Assistant Professor of Literature and Film at Xavier University-Ateneo de Cagayan (Philippines) where he serves as Deputy Director of Kinaadman: University Research Office and Associate Editor of *Kinaadman: A*

Journal of the Southern Philippines. His works center postcolonial theory, ecocriticism, Indigeneity, and Global South cinema.

Andrew Hageman is the Director of the Center for Ethics and Public Engagement and an Associate Professor of English at Luther College (United States), working at the intersections of technology, ecology, and anti-racism. His publications range from Lynchain cinema/ecohorror to transnational literature, blockchain, speculative fiction, and Stephen King's fiction.

Cajetan Iheka is a Professor of English at Yale University (United States). He has authored *Naturalizing Africa: Ecological Violence, Agency, and Postcolonial Resistance in African Literature* and *African Ecomedia: Network Forms, Planetary Politics.* He is the editor of *Teaching Postcolonial Environmental Literature and Media.*

Manel Jiménez-Morales is the Vice-Rector for Educational Transformation, Culture, and Communication and a Lecturer in Communication at Pompeu Fabra University (Spain). Jiménez-Morales has been a Visiting Professor at the University of Oxford, UCLA, and the British Film Institute, among others. He researches narrative and audiovisual aesthetics and new educational and cultural formats.

Aarón Lacayo is an Assistant Professor in the Spanish Department at Gettysburg College (United States). Published in *Comparative Literature Studies* and *Teaching Central American Literature in a Global Context,* his current project focuses on intersections of ecology, politics, and violence in postwar Central American cinema. He has translated two fiction books.

Angelica Lawson (Northern Arapaho) is an Assistant Professor of Cinema and Ethnic Studies, specializing in Indigenous Studies at the University of Colorado-Boulder (United States). Lawson's publications include contributions to *Ecocriticism and Indigenous Studies: Conversations from Earth to Cosmos* and a *Studies in American Indian Literatures* special issue on Indigenous digital media.

Anthony Lioi is a Professor of English at the Juilliard School (United States) and teaches composition, American literature and culture, and environmental humanities. He is the author of *Nerd Ecology*, a past president of ASLE, and an editor of *Resilience: A Journal of the Environmental Humanities.*

Marta Lopera-Mármol is a PhD candidate in Communication at Pompeu Fabra University (Spain) and Visiting Scholar at the University of Cambridge at King's College with an MRes in Social Communication and publications in several top-tier journals and publishers. Her lines of research are mental disorders, television series, and media sustainability.

Salma Monani is a Professor of Environmental Studies at Gettysburg College (United States). She is writing *Indigenous Ecocinema: Decolonizing Media Landscapes* and is co-editor of three ecocritical media anthologies, including *Ecocinema Theory and Practice*. She has published extensively on Indigenous cinema and ecomedia.

Debashree Mukherjee is an Associate Professor in the Department of Middle Eastern, South Asian, and African Studies at Columbia University (United States) who researches media histories of indentured plantation labor and South-South oceanic migrations. She authored *Bombay Hustle: Making Movies in a Colonial City* and edits *BioScope: South Asian Screen Studies.*

Christian Quendler is a Professor of American Literature, Film, and Media, and Chair of the American Studies Department at the University of Innsbruck (Austria). He is the author of *The Camera-Eye Metaphor in Cinema* and the principal investigator of "Delocating Mountains: Cinematic Landscapes of the Alpine Model" (Austrian Science Fund).

Emily Roehl is an Assistant Professor of English and Journalism at Augustana University (United States) and the co-founder of Mystery Spot Books. Her work has appeared in *Environmental History, Southern Cultures,* and *Jump Cut.* She has also produced a series of events on energy justice, place-based research-creation, and lower-carbon research methods.

Stephen Rust is a Senior Instructor of English at the University of Oregon (United States). He is co-editor of *Ecomedia: Key Issues* and *The Routledge Handbook of Ecomedia Studies,* an advisory board member of the journals *Media+Environment* and *Journal of Environmental Media,* and author of several articles on cinema and the environment.

Regina Kanyu Wang is a PhD candidate at the University of Oslo (Norway). Also a writer and researcher with a fellowship at Arizona State University (United States), she is co-editor of *Vector, The Way Spring Arrives and Other Stories,* and *The Making of The Wandering Earth: A Film Production Handbook.*

Mila Zuo is an Assistant Professor of Cinema and Media Studies at the University of British Columbia (Canada). She is the author of *Vulgar Beauty: Acting Chinese in the Global Sensorium.* Her creative works include *Carnal Orient* (2016), *Détourning Asia/America with Valerie Soe* (2019), and *Kin* (2021).

ACKNOWLEDGMENTS

The editors wish to thank our contributors for their time and dedication to this collection, especially given the conditions we have been working under. Soon after we began work on this collection in early 2020, COVID-19 and its consequences (including lockdowns, disruptions to teaching and research, and widespread illness and death) began to take their history-changing toll across the world. Despite this unexpected and unprecedented challenge, our contributors somehow managed to meet their deadlines, peer review each other's chapters, and exceed our expectations for this collection. We are grateful beyond words for their efforts and those of our families, students, and, of course, all the frontline care providers and essential workers who made it possible for us to complete the project in a timely manner.

We extend hearty thanks and cheers to a great many colleagues and friends at the institutions where we teach and the organizations where we work for their support and encouragement. We haven't necessarily been able to meet in person at conferences like the Society for Cinema and Media Studies and the Associate for the Study of Literature and Environment, but these are the spaces that have continued to support our research and our efforts to grow the field of ecomedia studies since the mid-2000s.

We are also grateful for the work of our assistant editor Matthew Bicakci, who helped us format the manuscript during the final stages of the project and provided sharp-eyed copy editing. And, to our Routledge editor, Emma Sherriff, who has kept us in line and on time.

Thanks to the generous support provided by a University of Oregon Libraries Open Access Publishing Award and the School of Culture and Communications at the University of Melbourne, we are pleased to publish this volume simultaneously in print and open access formats so that cost will never be a barrier for anyone interested in ecocinema studies.

INTRODUCTION

Cut to Green: Tracking the Growth of Ecocinema Studies

Stephen Rust, Salma Monani and Seán Cubitt

It has become increasingly clear, in the decade since our first volume of *Eco-cinema Theory and Practice* appeared in late 2012, that film can no longer be considered apart from its imbrication in the fabric of the world. Until the close of the twentieth century, it may have been possible to ignore the material connection of celluloid reels with the oil industry, or the fact that drive-in movies depended on paving large tracts of ground. Even then, however, it was difficult to miss the insistent ecological themes that filmmakers returned to over and over in their onscreen messaging. We follow Hegel's old edict about Minerva's owl that only flies at dusk ([1820] 1991) when our hindsight helps us understand how the ruin of "first nature" becomes really apparent only when cinema, along with much of our culture, economy, and politics, moved into the "second nature" of virtual data. The majority of ecocritical cinema and media studies conducted so far has come in this century when, arguably, cinema and other media seemed to have finally severed the indexical umbilical that attached it to the physical world and become digital information. While Rachel Carson's book *Silent Spring,* published in 1962, gives a respectable start date for the modern environmental movement, cinema studies has taken a considerable amount of time to catch up.

Ironically, in the 1970s cinema was considered the privileged site where technology and human subjectivity produced one another; yet, as products of "culture," neither were necessarily associated with "nature." It wasn't until this new generation of ecocritical scholars – who insisted that the cinematic apparatus, far from being divorced from nature, is in fact profoundly ecological – that ecocinema studies took root. Cinema has become unthinkable apart from its dependence on mining, electricity generation, and fabrication with their attendant pollution, on global logistical operations and supply chains with

DOI: 10.4324/9781003246602-1

massive ecological footprints, on material and technical infrastructures with direct consequences in the physical world, and on the problem of waste. For film scholars and filmmakers, the scale of this collective realization produces a specific challenge for ecological thought. Ontologically, it is clear that like human beings, media technologies and screenings are only thinkable as permeable congregations of materials and energies suffused by flows and affects coursing through the wider world as cells and neurons, chips, and datastreams. But historically, since the 1970s (at least), it has become equally clear that the three orders – ecologies, technologies, and societies – are profoundly alienated from one another.

A shadow of this problem is dimly, though rarely systematically, reflected in the way we understand the words "environment" and "ecology" as terms that construct our worlds and our storyworlds. Ecology is usually defined as referring to a system or fluid field of interactions involving everything, at every scale, connected to Planet Earth – animate and inanimate, from oxygen to the machinations of the United Nations – so that we cannot think of a phenomenon like the Los Angeles freeway system apart from its interwoven human, technical, and natural components. An environment, on the other hand, materially environs: it is constructed in a historical moment – endlessly repeated – of exclusion. Like "nature," the word "environment" appears as the negative of a positive term. Here is our vaunted civilization, over there is nature. Here is social and technical order, over there is what environs us – the merely physical and less-than-human noise to be excluded from the rationality of technological signals. Alas, history tells us that equating nature with less-than-human also reduced women, enslaved and colonized peoples, brutalized animals, and despoiled environments all to the same level of raw materials to be exploited.

Drawing this distinction between an ontology of ecological flows and a history of environmental alienation cannot provide a technical vocabulary for ecocriticism; instead, we draw on it to make explicit the consequent ethical and political relevance of ecocinema studies. From the ecological ontology of mutual implication in planetary flows, we take the utopian path. As Jennifer Fay writes, the love of film and the love of nature, cinephilia, and ecophilia are

> forms of love that intensify when celluloid and certain ecosystems draw near their moment of disappearance. The latter expresses a love of dwelling in the world, the former a desire to dwell in the image. Or, taken together, they express a singular love of dwelling in the world *through* the image.
>
> *(2018, 163)*

In this utopian current, film as medium and cinema as a mode of experience are mediations that suture us back into a world that otherwise slips away. On the other side of love stands the pedagogical and political compulsion to point out that the worst environmental damage has already happened or is about to happen, and cinema's obligation is to horrify its audiences, to force them to change or to help them envision some form of survival. Just as it is hard to discern our contributors making hard and fast distinctions between ecology and environment, it is impossible to unpick their commitments to radical change and to the celebration of wholeness. This ambivalence is not a failing: it is integral to the practice of ecocinema studies in the present moment.

A Montage: The Collective Work of Ecocinema Studies

Ten years ago, *Ecocinema Theory and Practice* was published as part of the American Film Institute Readers Series by Routledge to introduce a then-nascent field. In the subsequent decade, ecocritical cinema studies have matured and proliferated, most of all in relation to new kinds of attention applied to new areas of practice. *Ecocinema Theory and Practice 2* speaks first and foremost of, to, and from practice. By collaborating in collective practices that embrace not only humans but also non-human partners in cultural making, a new aesthetic comes into view. It is still vital to maintain fierce criticism of the performative power of old, bad theories and practices. But it is equally essential to make possible new practices and ideas, the collective endeavor we undertake in this collection. By engaging in and thinking through such emergent modes of practice as those exemplified by our contributors, ecocinema scholars worldwide have sought to overcome the historical legacy of binary thinking and intellectual norms criticized by new ecocritical, intersectional, decolonial, queer, feminist, Indigenous, vitalist, and other developing theoretical, cinematic, and social practices. A significant goal of the collection is to demonstrate the unique ways that cinema studies scholarship can address environmental injustices and global environmental change. Organized around the themes of cinematic materialities, discourses, and communities, the essays in *Ecocinema Theory and Practice 2* have benefitted from peer reviewing between authors and feedback from multiple editors, encouraging a stronger sense of "the book" as a collaborative process appropriate to our field of study.

Since the publication of *Ecocinema Theory and Practice* and our related collection *Ecomedia: Key Issues* (Rust, Monani, and Cubitt 2016), a tide of new journals (among them *Environment and Planning: E: Nature and Space*, *Media+Environment*, and the *Journal of Environmental Media*, launched in 2018, 2019, and 2020 respectively), books, articles, and conferences confirm the growing impact of environmental discourse across the field of cinema and media studies. Things are moving so quickly that whole new fields and subfields of inquiry have opened up. Richard Maxwell and Toby Miller's *Greening the Media* (2012) kickstarted ecological studies of media infrastructure (also

Maxwell et al., 2015; Cubitt 2017), and Nadia Bozak's *The Cinematic Footprint* (2012) introduced ecocritical production studies, while Alexa Weik von Mossner (2014), Adrian Ivakhiv (2013), Nicole Seymour (2013), E. Ann Kaplan (2016), and Sylvia Bissonnette (2019) turned our attention to affect studies. Pietari Kääpä (2013), Pat Brereton (2016), Weik von Mossner (2017), and others inspired audience research and empirical ecocriticism. Robin Murray and Joseph Heumann (2014, 2016, 2017), Stephen Rust and Carter Soles (2014), Bridgette Barclay and Christy Tidwell (2018), Tidwell and Soles (2021), Jennifer Fay (2018), Helen Hughes (2014), Anil Narine (2015), and many others worked to expand genre studies. Kääpä and Tommy Gustaffson (2013), Anat Pick and Guinevere Narraway (2013), Jussi Parikka (2015), Scott MacKenzie and Westerståhl Stenport (2015), Nicholas Mirzoeff (2014, 2015, 2016), Ellen Moore (2017), Debashree Mukherjee (2020), Elena Past (2019), Gabriella Blasi (2019), Nikola Lübecker and Daniele Rugo (2017), Hunter Vaughan (2019), Ivakhiv (2018), Seán Cubitt (2020), Cassandra Guan and Adam O'Brien (2020), O'Brien (2016, 2017), Catherine Elwes (2022), and many more have significantly extended the historical and theoretical reach of ecocritical film and media studies. Melody Jue (2020), John Durham Peters (2015), Janine Randerson (2018), and Nicole Starosielski (2015) have explored elemental media, while Kristi McKim (2013) and others (for example, Cahill, Jacobson, and Bao 2022) have considered cinematic representations of weather and climate. Anna Tsing et al. (2017), Laura McMahon (2019), and Belinda Smaill (2016) have opened new dimensions of interspecies communication studies for students of film and media, and Sheldon Lu (Lu and Mi 2009; Lu and Gong 2020), Cajetan Iheka (2021), Salma Monani and Joni Adamson (2018), Sean Rhoads (2018), Chia-ju Chang (2019), and Rayson Alex and Susan Deborah (2016) have challenged the Eurocentrism of early ecocinema studies. What was a new field in 2012 has become a bustling global crossroads for a radical rethinking of media and ecology engaged not only with intersectional questions of race, class, disability, gender, and sexual identities but also with the new configurations of social justice and the information economy.

The emergent cinema of the twenty-first century is embedded in economic, social, technological, and ecological supply chains of materials and services. In 2010, when we embarked on our first volume, the most urgent task seemed to be to create a theoretical and aesthetic vocabulary for addressing films with explicit ecological themes. Today, ecocinema studies has followed the lead of feminist film scholars who have illuminated not only films by, for, and about women but also bring a feminist lens to every aspect of cinema. The ambition of this collection is as wide. To set about this task is, however daunting in its ambition, not least because ecological thinking demands connecting the objects of our studies – films and the practices surrounding them – with so many other factors.

Aspirations of Ecocinema Studies: Everything Everywhere

We present here a book full of critical writing about audiovisual media. Writing, it has been said, is always after the event – critical writing follows after the event of thinking. Not necessarily so with film which, from the spectator's point of view, unfolds in the Now of viewing. But even the unfolding present bifurcates and multiplies. Lyotard (1994) distinguishes between the happening of an event and the something that happens. Take, for example, a shot of a leaf falling from a tree. Every leaf that falls, falls uniquely. Many millions of leaves fall every autumn, but each leaf falls in its own way. When we write "a leaf," each of us imagines a different leaf falling differently, but the word "leaf" remains generic: any leaf, not the discrete, irreplaceable, one-off leaf that cinema is condemned to capture.

The shot of an individual falling leaf is firstly motion itself, then it is the motion of the leaf, but almost inevitably, as the shot ends and is replaced by another, it arrives at significance. Perhaps the shot leads us to imagine the leaf shouting out "Freedom!" as it parts from the branch, or we get the feeling that "Autumn is sad" and perhaps elaborate on that emotional response with a verbal one like "Falling leaves are the way deciduous trees cry," before we then reflect with the thought that evergreens can't really cry, even though we know, metacognitively, that cypress trees, for example, have long emblematized mourning since the ancient Greeks. These more or less critical thoughts are always subsequent to the shot as event in the Now, the shot as pure motion, which itself precedes our perception that this is the motion *of* a leaf, and our understanding that its motion is one of falling. In other words, placing this shot of a leaf falling among other thoughts and shots that precede and follow it can place the individual falling leaf into something akin to discourse but only because we have become savvy about the way films are constructed aesthetically and historically. To write critically about cinema is always to reprise our experience of this initial sequence of sensations, affects, and thoughts that we percolate nearly simultaneously (as rapidly as human senses and brains are capable), and to retrace them, albeit more slowly. If watching a film is (nearly) *immediate*, writing about it is to meditate and *mediate* a process of understanding the relations between shot, experience, and communication, since writing entails communicating ideas in a way that thinking them does not.

The task of writing ecocritically about cinema is to mediate the experience of cinema in such a way as to evoke the near-immediacy of the filmic experience while emphasizing that the shot itself and our sensory, emotional, and intellectual responses to it are also processes of mediation. Once we start down this ecocritical path, it is impossible not to confront intricate networks radiating from the shot to how it was produced: not only where, when, and often why, but also with what devices it was made, from what materials, in what organizational and economic form, in which format and at what scale over which lapse of time arriving to us. Ecocinema studies invoke where films come from and where they are going, as physical objects and as cultural forms, together with a series of cultural, economic, and ecological considerations of how they travel through time and space to reach us. The astute reader will already have noticed that this implies that writing critically about ecocinema is therefore about everything everywhere all the time. And that it wants to loop all of that accumulation of experience back into the Now of our initial viewing.

Ecocinema studies aspire to total knowledge of texts and contexts, which is both true and either absurdly ambitious or completely unachievable. That ambition is not as lunatic as it sounds, however, for that is also the goal of information capital in the age of network databases. The difference between cinema's ecocritics and the BAT/FAANG corporations (Baidu, Alibaba, Tencent/Facebook, Amazon, Apple, Netflix, and Google) that dominate network commerce is not only that the latter treat knowledge as information and instrumentalize information as a commodity but also that they genuinely act (since as corporations they cannot really be said to "believe") as if total knowledge can be accomplished. Ecocinema studies scholars acknowledge not only the endlessness but also the practical incoherence of total knowledge, always understanding that while even a simple shot of a leaf falling, unique as it is, is already implicated in a universe of seasons and arboreal evolution, film financing, camera lens manufacturing, and cinematic exhibition so vast and complex as to render any attempt to achieve total understanding of even a single frame of such a film ultimately fruitless.

As a collaborative venture, ecocinema studies can at least point in the various directions from and toward which that shot travels. It makes a fundamental point about the ontology of the moving image: that no image is complete in and of itself, autonomous from the rest of the world, either as pure art or pure commodity. Even the simplest shot already implicates an entire planet, a solar system, and perhaps forces far beyond it ("we are all made of star stuff" as Carl Sagan said in *Cosmos*). The physical laws of mechanical operation guiding the histories of media imaging, projecting, and archiving technologies precede the emergence of life, let alone the beginnings of humanity. This grounding insight into connectivity and the impossibility of ever knowing how it all works allows ecocinema scholars to understand that the already complex mediation of a simple shot implies that it is not self-identical. The leaf falling and the shot of the leaf falling are already at odds. The event of motion caught on film is not the same as the viewer's perception that the motion belongs to the leaf (perhaps you sense the tree falling upward leaving the leaf behind?). Any intuition as to what that perception feels like emotionally or means intellectually to each viewer, however swiftly such affects arrive, are always other than either the leaf or its image. And the leaf, let's recall, is after all only one of the millions falling every year, and the uncounted, unperceived, and unthought billions that have fallen or will fall. The shot is incomplete because it cannot even catch every angle of this one event, let alone the billions of broadly similar but actually very different leaf events. The shot may draw together these various aspects of the moment of projection, but the understanding that every shot is preceded and followed by others (even the last frame of any moving image is inevitably followed by the first frame of another), and that audiences respond perceptually, emotionally, and intellectually, demonstrates that the shot is radically incomplete, triggering all kinds of work, from editing to critical writing, that seeks to produce what the image implies but can never deliver: totality. Despite recognizing that in the networked multitude of the universe, a single shot is incoherent and incomplete, ecocinema studies pursue collectively the critical change that the radical incoherence and incompletion of film brings into cultural life. The inevitable disjuncture between the experience of images and written communiqués that try to capture both the images and the experience is part of ecocriticism's aspiration to universality and its refusal of totality.

Cinema, Ecological Crisis, and Social Justice

The contributors to *Ecocinema Theory and Practice 2* share a sense of global ecological crisis, of intellectual and eco-political urgency. Anthropogenic climate change is only one environmental factor radically altering ecological relationships across our planet. Enclosure of Indigenous lands, clear-felling ancient-growth forests, animal mistreatment, petrochemical infrastructures endangering land and people, the recycling crisis, and oceanic plastic pollution have generated major political protests and new films and ways of making them. They have also propelled new modes of thinking, learning from colonized and Indigenous experiences how to reflect critically on globalization, colonialism, capital, and the European enlightenment tradition in science, engineering, philosophy, and politics (Tung 2020). Ecocritical thinking in cinema studies as elsewhere no longer believes in the kind of binary oppositions that once separated humans from nature. Instead, as we first noted in *Ecocinema Theory and Practice*, ecocinema studies is keen to show how film – from its production to its post-consumption – mediates the inevitable entanglements of humans and nature. We understand that films can themselves be critical of these entanglements. As events, films participate in but also bear witness to local and planetary ecological crises, as well as to the care that such crises instill in filmmakers, their filmed subjects, and their audiences.

New understandings of environmental injustices and ecological crises have emerged in the twenty-first century and with them new forms of care. In the current decade, in which neo-nationalist projects have become core political ideologies in many of the world's most populous nations, the capitalist economic structures of globalization still govern much of the supply of media, whether we speak of content, audiences, or devices. Where scholars of globalization have been forced to confront the reality of what was often disingenuously called "uneven development" with demands for social justice, environmental studies scholars have tended to place the health of the planet first, in the fond belief that restoring and conserving the natural would automatically lead to political and economic equity. Among many writings from the Global South, Sharachchandra Lele (2020) makes us confront two presumptions of neoliberal thinking: one, that technical and economic solutions such as reforestation and carbon credits are presupposed to produce and prioritize "sustainable" economic growth, not to sustain an ailing ecology, and that, therefore, nature can be made to pay its way, like any other activity under capital; and two, that the bulk of the land and oceans to be restored are far from the Global North, whose metropolitan centers consume the vast majority of resources, produce the most pollution, and have demolished the greatest proportion of the world's natural environments. Since the time of Malthus, colonized and minoritized populations have been expected to bear the brunt of the presumed limits to growth (Meadows et al. 1972). Many of the contributions to this volume contest both the fiscal account of nature and the presumption that the poor must pay for its restoration. This marks a significant development since the first volume of *Ecocinema Theory and Practice*.

Learning from queer activists (e.g., Seymour 2018), ecocritical thinking in film studies no longer believes in the kind of binary oppositions that once separated humans from nature and divided "races," genders, sexes, and sexualities. In this collection, our contributors provide rich intersectional analyses to demonstrate the multiple ways in which motion pictures can be understood not only as keenly ecological but also as spaces to contest neoliberal thinking. They provide new or revivified means to engage with objects of study currently emerging, especially in the fields of visual effects, sound studies, the intersections of film and avant-garde art, and the new relationships formed in digital media. Many of the essays gathered here respond to and feedback on recent developments in contemporary critical theory including vitalist film philosophy (e.g., Brown 2018), feminist epistemologies (e.g., Barad 2017), epistemologies of the South and decoloniality (e.g., Tuck and Yang 2012; Santos 2018), affect studies (e.g., Braidotti 2019), and phenomenologies of embodiment (e.g., Angerer 2016). This volume presents new discourses and emerging ecocinema communities that offer radical alternatives to the neoliberal capitalist status quo.

We should not mistake technical innovation, a keyword of neoliberalism, for a radical alternative. The ecocritical lesson we should take from the recent history of technological development is to not just focus on what can now be included or enclosed by cinema but also on what has been further excluded and naturalized. High-resolution digital cameras and projectors have indeed offered new ways of seeing with and behind the veil of cinema. Other novelties that have impacted the recent history of cinema include the ubiquitous cameras/computers in our pockets, buildings, and vehicles, the flexible but decidedly anthropocentric vision afforded by Steadicam since 1975 and, in the opposite direction, the distinctly non-human gaze and independence from gravity that drone photography has made cheap and accessible. The twin tendencies of anthropomorphism and allomorphism engendered by motion pictures, of becoming human and becoming other, should not necessarily be seen as forming a binary opposition. Through seeing and hearing with cinema, each can produce its own negative (becoming inhuman, becoming the same). Rather, the relation between them forms a terrain of mediation – of experience, as Belton (2014) demands, and of imagination.

Brakhage's *Act of Seeing with One's Own Eyes* (aka "the autopsy film," 1971) raised the question of whether it is possible to see the grinding visual truth of mortality and whether death, the most inevitable truth of nature, might escape not only cinema (which, as quasi-autonomous apparatus, can observe what we cannot perceive) but also the human vision itself (Miller 2018). It has been said that digital cinema reduces light to data. We have become all too familiar with mortality data during the COVID-19 pandemic. But death is not merely datum: it is an event that evades picturing and datafying. The best that data visualization can do is to try to represent time, as it does in weather reports and stock market feeds. Alternatively, it might be argued that in place of events, contemporary audiences experience only a narrow vocabulary of swipes, clicks, likes, and recommendations. We are reduced to behaviors. Because human action is so diminished, humans are becoming data. On the downside, as data, we act as functionaries of a cyborg data system (Flusser 2000). But on the upside, whatever cannot be harvested from the human population as data is left to become environmental: the raw material surrounding a vast technological empire, bringing greater possibilities for the alliance between the residual humanity left behind by information capture and the natural world left behind by the extraction industries. In the latest twist to this saga, left-over humans and nature, notably in the form of unpredictable storms and fire seasons, have become essential components of an economic system that thrives on contingency and disaster (Klein 2007, 2014; Ayache 2010). Contemporary cinema, and thus ecocinema studies, works at this fault line between enclosure and escape, to evolve new alliances between humans, technologies, and ecologies beyond the economic evolutions of profit-driven anthropocentrism.

Conclusion and Overview of Chapters

To the extent that film is digital, it is integral to the entire technological apparatus of contemporary social, political, and economic life. It can be seen as the servant of economic and socio-political forces that care no more for human populations than for ecologies. But it can also be seen as both the screen between us and nature, and as the screen on which nature projects itself, just as we project ourselves onto nature. Contemporary cinema has the potential to become a mediating interface that at last allows us to comprehend what we have done, to the world and ourselves, but also how and where we might begin remaking that relation: in the image, in the imagining, of a healed world. But before we can heal, we need diagnoses, and we need to understand the pharmacopoeia that cinema provides us with to set about treatment. In this spirit, we have organized the book around three themes.

The section on Materialities opens with Cubitt's global overview of the competition between economy and ecology in cinema's supply chains of services and materials. We then turn to more local and specific accounts of such tensions to tease out particular resonances in specific regions of the globe. Carolyn Fornoff's chapter explores production and exhibition practices in Mexico, spotlighting bike-powered green alternatives designed to bring cinema to underserved rural areas. Marta Lopera-Mármol and Manel Jiménez-Morales' chapter analyzes green filmmaking in Catalonia and proposes strategies for extending the reach of such practices. Debashree Mukherjee turns our attention to Bollywood melodrama to reveal the links between India's coal and cinema industries of extraction and exhaustion.

The Discourses section introduces analytical frames and new keywords by which to engage in ecocinema studies. Catejan Iheka develops a concept of "wild cinema" from narratives of land depletion and repair in two African films and Elio Garcia coins the term "polytemporalities," extending ecocritique from places to times by analyzing climate trauma in the slow cinema of Filipino director Lav Diaz. Andrew Hageman and Helen Wang offer a model for comparative ideological ecocritique, using as their case studies two popular US and Chinese science fiction films, while Christian Quendler proposes a queering of comedic ecocinema by way of analyzing Buster Keaton's *Our Hospitality* (1923) as "chimera." Anthony Lioi rounds off the section by exploring the concept of "mesocosm"– bounded worlds – to help us understand how film and media fans collectively produce more-than-metaphorical ecological networks of cultural and material meanings.

Our concluding section on Communities further expands the scope of ecocinema studies by reminding us of how cinema, while often a communal practice (collaboratively produced by a film crew), can more intentionally be about and for community justice, aimed to elevate ecological and social justice. Angelica Lawson (Northern Arapaho) describes how animator Jonathan Thunder (Ojibwe) and media artist Missy Whiteman (Arapaho and Kickapoo) spotlight Indigenous cosmologies of human and more-than-human communities through digital media, Aarón Lacayo links disability and ecological toxicity through *Polvo* (*Dust*, Julio Hernández Cordón, 2012) a film about a Mayan community in the wake of the Guatemalan civil war (1960–1996), and Emily Roehl provides an account of Indigenous community-building and drone filmmaking as a response to the destructive colonialism of the Dakota Access

Pipeline. Scholar and filmmaker Mila Zuo critiques the rise of streaming film festivals during pandemic conditions, as a condition for dissipating community, while Mariam Abazeri's chapter on the Iranian participatory film production *Women of the Sun: A Chronology of Seeing* (2020), which Abazeri co-produced, provides the Persian concept of "adab" to show that the women working on the film discovered "the world around them not as a fixed state of values and behaviors but as a dynamic process." Ecocinema studies have no lesser ambitions; it welcomes the truth that film criticism, along with films and filmmaking, can be "wild," to use Iheka's term, or in Zuo's words, that "cinema like the coyote...be feral," such that it is always unknowable, not only as finished products but also at every stage of its coming to be.

Jennifer Fay's afterword punctuates this dynamism of cinematic community and wildness by further exploring the connections between the chapters and possibilities for advancing the field. As she suggests, there must be many critical sequels to this collection to come, and much research and communication left to do. Work on materialities could easily be expanded with ecocritical analyses of the governance of technical standards, economic policy, extra-territorial contract and intellectual property law, financial services, risk management, and policing the global trade in services, including the movement of engineering and design expertise. We acknowledge here emerging work in such areas as environmental management through policy and governance (Kääpä 2018; Kääpä and Vaughan 2022), data and other modes of knowledge (Bacevic 2021), the rise of carbon financing (Freidberg 2017; Field 2022), and the oscillations between global production (Yeung 2021) and the terrifying insights into "global destruction networks" offered by Wang et al. (2021). Similarly, interest in ecocinema discourses could easily expand upon our collection and previous work in the field through scholarship devoted to animation (Pallant 2015), musicals, speculative fiction, horror, and other significant genres, into sound (Smith 2015) and other cinematic technologies and aesthetics, topics such as ethics (Brereton 2016), philosophy (White 2018), and piety (McFarland Taylor 2019), and, of course, deeper inquiry into ecological entanglements and social justice. We further invite forays into the rich evolving scholarship of temporality studies connecting collapsing and expanding time frames in global media's new distributed and re-connected geographies to Deleuze and Guattari's (1987) deterritorializing and reterritorializing, while also reaching toward Kyle Powys Whyte's (2018) Indigenous notions of "spiraling" and intergenerational time (2018). We are privileged to publish, in the communities section, work that articulates Indigenous worldviews; yet we have so much to learn, as a community of scholars, from the lived experiences and cinematic expressions of these communities, not least about how media technologies from digital storytelling to lightweight and small-file movies can complete circuits of inclusion between a people and its places, about what it can still mean to inhabit. Ten years after our first collection, we dedicate this volume to the emerging voices of the next ten years, and to the startling, entrancing, and healing ideas they will develop in their scholarship, art, and activism.

Works Cited

Alex, Rayson K. and S. Susan Deborah, eds. 2016. *Ecodocumentaries: Critical Essays.* London: Palgrave Macmillan.

Angerer, Marie-Louise. 2016. *Ecology of Affect: Intensive Milieus and Contingent Encounters.* Translated by Gerrit Jackson. Lüneburg: Meson Press.

Ayache, Elie. 2010. *The Blank Swan: The End of Probability.* Chichester: John Wiley.

Bacevic, Jana. 2021. "Unthinking Knowledge Production: From Post-Covid to Post-Carbon Futures." *Globalizations* 18.7:1206–1218.

Barad, Karen. 2017. "Troubling Time/s and Ecologies of Nothingness: Re-Turning, Re-Membering, and Facing the Incalculable." *New Formations* 92: 56–86.

Barclay, Bridgitte and Christy Tidwell. 2018. *Gender and Environment in Science Fiction.* Washington, DC: Rowman & Littlefield.

Belton, John. 2014. "If Film Is Dead, What Is Cinema?" *Screen* 55.4: 460–470.

Bissonnette, Sylvia. 2019. *Affect and Embodied Meaning in Animation: Becoming Animated.* Boca Raton: CRC Press.

Blasi, Gabriella. 2019. *The Work of Terrence Malik: Time-Based Ecocinema.* Amsterdam: Amsterdam University Press.

Bozak, Nadia. 2012. *The Cinematic Footprint: Lights, Camera, Natural Resources.* New Brunswick: Rutgers University Press.

Braidotti, Rosi. 2019. "A Theoretical Framework for the Critical Posthumanities." *Theory Culture and Society* 36.6: 31–61.

Brereton, Pat. 2016. *Environmental Ethics and Film.* London: Earthscan/Routledge.

Brown, William. 2018. *Non-Cinema: Global Digital Film-Making and the Multitude.* London: Bloomsbury.

Cahill, Leo, Brian Jacobson, and Weihong Bao, eds. 2022. "Special Issue: Media Climates." *Representations*, 157. University of California Press.

Chang, Chia-ju, ed. 2019. *Chinese Environmental Humanities: Imagining Huanjing as a Critical Concept.* New York: Palgrave Macmillan.

Cubitt, Sean. 2017. *Finite Media: Environmental Implications of Digital Technologies.* Durham and London: Duke University Press.

———. 2020. *Anecdotal Evidence: Ecocritique from Hollywood to the Mass Image.* London: Oxford University Press.

Deleuze, Gilles and Felix Guattari. [1980] 1987. *A Thousand Plateaus.* Translate by Brian Massumi. Minneapolis: University of Minnesota Press.

Elwes, Catherine. 2022. *Landscape and the Moving Image.* Bristol: Intellect.

Fay, Jennifer. 2018. *Inhospitable World: Cinema in the Time of the Anthropocene.* London: Oxford University Press.

Field, Sean. 2022. "Carbon Capital: The Lexicon and Allegories of US Hydrocarbon Finance." *Economy and Society.* doi:10.1080/03085147.2022.2030606

Flusser, Vilém. 2000. *Towards a Philosophy of Photography.* Translated by Anthony Matthews. London: Reaktion Books.

Freidberg, Susanne. 2017. "Trading in the Secretive Commodity." *Economy and Society* 46.3–4: 499–521.

Guan, Cassandra and Adam O'Brien. 2020. "Cinema's Natural Aesthetics: Environments and Perspectives in Contemporary Film Theory. Special Dossier Introduction." *Screen* 61.2: 272–279. doi:10.1093/screen/hjaa014.

Hegel, G.W. F. [1820] 1991. *Elements of the Philosophy of the Right*, edited by Allen Wood and translated by H.B. Nisbet. Cambridge: Cambridge University Press.

Hughes, Helen. 2014. *Green Documentary: Environmental Documentary in the 21st Century.* Chicago: Intellect.

Iheka, Cajetan. 2021. *African Ecomedia: Network Forms, Planetary Politics.* Durham and London: Duke University Press.

Ivakhiv, Adrian. 2013. *Ecologies of the Moving Image: Cinema, Affect, Nature.* Ontario: Wilfrid Laurier University Press.

———. 2018. *Shadowing the Anthropocene: Eco-Realism for Turbulent Times.* New York City: Punctum Books.

Jue, Melody. 2020. *Wild Blue Media: Thinking Through Seawater.* Durham: Duke University Press.

Kääpä, Pietari. 2013. "Understanding the Audiences of Ecocinema." Special Issue Introduction. *Interactions* 4.2: 107–111.

———. 2018. *Environmental Management of the Media: Policy, Industry, Practice.* London: Routledge.

Kääpä, Pietari and Tommy Gustaffson. 2013. *Transnational Ecocinema: Film Culture in an Era of Ecological Transformation.* London: Intellect.

Kääpä, Pietari and Hunter Vaughan. 2022. "From Content to Context (and Back Again): New Industrial Strategies for Environmental Sustainability in the Media." In *A Companion to Motion Pictures and Public Value*, edited by Mette Hjort and Ted Nannicelli, 308–326. Chichester: Wiley-Blackwell.

Kaplan, E. Ann. 2016. *Climate Trauma: Foreseeing the Future in Dystopian Film and Fiction.* New Brunswick: Rutgers University Press.

Klein, Naomi. 2007. *The Shock Doctrine: The Rise of Disaster Capitalism.* New York: Henry Holt.

———. 2014. *This Changes Everything: Capitalism vs. the Climate.* New York: Simon and Schuster.

Lele, Sharachchandra. 2020. "Environment and Well-Being: A Perspective from the Global South." *New Left Review* 123 (May–June): 41–63.

Lu, Sheldon H. and Jiayan Mi, eds. 2009. *Chinese Ecocinema in the Age of Environmental Challenge.* Hong Kong: Hong Kong University Press.

Lu, Sheldon H. and Haomin Gong, editors. 2020. *Ecology and Chinese-Language Cinema: Re-Imagining a Field.* New York: Routledge.

Lübecker, Nikola and Daniele Rugo, eds. 2017. *James Benning's Environments: Politics, Ecology, Duration.* Edinburgh: Edinburgh University Press.

Lyotard, Jean François. 1994. *Lessons on the Analytic of the Sublime.* Translated by Elizabeth Rottenberg. Redwood City: Stanford University Press.

MacKenzie, Scott and Westerståhl Stenport, editors. 2015. *Films on Ice: Cinemas of the Arctic.* Edinburgh: Edinburgh University Press.

Maxwell, Richard, et al. 2015. *Media and the Ecological Crisis.* London/New York: Routledge.

Maxwell, Richard and Toby Miller. 2012. *Greening the Media.* Oxford/New York: Oxford University Press.

McFarland Taylor, Sarah. 2019. *Ecopiety: Green Media and the Dilemma of Environmental Virtue.* New York: NYU Press.

McKim, Kristi. 2013. *Cinema as Weather: Stylistic Screens and Atmospheric Change.* New York: Routledge.

McMahon, Laura. 2019. *Animal Worlds: Film, Philosophy, and Time.* Edinburgh: Edinburgh University Press.

Meadows, Donella H., et al. 1972. *The Limits to Growth: A Report for the Club of Rome's Project on the Predicament of Mankind.* New York: Universe Books.

Miller, Michael F. 2018. "Stan Brakhage's Autopsy: *The Act of Seeing with One's Own Eyes.*" *Journal of Film and Video* 70.2: 46–55.

Mirzoeff, Nicholas. 2014. "Visualizing the Anthropocene." *Public Culture* 26.2: 213–222.

———. 2015. *How to See the World.* New York: Pelican.

———. 2016. "It's Not the Anthropocene, It's the White Supremacy Scene, or the Geological Color Line." In *After Extinction,* edited by Richard Grusin, 123–149. Minneapolis: University of Minnesota Press.

Monani, Salma and Joni Adamson, eds. 2018. *Ecocriticism and Indigenous Studies: Conversations from Earth to Cosmos.* New York: Routledge.

Moore, Ellen E. 2017. *Landscape and the Environment in Hollywood Film: The Green Machine.* London: Palgrave Macmillan.

Mukherjee, Debashree. 2020. *Bombay Hustle: Making Movies in a Colonial City.* New York: Columbia University Press.

Murray, Robin and Joseph K. Heumann—. 2014. *Film and Everyday Eco-Disasters.* Lincoln: University of Nebraska Press.

———. 2016. *Monstrous Nature: Environment and Horror on the Big Screen.* Lincoln: University of Nebraska Press.

———. 2017. *Ecocinema in the City.* London/New York: Routledge.

Narine, Anil, ed. 2015. *Eco-Trauma Cinema.* New York: Routledge.

O'Brien, Adam—. (2016). *Transactions with the World: Ecocriticism and the Environmental Sensibility of New Hollywood.* New York: Berghahn.

———. 2017. *Film and the Natural Environment: Elements and Atmospheres.* London: Wallflower Press.

Pallant, Chris, ed. 2015. *Animated Landscapes: History, Form and Function.* London: Bloomsbury.

Parikka, Jussi. 2015. *A Geology of Media.* Minneapolis: University of Minnesota Press.

Past, Elena. 2019. *Italian Ecocinema Beyond the Human.* Bloomington: University of Indiana Press.

Peters, John Durham. 2015. *The Marvelous Clouds: Toward a Philosophy of Elemental Media.* Chicago: University of Chicago Press.

Pick, Anat and Guinevere Narraway, eds. 2013. *Screening Nature: Cinema Beyond the Human.* Oxford: Berghahn.

Randerson, Janine. 2018. *Weather as Medium: Toward a Meteorological Art.* Cambridge: MIT Press.

Rhoads, Sean. 2018. *Japan's Green Monsters: Environmental Commentary in Kaiju Cinema.* Jefferson: McFarland & Company.

Rust, Stephen and Carter Soles. 2014. "Living in Fear, Living in Dread, Pretty Soon We'll All Be Dead." "Ecohorror Special Cluster Introduction." *Interdisciplinary Studies in Literature and Environment* 21.3: 509–512.

Rust, Stephen, Salma Monani, and Sean Cubitt, eds. 2016. *Ecomedia: Key Issues.* New York: Routledge.

Santos, Boaventura de Sousa. 2018. *The End of the Cognitive Empire: The Coming of Age of Epistemologies of the South.* Durham: Duke University Press.

Seymour, Nicole. 2013. *Strange Natures: Futurity, Empathy, and the Queer Ecological Imagination.* Champaign: University of Illinois Press.

———. 2018. *Bad Environmentalism: Irony and Irreverence in the Ecological Age.* Minneapolis: University of Minnesota Press.

Smaill, Belinda. 2016. *Regarding Life: Animals and the Documentary Moving Image.* New York: SUNY Press.

Smith, Jacob. 2015. *Eco-Sonic Media.* Berkeley: University of California Press.

Starosielski, Nicole. 2015. *The Undersea Network.* Durham and London: Duke University Press.

Tidwell, Christy and Carter Soles, eds. 2021. *Fear and Nature: Ecohorror Studies in the Anthropocene.* University Park: Penn State University Press.

Tsing, Anna Lowenhaupt, et al. 2017. *Arts of Living on a Damaged Planet: Ghosts and Monsters of the Anthropocene.* Minneapolis: University of Minnesota Press.

Tuck, Eve and K. Wayne Yang. 2012. "Decolonization Is Not a Metaphor." *Decolonization: Indigeneity, Education & Society* 1.1: 1–40.

Tung, Charles M. 2020. "Time Machines and Timelapse Aesthetics in Anthropocenic Modernism." In *Timescales: Thinking across Ecological Temporalities*, edited by Bethany Wiggin, Carolyn Fornoff, and Patricia Eunji Kim, 79–94. Minneapolis: University of Minnesota Press.

Vaughan, Hunter. 2019. *Hollywood's Dirtiest Secret: The Hidden Environmental Costs of the Movies.* New York: Columbia University Press.

von Mossner, Alexa Weik, ed. 2014. *Moving Environments: Affect, Emotion, Ecology, and Film.* Ontario: Wilfrid Laurier University Press.

———. 2017. *Affective Ecologies: Empathy, Emotion and Environmental Narrative.* Columbus: The Ohio State University Press.

Wang, Kun, Junxi Qian, and Shenjing He. 2021. "Global Destruction Networks and Hybrid E-Waste Economies: Practices and Embeddedness in Guiyu, China." *Environment and Planning A: Economy and Space* 54.3: 533–553.

White, Daniel. 2018. *Film in the Anthropocene: Philosophy, Ecology, and Cybernetics.* London: Palgrave Macmillan.

Whyte, Kyle P. 2018. "Indigenous Science (Fiction) for the Anthropocene: Ancestral Dystopias and Fantasies of Climate Change Crises." *Environment and Planning E: Nature and Space* 1.1–2: 224–242.

Yeung, Henry Wai-chung. 2021. "The Trouble with Global Production Networks." *Environment and Planning A: Economy and Space* 53.2: 428–438.

PART I
Ecocinema Materialities

1

UNSUSTAINABLE CINEMA

Global Supply Chains

Seán Cubitt

Struggles over naming our epoch of climate change – Anthropocene? Capitalocene? – are symptomatic of the growing recognition that ecology and economy can no longer be separated: that indeed, they have always been implicated in one another. For film studies, this recognition necessitates adding to early ecocritical concerns with what film does, a renewed inquiry into how it works, what it is made of, and who pays for it. That "who", in the context of ecocritique, obviously includes non-humans. Twenty-first-century cinema and media are networked. This network is clearly the condition of distribution, a branch of the industry that has historically included the management of finite numbers of physical copies being transported to exhibition venues and returned to warehouses. Moving DCP (digital content packages) on portable hard drives is easier on projectionists' sciatica but does not fundamentally alter the logistics of moving films physically from place to place and the associated security required to protect intellectual property. Security remains a key concern in the delivery of files via digital networks, and though the restriction on numbers of copies is relaxed, the costs of shifting them from supplier to viewer are still real, and the energy and pollution outfall is only shifted from internal combustion to electricity grids. This chapter explores the geopolitical dimensions of the global film industry's supply chain networks at a time when digital production, distribution and exhibition are placing tremendous strains on human and non-human alike, asking whether human economies bound to the physical limitations of the earth can sustain our insatiable hunger for media entertainment.

DOI: 10.4324/9781003246602-3

Then and Now: Setting the Stage for Economic and Ecological Legacies

Some things have not changed. World War One decimated European film industries, and the rising hegemon across the Atlantic was swift to take advantage. Despite the various golden ages of German and Danish silent film, French cinema of the Popular Front and the popular success of British studios in the 1940s, Hollywood's ascendancy in European and global markets became a fact of cultural life. Giuseppe Richeri shows how network production and distribution has not altered the dominance of US movie product in the European market, citing 2015 figures indicating that even in countries with mature cinema industries like Germany, Italy and France, a US title is potentially more profitable than a European title (2020, 136).

Similar structural imbalances shape markets in Latin America and Australasia, with perhaps only India, among the major economies, enjoying mass popularity for home-grown films without resorting to import controls rationing the numbers of US movies entering the domestic market (e.g., on the Chinese model: Chow 2020). Graeme Turner and Jinna Tay proposed some years ago that "these days the answer to the question 'What is television?' very much depends on where you are" (2009, 8), to which Lobato and Lotz responded "the answer to the question 'What is Netflix?' clearly also depends on where you are" (2020, 133; see also Lobato 2019; McDonald et al. 2021), bearing out Richeri's observation on film availability in the European Union at the global scale. The answers to our question, "What are film production and distribution these days?" similarly depend on geography, which implicates the environment.

While cinema has migrated to digital, film production and network distribution environmental costs are not mitigated by the digitization of distribution and its informal sharing economies (e.g., piracy: Crisp 2015). Making the film industry "sustainable" has become the goal of significant and admirable institutional and organizational initiatives (wearealbert.org, greeningofstreaming.org, BFI 2020, green4ema.org), but when it circulates in financial, planning, development, and policy areas of the industry, the word can simply mean "likely to survive for a few years", and "compatible with maintaining profit levels, business practices and tax base". As Leerom Medovoi notes, "what corporate sustainability discourse cannot admit, therefore, and what the word 'sustainability' unfortunately helps it to disavow, is the prospect that [ecological] injury is a necessary and 'sustaining' feature of capital accumulation" (2009). To the extent that it is an industry and therefore bound to cycles of credit, risk and profitability, cinema finds itself pitched against the very environments that sustain it. Nonetheless, there remains the imperative voiced by economist Will Davies, "Anthropocenic utopias are urgently required" (2017, 1), accepting the argument that any planned utopia is an imposition of present thinking on the future; Davies nonetheless specifies that ecocritical utopianism commits to a commons protected from exploitation.

Many existing studies of materials and energy, infrastructures, and governance have investigated the new conditions of film production and distribution for two decades or more under the rubric of globalisation (e.g., Miller et al. 2001, 2005). Globalization has been characterised by the neo-liberal corporate seizure of nation states (Plant 2009) concentrating on the economic to the exclusion of the ecological, opening the gates for a new mode of ecological colonization. Raising economics to the dominant driver of policy was in itself a performative act (Callon 2006; Çalışkan and Callon 2009); the ubiquitous description of the film as a "creative industry" presumes the supremacy of economic interests. A key premise of this chapter is that "sustainability" (as figured by the corporate practices that dominate global economies, including the film industry) is a false reconciliation of economics and ecocritique and that Davies' Anthropocenic utopias can only become feasible if and when the divorce of ecology from economics is truly overcome. Cinema has as its urgent task not only to envision those utopias and to outline the devastation resulting from the lack of them but also to create models for ecological economies beyond sustainability. Of all the technologies that capital promises will avoid the coming cataclysm, the apparatus of the moving image, though bitterly compromised (as this chapter must argue), is also the beam of light that we can follow towards a new common hearth – whose Greek name was oikos, the root of both ecology and economics.

Physical Distribution

A good deal of ink has been spilt on the impact of streaming services on broadcast television (see notably Lotz 2014, 2018; Marks et al. 2020), and we can look forward to more writing on the long-term impact of streaming on cinema-going once the effects of the COVID-19 pandemic assimilate into everyday life (see Mila Zuo's chapter in this collection). The 90–180 minute feature film, which emerged in the 1910s, has survived as a cultural form through the long-term demise of the theatrical exhibition since the 1940s, weathering the challenges of over-the-air and cable television, rental (and sell-through) video, and internet streaming; bruised and bloodied it is still the dominant movie format. The appeal of short-form videos and the escalating production values of serial drama have whittled down its dominance through the seemingly opposed attractions of distracted and binge viewing. Nonetheless, the investment in theatrical releases in the months following pandemic lockdowns indicates that corporations still have faith in feature films, with spectacular productions like *Eternals* (Chloe Zhao), *The Last Duel* (Ridley Scott), *Dune* (Denis Villeneuve), and *No Time to Die* (Cary Joji Fukunaga) following each other on successive weekends during the last months of 2021. Each of these movies benefitted from distributed production, with second units shooting in diverse locations and studios, and (what are still called, rather inaccurately) pre- and post-production teams working simultaneously in globally distributed networks. How do cinema's global supply chains, linking location shoots with offshore effects houses and metropolitan distribution, stack up in the ecological economy?

Supply chains look different depending not only on where the viewer is or on the point-of-view of each worker playing a contributory role in the chain but also on the standpoint of an environment experiencing a film crew descending on a location or the view from the position of server farms delivering "screen traffic" (Acland 2003). Even as the geography of human and non-human components in the making and movement of films implies differential considerations given to metropolitan ecologies and employees compared to marginalized locations and workers, it also implies temporal differences. The duration of viewing on SVOD (streaming video on demand) services, including the selection of a title, pausing, commenting and recommending, produces data points that inform future production decisions. Other data prompt decisions on budgets for visual effects, soundtracks, release dates, and marketing campaigns. High-bandwidth communication networks enable 24-hour around-the-clock workshifts across different time zones, lengthening the working day, accelerating production, and enabling further geographical distribution of production tasks and real-time decisions that are equally driven by accumulated historical data on tastes and reactions, and by projecting trends into a plannable future.

Such network logistics have transformed the long history of runaway productions (Steinhart 2019) and transnational co-productions (Chan 2012). Trend projections based on accumulated data about prior experience can have lasting impacts. Governmental and cultural reactions against the abuse of local ecologies on location shoots can remove them from the list of potential locations for years at a time while recovering from that abuse can take even longer (Law et al. 2007; Cripps and Olarn 2019). Nonetheless, locations continue to attract producers, as do tax breaks, currency deals, and efficiency coefficients; a hundred less obviously creative determinants may also make a desirable site for directors unpalatable to producers. Like restoration of damaged local ecosystems, the operation of supply chains requires labor that extends not only to non-human work but also to human, technological, and environmental labor that is not deemed "creative" in standard economic and aesthetic accounting procedures. As Mezzadra and Neilsen phrase it, when work is reduced, for logistical purposes, to abstract operations, those operations simultaneously reduce "the complex interactions of space and time that occur between its seeming moments of cause and effect, input and output, to linear processes" (2019, 6; see also Nost and Goldstein 2022). Economic operations render human and non-human labor invisible, much like the contributions of land, air and water to the making and distribution of films.

Far from immaterial, the physical infrastructures and consumer devices that contemporary cinema depends on are assembled through extensive ocean-spanning trade networks of containerized shipping, one of the least regulated and most polluting of all industries, even as it is one of the most essential parts of the supply chain. When shipping is disrupted, components and finished consumer and professional equipment that sustain the film industry's global supply chain cannot circulate or even be produced. Yet, the ecological toll of such shipping networks is on par with the impacts of digitization (Sekula 1995). The International Energy Agency's 2021 report predicts maritime trade's fuel consumption will see global growth of 0.3 million barrels a day of bunker fuel, and the International Maritime Organization's recent regulation reducing the sulphur content of maritime diesel will not effect its carbon content (IEA 2021, 16). Shipping, like aviation, contributes around 3% of global carbon emissions. Fierce arguments as to whether air and sea transport should be covered by national targets or passed on to global bodies like the International Maritime Organisation – itself in hock to the major shipping companies and widely accused of greenwashing its unambitious COP26 targets (Container Management 2021) – contributes to the lack of oversight, especially in international waters. The perceived urgency of restoring global trade to pre-pandemic levels, not least to rebuild supply chains for consumer electronic equipment, blinds international bodies and governments to the physical challenge of reducing transport's environmental costs and encourages the shameful shell game of "net zero emissions". Further environmental impacts from spilled fuel and cargo and cleansing buoyancy tanks, often unreported, are further hidden costs of the supply chains feeding global cinema.

Unsustainable Networks: Shipping and Satellites

In recent years, streaming services have been charged with significant carbon footprints (Marks et al. 2020; Deneault 2021). Many providers and the telcos that handle their transmissions have moved to renewable energy and much more efficient storage and transmission, so that the greatest energy use tends to be in domestic equipment (routers, peripherals, and screens) with a marked move towards smaller screens (though it is unclear whether more people sharing a larger screen has less impact than the same number watching small individual screens) (The Carbon Trust 2021, 9). The carbon footprint of video streaming per individual viewer is in the range of 55 grams of carbon per hour of video streaming but given the huge numbers of people viewing both long-form (e.g., Netflix) and short-form (e.g., YouTube) video, the total figures are more dramatic. As *The Guardian* reported in October 2021, Netflix fans "clocked up more than 6bn [6 billion] hours watching the top 10 shows – which included *Squid Game*, *Stranger Things*, *Money Heist* and *Bridgerton* – in the first 28 days after each show was released" (Sweeney 2021). Scaling up for the long-tail economics of targeted viewing, adding in the more than 1 billion subscribers to streaming services globally, without considering the billions of hours of video viewed on social media platforms, those 55 grams begin to multiply towards huge tonnages of carbon, comparable to something in the range of 147,000 standard gas canisters every hour.

The quantities of materials and energy required to freight ostensibly intangible goods and services are deliberately obscured by the language of "cloud computing" and "server farms" with their atmospheric and pastoral connotations. Ecologically, a picture is worth considerably more than 1,000 words. The phrase "A picture of a smiling child" contains six words yet a passport-sized digital image of the same subject takes the equivalent of 2,000 "words" of code. A single frame of high-resolution video of a child smiling is exponentially larger and needs far more bandwidth. In so-called "emerging markets" like Africa, the growth spiral of new formats and new demands for speed and coverage increases the need for infrastructural media of connection, now themselves increasingly a monopoly industry (Starosielski 2021). The e-waste disposal challenge of tens of thousands of kilometres of abandoned cable is only one result of this monopoly on subsea network infrastructure. The other is increased competition from near-Earth orbital satellites.

SpaceX's Starlink project is intended to supply those developing markets with infrastructures sufficient to meet increasing demand for entertainment and information media but is also being pitched as a fast and efficient networking solution for investment capital from the Global North, which will include supply chains and logistical services. SpaceX ultimately intends a network of 42,000 geostationary satellites (Mann 2021). A satellite launch only uses about the same amount of fuel as a trans-Atlantic flight, the SpaceX vehicles carry several satellites per trip and the launch capsules are reusable, so there is some mitigation of the normal environmental impact of space vehicles. But satellites have a finite lifetime, limited by the amount of gas or liquid fuel they can carry for adjusting their position (critical to their orientation to incoming and ongoing signals), which is continuously affected by heating, cooling and the tidal pulls of gravity. Their thermoelectric generators, typically fuelled by plutonium to power transponders and navigation systems, also have a finite lifespan, and though each satellite carries only tiny quantity of radioactive isotopes, 42,000 satellites use an appreciable amount. Antennae and transponders, like most electronic components, are made from some common but also some rare minerals, with all the problems they pose for the lands they were mined on. If the problems of space debris from decommissioned satellites are ever solved, that too will have significant environmental costs (Undseth et al. 2020). Extracting, refining, and fabricating advanced technologies from the resultant metals are all work, and though the forces of gravity and radiation appear entropic from the standpoint of capital, they too are energies at work in the supply chain of global cinema. The result of their labor may be a long, drawn-out scattering of molecules through the upper atmosphere and back to the surface of the Earth decades or centuries hence, with unknown effects, in orbit or in the air, on the planet's albedo, the chemistry of the atmosphere, and the kinds of allergies described in Aarón Lacayo's chapter in this volume. This too is work as defined by the laws of thermodynamics.

That we do not have to wait for thousands of years while molecules from abandoned satellites settle on the ground or ocean is surely clear from the international trade in waste electronics (Szasz 1994; Grossman 2007; Gabrys 2010). As the Basel Action Network reports (2002, 2005), much work has been done on the human and environmental impacts of recycling waste electronics from the Global North to the Global South. As in production, the post-consumption disposal of unwanted devices is organized in global supply chains feeding recycling zones throughout the South, from Agbogbloshie to Chittagong (Amuzu 2018; Mah 2021). A major challenge is that the supply to end-users of waste materials depends on a mixture of formal (governmental or commercially regulated) and informal brokers. Unregulated waste brokers operate at or beyond the fringes of the law and are likely to dismiss the claims of workers and local ecologies for protection from the toxins involved in both the valuable recycled materials and the valueless ones burned or otherwise left to rot. Extensive efforts to control the informal sector (Baidya et al. 2020) often break down under the demands for cheap, quick and relatively high-quality waste (e.g., stripped of unprofitable plastics). Not only is the labor of both formal and informal waste industries invisible, but the toxins they scatter are also tucked away, unseen by the wealthy world unless exposed by a documentary like Kern Konwiser and Mago Nagasaka's *Still a Black Star* (2022, http://www.stillablackstar.net/). Audiences – ecocritically aware audiences – must draw out the implications, perceiving the depths of such labor as that produced by e-waste, on flat screens. Even when "reality is freed to exhibit itself" (Cavell 1979, 166), its self-presentation implies the work and environmental impacts of production, distribution, and waste and demands a parallel work of perception and understanding from its viewers.

Network Transport: The Labor of Digital Special Effects

The link between the work performed by what accountants refer to, embarrassingly without irony, as "environmental services" and the labor implicit in supply chains appears discontinuous partly because of the disjuncture between scales and times of operation, and partly because the whole purpose of capitalist supply chains, as Sekula, Orenstein and Mezzadra and Neilsen have variously proposed, is to hide labor (as well as to minimise the wages paid for it). Films too are devices for hiding the labor, human and non-human, required to make them. Contemporary supply chains, notably in the visual effects sector, are not simply an efficient use of digital networks, although the move to digital filmmaking has certainly improved the relative ease and speed of delivery of film services from remote workplaces to Hollywood productions via commercial internet channels. The effects professionals interviewed in Michael Curtin and Kevin Sanson's *Voices of Labor* (2017) repeatedly indicate the power of six major studios' effective monopsony in relation to more than 500 significant effects shops around the world, the effects of deregulation of labor, targeted investment in sunrise industries (including effects and the creative industries generally), tax rebates and subsidies from national and local governments, and the effects of purchasing power in fluctuating currencies. Increasingly precarious employment opportunities drive effects artists to migrate to offshore production centres following the work, or to stay in the major production centres competing in a race to the bottom on price, quality, and speed.

The golden rule of filmmaking "You can have it fast and cheap but it won't be good, or good and fast but it won't be cheap" no longer works when the market is so severely imbalanced in favour of fast and cheap. As Curtin and Sanson observe,

> Firms bid for work with fixed prices, meaning they enter into a contractual agreement with producers to deliver the required imagery on a fixed deadline at a guaranteed price. There are no allowances for the additional time or resources a firm may require because of production delays or requested changes.
>
> *(2017, 201)*

Instead, they overwork existing staff or hire extra staff on short contracts to complete the work, including tweaks to existing effects plates demanded by their buyers, without extra cash, in the hopes that completing their contracts will get them the next job, when they can make good their losses. The result is increasing precarity not only for workers but also for shops. The major shops extend the practice by establishing branches globally, wherever subsidies and talent combine, thus hollowing out any possibility of union organization, while also sub-contracting to smaller firms for specific shots or layers. These small firms then carry the highest financial risks and offer the worst employment conditions (Curtin et al. 2014; Curtin and Sanson 2016).

This economic deracination of the effects supply chain not only disconnects filmmaking from lived spaces and ecologies: there are profound geopolitical aesthetics involved. The financial structure of Tsui Hark's 2005 hit *Seven Swords* (Qī Jiàn) and its integrated supply chain of visual effects, for example, drove the subsequently political choice to shoot much of the live action on location in Xinjiang (Cubitt 2019). The aesthetics of wuxia (martial arts) movies includes the diegetic world of jianghu – the "rivers and lakes" world of martial arts, equivalent to the storyworlds of pirate films and westerns – that Stephen Teo describes as marginal, illicit, and abstract (2009, 18). Such abstracting of settings from the labor of localities, also characteristic of contemporary Hollywood's displaced geographies, removes any impetus for any actual location to represent itself rather than, say, Mars, Asgard, or even Boston (impersonated by New York in *The Departed* [Martin Scorsese, 2006]). This aesthetic is not just a product of economics – though it certainly is that – nor a standard practice that ecocriticism can therefore ignore. It is a symptom of a profound de-localisation that bleeds across contemporary culture, from our collective ignorance of the provenance of our everyday foods to our cheerful disregard for the destination of our waste.

The abstraction of aesthetics from human and non-human labor is an integral part of the abstraction of all human life from its local and planetary ecology. Film production has long screened off the outside world as much as it has created fictional ones. Compositing – layering foregrounds and backgrounds, only some of which are photographed – began with Méliès' painted backdrops in the first decade of the twentieth century. More recently, Industrial Light and Magic built a virtual set for the Lucasfilm/Disney+ series *The Mandalorian*, powered by Epic Games' aptly named Unreal Engine (Axon 2020), an installation now being eagerly internationalized (Hopewell 2020; Austin 2021). We should recall that every screen is not only a display mechanism but also a device for screening out an exterior world from a viewer's perception and screening of the privileged site of viewing from the global supply chain and labor that make such viewing possible. The obverse of the delocalising of locations promised in the Dubai Film Commissions slogan "Make it what you want it to be" (Dickinson 2020) is the universalisation of the screen itself, not just as an interface but as a dividing line between humans and their natural and technological ecologies. It demonstrates not only the sustainability of illusion but also the illusion of sustainability.

Alienating screens and screen products is not without human cost. Kay Dickinson (2021) emphasises the participation of governments and higher education providers in producing the skilled technical and creative workers that the globalised film industry requires. This support includes not only skills training but also attuning attitudes to the requirements of a project-based (rather than employment-based) model of labor, an entrepreneurship of the self (Foucault 2010, 226). Readied to consider themselves not as employees at all but as mini-enterprises ready to compete on quality, speed, price, and flexibility, such workers are decreasingly likely to organize in the traditions of cultural sector guilds and trades unions or to dispute capitalist accountancy's disdain for the environmental costs of its activities (shifting such costs, if acknowledging them at all, to marketing departments).

While the impacts of the New International Division of Cultural Labor (Miller et al. 2005) are perhaps less obviously implicated in environmental concerns than location shooting, they compound the impacts of the runaway film model increasingly typical of Hollywood products (as well of the Hong Kong film industry among others [Yeh and Chao 2018]). The same supply chain logistics that govern the extraction, shipping, and manufacture of electronics and the shipping of e-waste also govern the effects industry. The globalization of visual effects is embedded in supply chain capitalism or in Anna Tsing's (2009) phrase the "technical architectures of biopolitical control" that, as Ned Rossiter describes, "register an epochal shift of geopolitical proportions as automation increasingly takes command" (2021, 132). The articulations of biopolitics and geopolitics concern not only humans but also the historical specificity of the alienation of humans from a planet increasingly composed of visited film sites and locations, not of ecologically sustainable co-habitation.

Maintaining systemic competition between suppliers, and between creatives bargaining for employment on projects secured by suppliers, also maintains the critical differences between suppliers that buyers can parley into profit. Differences are key sources of wealth, but from the standpoint of major studios, those differences must be reduced to numbers, not qualities. Factors such as tax regimes, transaction and translation costs can be accounted for. It is almost a given that quality can be dictated at the level of contracts, and that suppliers are legally obliged to provide the same quality, so that costs become the critical factor in purchasing. Buyers – the studios – need only concentrate therefore on price, and on ensuring that suppliers are kept in a position of weakness in order to maintain buyer control (Skilton 2014). This practice, however, combined with the brevity of contracts in a project-based industry, leads to the situation described by Jennifer Loy:

> The stresses of a condensed time frame for project delivery, and the bespoke nature of the props and construction required, driven by management teams often brought specifically for a project, mean it is likely there is little appetite for pre-empting regulatory change by collaboratively updating industry practices.
>
> *(2020, 46)*

The reduction of difference in price is integral to the exclusion of environmental concerns from both film industry economics and its aesthetics.

Conclusion: Supply Chain Aesthetics

Films tend to disguise their production under the veneer of entertainment (taken in the broadest sense to include the spectrum from amusement to profundity that characterises escapist and utopian, emotional and intellectual, poetic, and political pleasures of cinema). Similarly, producers externalize the economic and ecological effects of film-*making* from the experience of viewing movies. Ecocritical examination needs to unearth the hidden dimensions folded into the paradise garden of a given film. Jennifer Fay's analysis of Buster Keaton's

Steamboat Bill Jr. (1928) (2018, 23–58) and Hunter Vaughan's of *Singin' in the Rain* (Gene Kelley and Stanley Donen, 1952) (2019, 71–90) are exemplary of studies that approach the materialities of film not as enclosed in the aesthetics of formalism that attends only to the audiovisual fabric of the movie and, in some instances, the viewer's engagement in it, but as extending to what we know about a film when we see it, and what we find out about it subsequently. This form of critique is not solely about interpretation. Film analysis is interminable, although an ecological frame does lead the inquiry in particular directions. On the one hand, there is no end to the connections cinema must make to the world that produces it and the world that receives it. Any one act of analysis is, on the other hand, finite; we chose what to attend to and for how long. If we were to expand the concept of supply chains metaphorically, then the entire history of the world and its cultures exist, as Stéphane Mallarmé might have said, to complete themselves in a movie. Restricting ourselves to the geopolitical economy of global supply chains in the movie industry since the beginning of this century is already a vast enough topic. The fact that audiences cannot clearly see or hear supply chains on screen or in the soundtrack should be itself an object of inquiry.

An audience must begin with what we hear and see, using the skills we have acquired from film viewing in various modes (theatres, televisions, handhelds, etc.) and the traditions of film criticism to take a step back from the entertainment and our enjoyment of it to see how it operates materially in the here and now. As we have developed our understanding of the tools of narrative, imaging and scoring for more than a century and learned to analyse continuity and synchronisation, so we need now to learn to unpick compositing. And as audiences learned to trace the history of studios, directors and stars, now we need to track the new configuration of transnational film production and distribution. Just as special effects inspired fan cultures fascinated by screen illusions, and continuity yielded up its secrets to close readings of editing practice, so too the disjunctures of supply chains will become increasingly apparent as we track locations – often quietly referred to in credit sequences with acknowledgement to regional film bodies and government schemes – and pick up on suppliers of visual and special effects listed on easily accessed professional sites and the trade press. There will be harder roads to travel where ecological impacts are concerned; few trade reporters and very few corporate employees are interested in these aspects of sustainability, not least because the only route to addressing them, global organization, would wreck the economics of micro-differences in working conditions. In this light, it is clear that unionisation and environmental protection are equally at odds with the supply chain strategy of anarchic competition. Film appreciation and film aesthetics cannot be separated from either struggle.

In a time when apocalyptic forces of war, pestilence, and famine tie us ever more closely to a planet in crisis, this chapter cannot but convey the sense that economies and ecologies are time-critical as well as geographical. Many global leaders admit their weakness in the face of a system that gives them no leeway to bring about change. The entrenched power of fossil-based industries, whose CEOs claim they too are powerless in the face of market forces, overpowers governments. Commerce itself fails preposterously to plan for its own destruction (Collier et al. 2021). Capital no longer operates according to the will of even the world's 2,153 kleptocrats, who own more wealth than the poorest 60% of the planet's population (Oxfam 2020). The alienation enacted on and by screens has to be unpicked, with patient labor, so that we humans do not find ourselves crushed in a pincer movement between two seemingly unstoppable forces: a cyborg economy out of control and a planet rebelling against market anarchy. Ecocritical film studies, like any other niche, are intimately connected to the economic, political, technical, and ecological forces that give it its object and sustain its activities. By intervening in the intervals left vulnerable by the inevitable incompleteness of cinematic illusion on screen and in the experience of the viewer, we can begin to lever open a cultural and organizational pathway to ending the catastrophic impasse of the present. We should learn from the disastrous logistics of the cinematic supply chain how to design intelligent and collaborative human–technical–ecological logistics of our own.

Works Cited

Acland, Charles R. 2003. *Screen Traffic: Movies, Multiplexes and Global Culture.* Durham: Duke University Press.

Amuzu, David. 2018. "Environmental Injustice of Informal E-Waste Recycling in Agbogbloshie-Accra." *Urban Political Ecology Perspective. Local Environment* 23.6: 603–618.

Austin, Madeleine. 2021. "Film Industry Makes Bold Pitch for Canberra to Be Australia's Next Hub for Producing Feature Films." *ABC News.* July 9, 2021. https://www.abc.net.au/news/2021-07-09/sound-stage-to-set-canberra-up-as-feature-film-hub/100278742. Accessed 1 November 2021.

Axon, Samuel. 2020. "The Mandalorian Was Shot on a Holodeck-Esque Set with Unreal Engine, Video Shows." *Ars Technica.* February 22, 2020. https://arstechnica.com/gaming/2020/02/the-mandalorian-was-shot-on-a-holodeck-esque-set-with-unreal-engine-video-shows/

Baidya, Rahul, Biswajit Debnath, Sadhan Kumar Ghosh, and Seung-Whee Rhee. 2020. "Supply Chain Analysis of E-Waste Processing Plants in Developing Countries." *Waste Management & Research.* 38.2: 173–183.

Basel Action Network. 2002. "Exporting Harm: The High-Tech Trashing of Asia." http://www.ban.org/E-waste/technotrashfinalcomp.pdf. Retrieved 17 March, 2009.

Basel Action Network. 2005. "The Digital Dump: Exporting High-Tech Re-Use and Abuse to Africa." http://www.ban.org/BANreports/10-24-05/index.htm. Retrieved 17 March, 2009.

BFI. 2020. *A Screen New Deal: A Route Map to Sustainable Film Production.* London: BFI.

Çalışkan, Koray and Michel Callon. 2009. "Economization, Part 1: Shifting Attention from the Economy towards Processes of Economization." *Economy and Society* 38.3: 369–398.

Callon, Michel. 2006. "What Does It Mean to Say That Economics Is Performative?" CSI Working Papers Series 005. <halshs-00091596>. Reprinted in *Do Economists Make Markets?: On the Performativity of Economics*. 2007, edited by Donald MacKenzie, Fabian Muniesa, and Lucia Siu, 311–356. Princeton: Princeton University Press.

Cavell, Stanley. 1979 [1971]. *The World Viewed*. Enlarged edition. Cambridge: Harvard University Press.

Chan, Kenneth. 2012. "Asia." In *The Wiley-Blackwell History of American Film. Volume IV: American Film, 1976 to the Present*, edited by Cynthia Lucia, Roy Grundmann, and Art Simon, 406–426. New York: Wiley-Blackwell.

Chow, Thomas. 2020. "Hollywood in China: A New Film Central – Opportunities and Challenges for International Filmmakers in China." *US-China Today*. July 14, 2020. https://uschinatoday.org/features/2020/07/14/hollywood-in-china/

Collier, Stephen J., Rebecca Elliott, and Turo-Kimmo Lehtonen, eds. 2021. "Special Section: Climate Change and Insurance." *Economy and Society* 50.2: 158–296.

Container Management. 2021. "IMO Accused of "Greenwashing" by Environmental Campaigners. Container Management 21 June." https://container-mag.com/2021/06/21/imo-accused-of-greenwashing-by-climate-campaigners/. Accessed 4 November 2021.

Cripps, Karla and Kocha Olarn. 2019. "Thailand Bay Made Popular by 'The Beach' to Remain Closed for Two More Years." *CNN*, May 11, 2019. https://edition.cnn.com/travel/article/thailand-maya-bay-reopening-date/index.html

Crisp, Virgina. 2015. *Film Distribution in the Digital Age: Pirates and Professionals*. London: Palgrave.

Cubitt, Sean. 2019. "Mediating Xinjiang: For an Aesthetic Politics." *Journal of Asia-Pacific Pop Culture* 4.1: 5–25.

Curtin, Michael, Jennifer Holt, and Kevin Sanson, eds. 2014. *Distribution Revolution: Conversations about the Digital Future of Film and Television*. Berkeley: University of California Press.

Curtin, Michael and Kevin Sanson, eds. 2016. *Precarious Creativity: Global Media, Local Labor*. Berkeley: University of California Press.

Curtin, Michael and Kevin Sanson, eds. 2017. *Voices of Labor: Creativity, Craft, and Conflict in Global Hollywood*. Berkeley: University of California Press.

Davies, William. 2017. "Moral Economies of the Future: The Utopian Impulse of Sustainable Prosperity." CUSP Working Paper No 5. Guildford: University of Surrey. https://cusp.ac.uk/wp-content/uploads/WP05-WD-2017-Moral-Economies-of-the-Future.pdf

Deneault, Tessa Perkins. 2021. "The Growing Carbon Footprint of Streaming Media." *Phys.org.* July 27, 2021. https://phys.org/news/2021-07-carbon-footprint-streaming-media.html

Dickinson, Kay. 2020 "Make It What You Want It to Be: Logistics, Labor, and Land Financialization via the Globalized Free Zone Studio." In *In the Studio: Visual Creation and Its Material Environments*, edited by Brian R. Jacobson, 261–280. Berkeley: University of California Press.

Dickinson, Kay. 2021. "Supply Chain Cinema, Supply Chain Education: Training Creative Wizadry for Offshore Exploitation." In *Assembly Codes: The Logistics of Media*, edited by Matthew Hockenberry, Nicole Starosielski, and Susan Zieger, 171–187. Durham: Duke University Press.

Fay, Jennifer. 2018. *Inhospitable World: Cinema in the Time of the Anthropocene.* London: Oxford University Press.

Foucault, Michel. 2010. *The Government of the Self and Others: Lectures at the Collège de France 1982–1983*, edited by Frédéric Gros. Translated by Graham Burchell. Basingstoke: Palgrave Macmillan.

Gabrys, Jennifer. 2010. *Digital Rubbish: A Natural History of Electronics.* Ann Arbor: University of Michigan Press.

Grossman, Elizabeth. 2007. *High Tech Trash: Digital Devices, Hidden Toxics, and Human Health.* Washington, DC: Shearwater.

Hopewell, John. 2020. "'Mandalorian'-Style Virtual Technology Sound Stage Orca Studios Opens in Spain." *Variety*, June 3, 2020. https://variety.com/2020/tv/global/mandalorian-style-led-volume-orca-studios-opens-spain-1234624036/. Accessed 1 November 2021.

IEA. 2021. "Global Energy Review 2021: Assessing the Effects of Economic Recoveries on Global Energy Demand and CO_2 Emissions in 2021." Paris: International Energy Agency.

Law, Lisa, Tim Bunnell, and Chin-Ee Ong. 2007. "The Beach, the Gaze and Film Tourism." *Tourism Studies* 7.2: 141–164.

Lobato, Ramon. 2019. *Netflix Nations: The Geography of Network Distribution.* New York: New York University Press.

Lobato, Ramon and Amanda D. Lotz. 2020. "Imagining Global Video: The Challenge of Netflix." *Journal of Cinema and Media Studies* 59.3: 132–136.

Lotz, Amanda D. 2014. *The Television Will Be Revolutionised* (Second Edition). New York: New York University Press.

Lotz, Amanda D. 2018. *We Now Disrupt This Broadcast: How Cable Transformed Television and the Internet Revolutionized It All.* Cambridge: MIT Press.

Loy, Jennifer. 2020. "Project-Based Supply Chain Intelligence and Digital Fabrication for a Sustainable Film Industry." In *Supply Chain Intelligence – Application and Optimization*, edited by Kaushik Kumar and J. Paulo Davim, 37–59. Cham: Springer.

Mah, Alice. 2021. "Toxic Legacies and Environmental Justice." In *Environmental Justice: Key Issues*, edited by Brendan Coolsaet, 121–131. New York: Routledge.

Mann, Adam. 2021. "Starlink: SpaceX's Satellite Internet Project." *Space.com*, May 29. https://www.space.com/spacex-starlink-satellites.html. Accessed 31 October 2021.

Marks, Laura U., et al. 2020. "Streaming Media's Environmental Impact." *Media+Environment* 2.1. https://doi.org/10.1525/001c.17242.

McDonald, Paul, Courtney Brannon Donoghue, and Timothy Havens, eds. 2021. *Digital Media Distribution: Portals, Platforms, Pipelines.* New York: New York University Press.

Medovoi, Leerom. 2009. "A Contribution to the Critique of Political Ecology: Sustainability as Disavowal." *New Formations* 69: 129–143.

Mezzadra, Sandro and Brett Neilson. 2019. *The Politics of Operations: Excavating Contemporary Capitalism.* Durham: Duke University Press.

Miller, Toby, Nitin Govil, John McMurria, and Richard Maxwell. 2001. *Global Hollywood.* London: BFI.

Miller, Toby, Nitin Govil, John McMurria, Richard Maxwell, and Ting Wang. 2005. *Global Hollywood 2.* London: BFI.

Nost, Eric and Jenny Elaine Goldstein, eds. 2022. Theme Issue: Politics of Environmental Data. *Environment and Planning E: Nature and Space* 5.1: 3–145.

Oxfam Canada. 2020. "Time to Care: Unpaid and Underpaid Care Work and the Global Inequality Crisis." Oxford: Oxfam. https://www.oxfam.ca/publication/35449/

Plant, Raymond. 2009. *The Neo-Liberal State*. Oxford: Oxford University Press.

Richeri, Giuseppe. 2020. "The Audiovisual Industry and the Structural Factors of the Television Crisis." In *A Companion to Television* (Second Edition), edited by Janet Wasko and Eileen R. Meehan, 129–144. New York: Wiley-Blackwell.

Rossiter, Ned. 2021. "Logistical Media Theory, the Politics of Time, and the Geopolitics of Automation." In *Assembly Codes: The Logistics of Media*, edited by Matthew Hockenberry, Nicole Starosielski, and Susan Zieger, 132–150. Durham: Duke University Press.

Sekula, Allan. 1995. *Fish Story*. Rotterdam: Witte de With. Düsseldorf: Richter Verlag.

Skilton, Paul F. 2014. "Value Creation, Value Capture and Supply Chain Structure: Understanding Resource-Based Advantage in a Project-Based Industry." *Journal of Supply Chain Management* 50.3: 74–93.

Starosielski, Nicole. 2021. "The Politics of Cable Supply from the British Empire to Huawei Marine." In *Assembly Codes: The Logistics of Media*, edited by Matthew Hockenberry, Nicole Starosielski, and Susan Zieger, 190–205. Durham: Duke University Press.

Steinhart, Daniel. 2019. *Runaway Hollywood: Internationalizing Postwar Production and Location Shooting*. Berkeley: University of California Press.

Sweeney, Mark. 2021. "Streaming's Dirty Secret: How Viewing Netflix Top 10 Creates Vast Quantity of CO_2." *The Guardian*. October 29, 2021. https://www.theguardian.com/tv-and-radio/2021/oct/29/streamings-dirty-secret-how-viewing-netflix-top-10-creates-vast-quantity-of-co2. Accessed 30 October 2021.

Szasz, Andrew. 1994. *EcoPopulism: Toxic Waste and the Movement for Environmental Justice*. Minneapolis: University of Minnesota Press.

Teo, Stephen. 2009. *Chinese Martial Arts Cinema: The Wuxia Tradition*. Edinburgh: Edinburgh University Press.

The Carbon Trust. 2021. *Carbon Impact of Video Streaming* [White Paper]. London: The Carbon Trust. https://www.carbontrust.com/resources/carbon-impact-of-video-streaming. Accessed 21 June, 2022.

Tsing, Anna. 2009. "Supply Chains and the Human Condition." *Rethinking Marxism* 21.2: 148–176.

Turner, Graeme and Jinna Tay. 2009. "Part One – What Is Television: Introduction." In *Television Studies after TV: Understanding Television in the Post-Broadcast Era*, edited by Graeme Turner and Jinna Tay, 7–8. London: Routledge.

Undseth, Marit, Claire Jolly, and Mattia Olivari. 2020. "Space Sustainability: The Economics of Space Debris in Perspective." OECD Science, Technology and Industry Policy Papers, No. 87, Paris: OECD Publishing. https://doi.org/10.1787/a339de43-en.

Vaughan, Hunter. 2019. *Hollywood's Dirtiest Secret: The Hidden Environmental Costs of the Movies*. New York: Columbia University Press.

Yeh, Emilie Yueh-yu and Shi-yan Chao. 2018. "Policy and Creative Strategies: Hong Kong CEPA Films in the China Market." *International Journal of Cultural Policy* 26.2: 109–123.

2

GREENING MEXICAN CINEMA

Carolyn Fornoff

In the summer of 2021, a snappy Mexican web series debuted on YouTube titled *El tema* (*The Issue*), organized around the tagline "el tema es el clima" (the issue is the climate). Spearheaded by movie star Gael García Bernal in collaboration with climate activist Pablo Montaño Beckmann, the series makes the case that climate change is "el tema," *the issue* that Mexico faces in the twenty-first century. Each of the six ten-minute episodes is oriented around a specific topic (another possible translation for *tema*) and place: from water in Chihuahua to carbon in Coahuila. In each installment, García Bernal and his co-host, Mixe public intellectual Yásnaya Elena Aguilar Gil, guide viewers through the issues, speaking on the ground with activists, scientists, and engaged citizens. The series mobilizes tropes characteristic of contemporary eco-documentary, like García Bernal's star power and aerial shots of denuded forests, to make the case that the environmental crisis has not yet received enough mainstream attention in Mexico, while at the same time highlighting the relentless efforts of those already advocating for better presents and futures for their communities.

Most interesting for the purposes of this chapter is *El tema*'s format. Two decisions, in particular, stand out. First, even though its content collectively clocks in around 90 minutes, *El tema* was not released as a feature-length film, but as a series of bite-sized episodes. Second, *El tema* debuted directly on YouTube rather than through distribution channels commonplace to Mexican environmentalist cinema such as specialized festivals, art house movie theaters, or cable TV. Often, YouTube, or Vimeo, is the final destination for such films, where they are uploaded either licitly or illicitly to reach a wider range of public after traversing the festival circuit. Yet thanks to backing from its production house, La Corriente del Golfo, *El tema* shortcut this circuitous route, landing directly online, where it was released in free weekly installments between

DOI: 10.4324/9781003246602-4

April and May of 2021. This distribution strategy maximized the series' reach, enabling viewers to easily share it with their networks on social media. As of December 2021, the first episode had garnered over 85,000 views, a sizeable audience for the genre of Mexican eco-documentary.

La Corriente del Golfo's decision to produce and distribute *El tema* as a web series responded not only to ongoing pandemic-related health concerns associated with enclosed exhibition venues in the summer of 2021 but also to the realities of film consumption in twenty-first century Mexico. Although Mexico has the world's fourth largest film exhibition infrastructure in terms of the sheer number of screens, 90% of movie theaters in Mexico are owned by just two companies, Cinépolis and Cinemex (Rosas Mantecón 2017, 235). As a result of the deregulation of film distribution codified into law by NAFTA, these companies are beholden to contracts that require that nearly 90% of screened films are Hollywood productions. This arrangement allows Hollywood to leverage captive global markets in places like Mexico to recoup costs for domestic flops like *Sonic the Hedgehog*, the most widely seen movie in theaters in Mexico in 2020 (IMCINE 2020, 88). Cinépolis and Cinemex theaters are consolidated in urban, upper-middle-class neighborhoods. The elevated cost of a movie ticket, ~70% of a day's earnings on minimum wage, accounts for the saturated spatialization of exhibition infrastructure. All of this has made moviegoing in twenty-first century Mexico highly regionalized and classed, or what Juan Llamas-Rodríguez characterizes as a globalized luxury experience (2019). By contrast, most Mexicans consume Mexican cinema on television, pirated DVDs, BitTorrent downloads, or YouTube. In this context, *El tema*'s free online distribution was a choice that aligned with its activist messaging of environmental justice as an intersectional issue of equity and access. Even so, access to high-speed internet capable of streaming content like *El tema* is far from democratic in Mexico, mapping onto similar spatialized socioeconomic inequities. Considering environmental media like *El tema* in tandem with the infrastructures of film distribution helps bring into focus a key question about ecocinema: who is it for? And what does the increasingly atomized consumption of cinema mean for the environment?

Taking *El tema* as its point of departure, this chapter argues that thinking about ecocinema in Latin America requires that scholars not only reckon with questions of representation but also with questions of praxis and industry, that is, with the material realities of film production, distribution, and exhibition. Within the field of Latin American film studies, these questions have been siloed. The growing body of scholarship that attends to environmental cinema and media in Latin America has primarily focused on how cinema helps visualize and narrate environmental crises. Such a focus sheds light on how cinema operates in tandem with environmental activism or makes nonextractivist ontologies palpable (Forns-Broggi 2013; Marcone 2015). Yet when we think about the relationship between the environment and cinema, it isn't just representation that matters. Scholars of ecocinema are increasingly interrogating the materiality of cinema as an industry, a move that recognizes that cinema is "culturally *and* materially embedded" (Rust and Monani 2013, 3). Illustrative of this material turn is Jussi Parikka's use of the portmanteau "medianatures" to underscore that these two terms are inextricable and co-constitutive; media does not just shed light on nature, it is made possible by nature and leaves long-lasting material legacies in its wake (Parikka 2012).

The fact that the minerals and raw materials that have made cinema possible have been largely sourced from the Global South makes thinking about materiality particularly relevant for scholars of Latin American cinema. Here I follow Cajetan Iheka's observations about Africa, where the promise of media—as a mechanism of cultural expression and critique, as connective of peoples and cultures, and as a sign of modernity—coexists with the devastating realities of its ecological costs and consequences. The tension between "the possibilities and problematics of media," Iheka posits, is central to rethinking "ethical living and media production in a time of finite resources" (2021, 3–4). The same is true in the context of Latin America, where cinema has diversified and proliferated as the technologies of filmmaking and film watching have become more portable and affordable, opening the field to historically marginalized filmmakers, and allowing viewers to engage with content that has been sidelined by the mainstream media (like *El tema*) without needing to traverse formal distribution routes, bringing important conversations about environmental justice to new viewers. At the same time, the global transformation of exhibition infrastructure from collective consumption in movie theaters to individual, private consumption through handheld devices, laptops, or flat-screen TVs, brings with it additional socioecological consequences for Latin America that have yet to be foregrounded by scholars.

While there has yet to be a rigorous ecocritical accounting of "the possibilities and problematics of media" (to borrow Iheka's terms) in Latin America, the field has long attended to the structures of coloniality and uneven global dynamics embedded in cinema. Industry studies scholars have demonstrated that cinema, like other industries, operates within national and transnational flows of culture and capital (Falicov 2019). On a parallel track, Marxist scholars have shed light on cinema's social reach, as well as its dependence on institutional infrastructures of the state and of capital. If a recurrent question for Marxist interpretation has been the relationship between cinema and socioeconomic conditions, ecocritical engagements with this tradition extend such questions to the role of resource extractivism in these circuits. Recent examples of such work include Santiago Acosta's (2020) consideration of how the influx of oil in the seventies transformed Venezuelan cultural production, Sebastián Figueroa's (2022) discussion of the overlap between nitrate extraction in Chile and the global emergence of cinema, and Héctor Hoyos' (2018) argument that centering the materiality of cultural production "cultivates a different ethos… one of thinking with, not past, imbrication" to elucidate embodied, uneven global relations of production (114). Following such efforts, this chapter interrogates how thinking *materially* about Mexican cinema—in both the ecocritical and Marxist senses of the word—reveals the organizing forms of production and consumption that film fosters.

In what follows, I lay out an abbreviated materialist sketch of Mexican cinema. First, I examine how the infrastructures of cinema have intersected with those of oil. I then turn to access, the biggest problem facing Mexican cinema today. I ask what is lost when cinema becomes increasingly atomized through consumption regimes that mimic capitalism's focus on surplus and the individual. Finally, I look at Cine Móvil ToTo, a post-carbon cinema exhibition initiative that makes visible the connections between cultural consumption and energy production.

Cinema and Energy

The fourth episode of *El tema*, "Energía," ("Energy") focuses on the coastal state of Tabasco, home to numerous oil fields and the under-construction Dos Bocas refinery managed by state-owned oil company Petróleos Mexicanos (Pemex). The episode narrates how Pemex has transformed the region into a sacrifice zone: endangering mangroves, polluting waterways, and jeopardizing fishing. A title card explains that climate change compounds this vulnerability; sea level rise threatens to flood nearly a quarter of the state over the next 30 years, including the controversial Dos Bocas refinery. This juxtaposition underscores the impasse between short-term investment in energy infrastructure and the territory's long-term future, jeopardized by the very emissions that this infrastructure makes possible. The episode highlights local efforts to combat regional foreclosure, including the restoration of mangroves (a key regulator of flooding) and advocacy for renewables. As host Yásnaya Elena Aguilar Gil explains, these activists promote "alternative forms of clean energy that might be managed other ways, not just through capitalism or the state," but through small-scale, community-driven initiatives like solar power that "bet on life," rather than death. The episode calls upon the audience to join in this collective task of post-carbon imagining of infrastructure that might sustain life in Tabasco.

El tema illustrates how cinema can shed light on the socioenvironmental toll of extractivism and amplify activist calls to imagine energy sovereignty beyond fossil fuels. But what if we reverse the terms of this equation? Rather than consider how cinema illuminates energy, how might thinking with energy allows us to see cinema differently? And how might the call for post-carbon energy production coincide with the imperative to reimagine the distribution and production of cinema? Such questions signal an "opportunity to think through what the age of oil brought us, what we want to salvage and maintain, and where we want to work to construct more equitable and just social relations," as the Petrocultures Research Group puts it (2016, 16).

There is much to be gained by considering the structural ties between Mexican cinema and state oil revenues (Fornoff 2021). While to a less comprehensive extent than in countries like Venezuela or Nigeria, oil has buoyed cultural production in Mexico. Ever since the industry was nationalized in 1938—a radical gesture that wrested control of subsoil resources from U.S. oil companies back to the people of Mexico—hydrocarbons have underpinned dreams of national development. Pemex has functioned "as the government's cash cow," steadily providing close to 40% of the federal government's operating revenue (Hernández Ibarzábal, and Bonilla 2020, 672). This financial reliance on subsoil energy reserves means that any state-funded enterprises, including cultural industries, are enmeshed in the waxing and waning of global energy prices and supply. Put differently, oil has mediated the shape and scope of cultural industries in Mexico.

Like other countries in Latin America and around the world, the Mexican film industry has been historically sustained by state funding. However, since the 1980s, the private sector has gained a strong foothold. Today, only about half of all Mexican productions receive some form of state support (IMCINE 2021). The neoliberal shift of the film industry away from public funding was triggered by the 1982 debt crisis catalyzed by plummeting global oil prices and demand, which punishingly hit Mexico because of its economic reliance on oil exports and its indebtedness to investments in costly extractive technologies.

In the wake of the oil crisis, the Mexican film industry was radically transformed by austerity measures. Up until that point, cinema in Mexico was characterized by "a sprawling State-centered infrastructure, sustained by a network of government-owned theaters, strict controls on ticket prices, mandated percentages of screen time for Mexican films, and vast subsidies for film production" (Sánchez Prado 2014, 6). This infrastructure reinforced a philosophy of cinema as a shared social and cultural experience that cut-across demographic and geographic differences, which transmuted as the industry underwent privatization. The deregulation of film admission prices, domestic distribution quotas, and exhibition management was later codified into law by NAFTA (North American Free Trade Agreement). As a result, the cost of attending a movie became prohibitively expensive for large swathes of the population. Ignacio Sánchez Prado has shown how these changes radically altered the trajectory of Mexican cinema, shifting its content to appeal to urban upper-middle class consumers who could afford to attend the movies.

Stratification and Access

One of the weightiest consequences of the neoliberal transformation of cinema in the wake of the oil crisis has been the stratification of access. According to IMCINE's (Mexican Institute of Cinematography) 2020 *Anuario Estadístico* (Annual Statistical Report), 88% of municipalities lack a movie theater, meaning that 40 million Mexicans are unable to easily access an exhibition space. This plays out across a center-*provincia* divide, with nearly a quarter of the nation's exhibition infrastructure located in Mexico City. Even within Mexico City, movie theaters tend to be concentrated in wealthier, centric areas, reflecting the tacit reframing of filmgoing as an activity for the middle and upper classes. In a recent assessment of this situation, the Cedecine (Community of Cinematographic Exhibition) Research Commission described "access" as "the most serious problem facing Mexican cinema," noting that most domestic film releases only debut in specialized theaters in upscale areas of Mexico City (IMCINE 2021, 138).

Stratification similarly characterizes Mexican films with environmentalist content, a genre that has exploded since 2010. One indicator of this stratification is the high levels of rural representation in Mexican environmental films that are made by, and circulate among, urban publics. What explains this disjuncture? Because unprecedented drought, deforestation, and extreme weather events are most keenly felt and readily visible in rural Mexico, Mexican environmental documentaries have tended to profile rural spaces and peoples. Feature-length films like *Cuates de Australia* (*Drought*, Everardo González, 2013), *Los hombres del pueblo que no existe* (*The Kings of Nowhere*, Betzabé García, 2015), *El Remolino* (*The Swirl*, Laura Herrero Garvin, 2016), and *Resurrección* (*Resurrection*, Eugenio Polgovsky, 2016), document developmentalism's harmful socioenvironmental impact on rural towns and highlight the efforts of those that choose or are forced to stay in situations of environmental crisis. These well-crafted films have been successful on both the domestic and international festival circuits, as well as at specialized environmentalist film festivals.

Despite the powerful representation performed by these films to raise awareness of the struggles of those who have been dispossessed or un-imagined by the state and global capital, the fact remains that rural peoples are largely unable to access exhibition spaces to see such films. Thus, while documentaries like these might be lauded for their ability to capture and communicate environmental crises, thinking at the level of exhibition infrastructure underscores how regimes of seeing are made possible for some and not for others. The above makes sense when we consider that the infrastructures of development that have caused environmental crises (oil pipelines, hydroelectric dams, deforestation, industrial contamination) have been imposed on the same areas where the infrastructures of film exhibitions have been removed. Cinema is therefore not just a modality of critique of the inequities that are structural to extractive capital, but it retraces and reifies these inequities through its transnational flows and infrastructures of production and consumption.

Another way of getting at the material tensions that characterize contemporary environmental cinema is by considering the proliferation of handheld devices for filmmaking and film watching. On the one hand, the expansion of affordable portable devices has made filmmaking more democratic (Arenillas and Lazzara 2016, 1). The explosion of Latin American documentary features and shorts dedicated to environmental issues can be linked to increased access to cheap filmmaking equipment, editing software, and so on, all of which have made it easier for neophytes and historically marginalized filmmakers to bypass traditional funding and production routes that have favored well-educated, urban, white men. On the other hand, the expansion of low-cost electronic equipment with short lifespans is correlated to the exponential growth of electronic waste (e-waste). The overwhelmingly informal disposal of e-waste in Latin America is accompanied by a slew of ills for the environment and human health, exposing the industry's laborers and their communities to harmful heavy metals. The transnational dynamics of e-waste disposal rehearse entrenched imperial logics, tracing an inverse trajectory that mirrors the extraction of minerals from the Global South that is the condition of possibility for industries like Hollywood. Mexico, for instance, is the primary global exporter of flat-screen TVs, and the top importer of used or defunct electronics like smartphones from the United States (Saldaña-Durán et al. 2020, 422). To think then with the global rise of streaming and smartphones in the twenty-first century as a technology with which to make and watch media also entails thinking about where these devices originate and end up: where they are shipped, sorted, resold, repurposed, deboned, smelted, and dumped. It is also to consider the environmental affects of media as not only effectively moving viewers to care about the environment through pathos but also as materially touching waste-workers, informal recyclers, and their families.

The steep decline of exhibition spaces in rural Mexico and the increased availability of handheld devices inevitably leads to the question of whether streaming has filled, or will fill, this void of exhibition access. Indeed, the expansion of information and communications technology infrastructures throughout Mexico has made the contemporary cinematic experience increasingly digital—as we see with *El tema* on YouTube, or with the state-run streaming platform FilminLatino, where many eco-documentaries and other domestic art house films can be viewed for an affordable fee. And yet telecommunications infrastructures and exhibition infrastructures are characterized by similar imbalances. According to INEGI (National Institute of Statistics and Geography), internet access in Mexico continues to operate along an urban-rural divide. Only 19% of homes in rural Mexico report internet connections, while 50% of rural inhabitants report internet access on their mobile devices (compared to 78% of urban inhabitants), which likely correlates to the increased availability of affordable or repurposed smartphones (INEGI 2021). Complicating the adoption of streaming are poor connection speeds, which are particularly problematic in southern Mexico, like the state of Tabasco that *El tema* profiles. What is worth underscoring here is that content like *El tema*, even with its democratic distribution strategy on YouTube, continues to primarily reach audiences that are Other to the subjects depicted on screen.

So what does the decline of movie theaters and the upswing in handheld devices mean for the film-watching experience and its ecological footprint? In her panoramic assessment of exhibition in Mexico, Ana Rosas Mantecón is quick to point out that cinema has not always been a collective experience. Cinematic precursors like the magic lantern and the kinetoscope were designed for individual viewership (Rosas Mantecón 2017, 19). And yet the contemporary global shift in film distribution and exhibition away from the theater and toward streaming is not only a return to a more atomized, stratified viewing experience but is also incomparably more carbon-intensive. In their discussion of the high level of emissions associated with high-resolution streaming, Laura U. Marks and Radek Przedpelski posit that although streaming is often described as decolonizing cinema in that it facilitates access to historically marginalized cinemas, in fact, the universalization of streaming is a form of "bandwidth imperialism" or prescriptive imposition of a resource-intensive model of cultural production and consumption (Marks and Przedpelski 2021). High-resolution streaming is a distribution model premised on the fantasy of limitless capacity and the denial of data's material costs. Marks and Przedpelski suggest that rather than take streaming as the gold standard that should be adopted by the Global South, the Global North should follow the lead of Global South filmmakers who have experimented with low-resolution, small file aesthetics. The future of cinema in the era of climate change, then, should be modeled on the ideals of equity in terms of access, as well as in terms of environmental footprint.

In Mexico, both cinema and infrastructure have been conceptualized as tangible signs of modernity. As this abbreviated account has shown, these two forms of production have frequently operated in tandem—with oil bolstering cultural industries, and cultural industries reinforcing the values of petroculture (consumption, growth, extractivism). The shrinking of exhibition infrastructure that has accompanied the waning of oil reserves underscores the contingent correlation between these two forms. Untangling the knot of cinema and oil, to take *El Tema'*s call one step further, requires conjuring up new forms of infrastructure and culture. Following Marks and Przedpelski's call for small-file media, Nadia Bozak's discussion of Inuk filmmaking as already modeling "an ecologically sound means of making and distributing digitally captured media" (2012, 192), and Cajetan Iheka's praise for Africa's "imperfect media" that illustrates "the creative, improvisational, and experimental impulses that scarcity engenders" (2021, 224), I turn to Cine Móvil ToTo as an example of how post-carbon cinema is being imagined in Mexico.

Exhibition for a Post-Carbon World

In response to the neoliberal consolidation of film exhibitions and the consequent crisis of access, communities, nonprofits, and filmmakers have patched together alternative exhibition infrastructures. Freya Schiwy explains that activists invested in reaching marginalized film audiences distribute their films in ways that blend "older with newer production and delivery platforms… screened in community centers; broadcast on terrestrial television; or streamed on YouTube, Vimeo, Indymedia, or other internet sites" (2019, 5). Cine Móvil ToTo is an analogous initiative that borrows established tactics from ambulant theater and updates them for the post-oil future.

Cine Móvil ToTo is a nonprofit that seeks to redress the lack of film distribution in rural Mexico and simultaneously decarbonize exhibitions. It does so by bringing bike-powered, open-air film screenings of Mexican movies to rural communities that lack movie theaters or streaming capabilities. Founded by Roberto Serrano and Diego Torres in 2013, Cine Móvil ToTo took off in 2019, when corporate sponsorships enabled them to scale up their efforts from 20 annual ambulant screenings to over 200 (Ramírez 2020). The organization's mission to bring Mexican cinema to rural populations was based on Torres' previous experience with Cine en tu Comunidad (Cinema in your Community), a now-defunct IMCINE (i.e. state-funded) ambulant exhibition program that similarly aimed to expand access to Mexican cinema. Serrano and Torres's twist on this model was to power it with renewable energy.[1] Serrano and Torres explain that the bike-powered model of Cine Móvil ToTo was inspired by a documentary, *Ginger Ninjas: Rodando México* (*Ginger Ninjas: Touring Mexico*, Sergio Morkin, 2012), about a rock band that toured California and Mexico by bike. The Ginger Ninjas used bikes to power their concerts, involving the audience in pedaling to charge the band's generators. To adapt this model for the exhibition, Serrano and Torres hired the band's engineer, Dante Espinosa, to create their first bike-converter prototype, funded through crowdsourcing in 2013 (Ramírez 2020).

The basic operations of Cine Móvil ToTo are as follows. A van-based team conducts regional tours with prescheduled stops for screenings in towns and villages. In conjunction with local governments and community organizations, the ToTo team determines the best space for the screening, typically a public plaza or open-air sports court with enough room to project a film for a seated audience. The outdoor nature of these venues has been a plus as Cine Móvil ToTo has continued to operate during the COVID-19 pandemic, in contrast with many traditional exhibition venues that have closed. The host community provides seating for the show in the form of benches or chairs. At the front of the audience, ToTo sets up four stationary bicycles. In advance of and during the show, community members, often children, pedal the bikes to power the exhibition equipment (Figure 2.1).

(a)

(b)

FIGURE 2.1   A Cine Móvil ToTo screening in Tabasco in 2021. Images courtesy of Rodrigo Soto.

The ToTo team drums up viewers through prior publicity, as well as on the day of the event through a loudspeaker attached to the van affectionately called the ToToneta. Armed with a catalog sponsored by IMCINE of a dozen domestic films, the team gives a brief synopsis of the available options to the audience. The public then votes on which film to screen. Often, family-friendly films prevail, like the animated film *La leyenda de la Llorona* (*The Legend of La Llorona*, Alberto Rodríguez, 2011), since Cine Móvil ToTo tends to draw families and young people. Other films featured in the 2021 offerings included

Tio Yim (2011), a documentary by Zapotec filmmaker Luna Marán, *Alamar* (Pedro González Rubio, 2009), a fictionalized eco-doc about a father who teaches his son to fish on Mexico's largest coral reef, and *El sueño del Mara'akame* (*Mara'akame's Dream*, Federico Ceccetti, 2016), a feature film that follows a Wixaritari teen torn between his dreams of becoming a rock star and his father's plans for him become a Huichol shaman. These offerings reflect efforts by the ToTo team to select films focused on rural populations and issues. These are also films that are unlikely to reach rural villages in the form of pirated DVDs, which tend to favor bigger-budget commercial films from Hollywood and Mexican studios.

Cine Móvil ToTo is the latest iteration in a long tradition of Latin American *cines móviles* (mobile cinemas), first launched in Cuba in the 1960s. Tamara Falicov explains that the model was based on Russian agitprop trains that toured the country after the 1917 October Revolution, bringing artists and actors to rural Russians to disseminate Communist policies and propaganda. In Cuba, *cines móviles* were similarly conceived as a crucial part of Fidel Castro's nation-building project. Films and projectors were transported to remote locations by "trucks, mules, and even fishing boats," to signal the Revolution's commitment to bringing modernity to rural regions, and as "a means of communication [for the new government] with a historically disenfranchised population" (Falicov 2012, 104). The program was a success, tripling the number of film viewers in Cuba within a decade.

Cine Móvil ToTo exemplifies how the ambulant model has been refashioned in the twenty-first century, when access to cinema continues to be a huge issue, but exhibition is no longer considered within the scope of the neoliberal state. If mobile cinemas have historically functioned as a means of spreading propaganda and consolidating sentiments of national belonging, Cine Móvil ToTo continues in this tradition. The state continues to underpin the initiative, from local governments who provide lodging and permit the use of public space, which allows local politicians to tout their support of their rural constituencies, to cooperation from IMCINE, which facilitates the licensing of state-funded domestic films for distribution. By limiting the films on offer to domestic cinema, Cine Móvil ToTo justifies its alignment with IMCINE's goal of fomenting national cultural production, essentially operating as an arm of this entity by filling the space of cut programs like Cine en tu Comunidad. In this sense, Cine Móvil ToTo is symptomatic of the privatization of cinema in Mexico, in that it is a nonprofit that has stepped in to redress the state's abandonment of the distribution and exhibition of domestic cultural production.

In addition to state support, Cine Móvil ToTo relies on corporate sponsorships to finance its tours. The website pitches its benefits to potential corporate partners in a variety of ways recognizable under the rubric of green capitalism. First as a form of image branding or greenwashing: "associate your brand with social responsibility... as a friend to the environment;" "make your brand the face of the United Nations' sustainable development objectives." Second, as a means of amplifying brand visibility in hard-to-reach areas: "Each tour generates 20,000 direct engagements and these are multiplied by the press and social media coverage, resulting in 8 million impacts over the course of five months." And finally, as a way of obtaining market research: "On each tour we can conduct activities like product sampling and demonstrations, as well as surveys of the audience in each community" (Cine Móvil ToTo website, my translation).

To illustrate how this works, a 2021 tour was sponsored by Mexico's largest beermaker, Grupo Modelo, best known outside of Mexico for exporting Corona. As part of the sponsorship package, ToTo screened a sponsored educational short about responsible drinking practices prior to the main feature and conducted surveys with attendees to gauge brand favorability (Neira 2021). These sorts of corporate partnerships have allowed ToTo to expand its scope and conduct multiple tours a year. Yet they also demonstrate how experiments in alternative and post-carbon exhibition structures must negotiate with the realities of funding in the context of limited state support. Grupo Modelo's relatively small investment in funding the ToTo tour reaps the company various rewards, including increased brand visibility and the opportunity to conduct focus groups with hard-to-reach publics; it also is a way to tout their support of national cultural production and their green credentials. The sponsorship allows Grupo Modelo to self-fashion its image in a way that we might describe as green corporate nationalism. In terms of actual carbon reduction, Grupo Modelo can make a much larger impact by making internal changes to its production model and energy usage. The company is making moves to do so by embracing wind power sourced from Puebla as of 2019 (albeit in partnership with Iberdrola, a wind developer that has been involved in land disputes with Indigenous communities in Oaxaca), and has plans to be totally reliant on renewables by 2025 (Iberdrola 2017). So Grupo Modelo's partnership with Cine Móvil ToTo, while illustrative of how green cultural initiatives strategically buoy brand visibility, is not necessarily a case of greenwashing (the superficial support for carbon reduction without structural change), but it does underscore how the possibility of post-carbon cultural production cannot be romanticized as somehow existing outside of neoliberal dynamics in which the infrastructures of culture are financed by capital.

Let's turn back to Cine Móvil ToTo. The bicycle is at the center of Cine Móvil ToTo's pitch to "green" expanded access to Mexican cinema, as the website puts it, "through the simple but powerful pedaling of a bicycle." Company imagery also orbits around the bicycle. In the logo, the two o's of "ToTo" are rendered as bike wheels that abstractly connect to a projection bulb through a looping yellow cord (Figure 2.2). This discursive and visual framing foregrounds the bicycle as ToTo's central powering device. Yet manually operated bicycles can only produce so much energy. Each stationary bike produces around 300–600 watts per hour according to Rodrigo Soto, Cine Móvil

FIGURE 2.2 The Cine Móvil ToTo logo.

ToTo's communication director. This output varies based on human capacity, error, and distractibility—variables that are particularly salient given the high involvement of enthusiastic youth. Because of these limitations, bikes are used to power the audio console, speakers, Blu-ray, and other equipment that do not require continuous high-volume energy. The projector, by contrast, has higher energy demands (400–500 watts) and is powered by solar panels to assure its seamless operation. These solar panels are strapped to the ToToneta (the van), where they charge during the trip, and are then placed near the venue to charge in advance of the show.

The bicycle is an effective shorthand for fossil fuel alternatives: a commonplace cheap technology. The widespread use of bicycles in rural and poor communities proves that post-carbon modes of social organization already exist. To associate the bicycle with futurity and technological innovation, as Cine Móvil ToTo does in its branding, scrambles the typical collapse of modernity with high-carbon lifestyles or expensive green technologies that are nonetheless reliant on the extractivist exploitation of minerals like lithium. The insights of Marxist philosopher Bolívar Echeverría help elucidate this point. Echeverría has argued that the idea of modernity has become so subsumed by capitalism and whiteness that they seem naturally coterminous. Yet modernity demands to be reimagined beyond its contingent capitalist iteration, which promises abundance yet undercuts this promise through the exploitation of human and nonhuman life (Echeverría 2019, 18). Modernity, Echeverría urges, should be conceptualized as the potential of technological change to serve principles beyond individual accumulation, like collaboration and community. From this vantage, the widespread use of bicycles in rural communities is not an indicator of belated modernity but a model of post-carbon living that is one path toward a planetary future.

While ToTo's visual and discursive focus on the bicycle reinforces its association with post-carbon technologies, the greater efficacy of solar panels at powering the high-volume energy requirements of film projection presents us with the question of why this technology is absent from ToTo's messaging. We might speculate that the bike is given greater weight than solar because pedal-powered machines require more active community involvement. Yet the disproportionate stress on audience participation in reducing emissions, when solar power is what truly undergirds ToTo screenings, reinforces the notion that the responsibility to reduce emissions lies with the individual. This is untrue on various levels. Mexico itself is only responsible for about 1% of global emissions, and the low-income communities that benefit from Cine Móvil ToTo already emit only one-seventh of the emissions of their wealthier counterparts (Santillán Vera and de la Vega Navarro 2018, 703). Thus, while the centrality of bikes in allowing individuals to power alternative exhibition infrastructures is a fantastic way to make the energy demands of cultural consumption visible, this visual shorthand obscures the fact that the solutions to the energy crisis are collective.

Unlike bikes, solar panels are expensive to acquire as well as to service. If a community were to want to make alternative exhibition structures permanent, they would need to fund the acquisition of a solar panel. The take-away here is that the transition to post-carbon cultural infrastructures requires resources and investment, as well as maintenance and training. Thus we might conclude that there should be less focus placed on the active involvement of rural participants in solving the climate crisis, and more focus placed on providing communities with the technologies that will allow them to sustain culture and create their own path to modernity, rather than rely on the fleeting presence of outside initiatives like Cine Móvil ToTo.

Cinema for the Post-Oil Commons

Over the past 15 years, Mexico has experienced a steady decline in crude output, which has halved since 2004. This drop is due to diminishing reserves, outdated technologies, and energy reform policies that have tipped the scales toward private transnationals. As a result, government revenue has suffered: in 2019, oil only accounted for about 17% of federal revenue, in sharp contrast to the 40% that has been the norm for decades. This steep reduction has again translated to significant cuts to state institutions, social programs, environmental agencies, and arts initiatives—meanwhile reinvestment in the petroleum industry in an attempt to revive it has increased. The film industry has been particularly affected: the total amount of state funds dedicated to cinema across the board was cut in half between 2012 and 2017; further austerity measures in 2019 slashed the remaining film sector budget by an additional 40%. What does this contingent proximity between the fate of oil and the fate of domestic cinema mean? And how does thinking about cinema as entangled with oil offer a way to rethink what modernity means and whether other modernities might yet exist? The historic inextricability of extractive and cultural industries in Mexico compels us to reimagine how the infrastructures of society can serve the commons in a way that is collaboratively imagined, equitable, and durable.

Cine Móvil ToTo represents just one example of an initiative that makes visible what the consumption of cinema actually entails. It brings cinema into view as a more-than-human assemblage that requires the exchange of energy among bodies. This revelatory gesture can be considered decolonial in its redress of "the dissociation of consumption from environmental impact," that Seán Cubitt notes "repeats the central structure of coloniality" (2014, 276). As a project that imagines alternative cinema infrastructures, strengthens distribution networks for national cinema, attempts to redress regional inequities, and offers corporations a way to signpost (albeit superficially) their green credentials, Cine Móvil ToTo activates divergent interest groups around a shared project. In this sense, Cine Móvil ToTo illustrates how politics can operate across divergence to imagine a world beyond fossil fuels.

Let us not romanticize what ecocinema can accomplish without also grappling with its structural limitations, circumscribed as they are by the long histories of colonial capitalism. I concur with Christian Sandvig's observation that attending to the "infrastructures of distribution," reveals "competing ideas about what content and which audiences are valuable, and indeed how culture itself ought to work" (2015, 226). When we think about Latin American ecocinema and particularly those films that profile rural peoples, it is not the only representation that matters. We should also consider who these programs and films are for. What does it mean to make and consume audiovisual content about subjects who cannot access it themselves because of the lack of exhibition spaces, insufficient streaming bandwidth, or prohibitively expensive tickets? Are handheld devices the only answer to this dilemma? Or might cinema spectatorship be reimagined? Questions like these point toward the importance of developing methods of scholarly inquiry that cultivate "the connections that inhere between media *about* the environment and media *in* the environment" (Walker and Starosielski 2016). The web series *El tema* and the Cine Móvil ToTo screening initiative offer different entry points to these questions. They both indicate that climate is "the issue" to address. This can be accomplished through content but also through format and distribution, whether it be the use of short, easily shareable videos on YouTube, or by powering film exhibitions for communities without access to exhibition spaces through the power of the sun. These alternative models of viewership indicate that Latin American eco-cinema is at the forefront of reimagining what cinema means and can do in the twenty-first century, a site of how cultural production might move away from the material reliance on fossil fuels.

Note

1 The cinema-by-pedaling model was pioneered in Latin America by the company Ecocinema in Uruguay (founded in 2010), with help from the Dutch foundation Solar Cinema. Uruguay is also home to the Festival Internacional de Cine a Pedal (International Festival for Cinema by Pedal), a three-day film festival powered by 22 bikes founded in 2013.

Works Cited

Acosta, Santiago. 2020. "We Are Like Oil: An Ecology of the Venezuelan Culture Boom: 1973–1983." PhD diss., Columbia University.

Arenillas, María Guadalupe and Michael J. Lazzara. 2016. "Introduction." In *Latin American Documentary Film in the New Millennium*, edited by María Guadalupe Arenillas and Michael J. Lazzara, 1–19. New York: Palgrave.

Bozak, Nadia. 2012. *The Cinematic Footprint: Lights, Camera, Natural Resources*. New Brunswick, NJ: Rutgers University Press.

Cubitt, Sean. 2014. "Decolonizing Ecomedia." *Cultural Politics* 10.3: 275–286.

Echeverría, Bolívar. 2019. *Modernity and "Whiteness,"* translated by Rodrigo Ferreira. Cambridge: Polity.

El tema, Episode 4, "Energía," directed by Santiago Maza, aired May 3 2021. https://lacorrientedelgolfo.net/proyecto/el-tema/energia/

Falicov, Tamara L. 2019. *Latin American Film Industries*. London: Bloomsbury.

———. 2012. "Mobile Cinemas in Cuba: The Forms and Ideology of Traveling Exhibitions." *Public* 40: 104–108.

Figueroa, Sebastián. 2022. "Apuntes sobre cine y extractivismo." *laFuga* 26. https://www.lafuga.cl/apuntes-sobre-cine-y-extractivismo/1100

Fornoff, Carolyn. 2021. "Mexican Cinema as Petrocinema." *Studies in Spanish and Latin American Cinemas* 18.3: 377–387.

Forns-Broggi, Roberto. 2013. "Ecocinema and "Good Life" in Latin America." In *Transnational Cinema: Film Culture in an Era of Ecological Transformation*, edited by Pietari Kääpä, Tommy Gustafsson, and Jelena Stanovik, 85–100. Chicago, IL: Intellect.

Hernández Ibarzábal, José and David Bonilla. 2020. "Examining Mexico's Energy Policy Under the 4T." *The Extractive Industries and Society* 7: 669–675.

Hoyos, Héctor. 2018. "Global Supply Chain Literature vs. Extractivism." In *Re-Mapping World Literature: Writing, Book Markets and Epistemologies between Latin America and the Global South*, edited by Gesine Müller, Jorge J. Locane, and Benjamin Loy, 88–117. Berlin: DeGruyter.

Iberdrola Press Release. 2017. "Grupo Modelo and Iberdrola Announce a Renewable Power Purchase Agreement." October 19, 2017. https://www. iberdrolamexico.com/en/press/grupo-modelo-and-iberdrola-announce-a-renewable-power-purchase-agreement/

Iheka, Cajetan. 2021. *African Ecomedia: Network Forms, Planetary Politics*. Durham: Duke University Press.

IMCINE: Instituto Mexicano de Cinematografía. 2021. "Beyond the Screen: The Film Exhibition Community." In *Anuario estadístico de cine mexicano 2020*, 137–145. http://anuariocinemx.imcine.gob.mx/Assets/anuarios/2020.pdf

INEGI: Instituto Nacional de Estadística y Geografía. 2021. *Comunicado de prensa* 352/21, June 22, 2021. www.inegi.org.mx.

Llamas-Rodriguez, Juan. 2019. "A Global Cinematic Experience: Cinépolis, Film Exhibition, and Luxury Branding." *JCMS* 58.3: 49–71.

Marcone, Jorge. 2015. "Filming the Emergence of Popular Environmentalism in Latin America: Postcolonialism and *Buen Vivir*." In *Global Ecologies and the Environmental Humanities: Postcolonial Approaches*, edited by Elizabeth DeLoughrey, Jill Didur, and Anthony Carrigan, 207–225. New York: Routledge.

Marks, Laura U. and Radek Przedpelski. 2021. "Bandwidth Imperialism and Small-File Media." *Post45*. https://post45.org/2021/04/bandwidth-imperialism-and-small-file-media/

Neira, Hidalgo. 2021. "Cine Móvil ToTo llevará cine, de manera sustentable, más allá de las grades ciudades." *Reporte Indigo*. August 18, 2021. https://www.reporteindigo. com/piensa/cine-movil-toto-llevara-cine-de-manera-sustentable-mas-alla-de-las-grandes-ciudades/

Parikka, Jussi. 2012. "New Materialism as Media Theory: Medianatures and Dirty Matter." *Communication and Critical/Cultural Studies* 9.1: 95–101.

Petrocultures Research Group. 2016. *After Oil*. Morgantown: West Virginia University Press.

Ramírez, Erick. 2020. "Disruptores: Cine Móvil ToTo, la pantalla nómada." *El Sol de México*. March 12 2020. https://www.elsoldemexico.com.mx/finanzas/disruptores-cine-movil-toto-la-pantalla-nomada-4959852.html

Rosas Mantecón, Ana. 2017. *Ir al cine: antropología de los públicos, la ciudad y las pantallas*. Mexico City: Universidad Autónoma Metropolitana.

Rust, Stephen and Salma Monani. 2013. "Introduction: Cuts to Dissolves—Defining and Situating Ecocinema Studies." In *Ecocinema Theory and Practice*, edited by Stephen Rust, Salma Monani, and Sean Cubitt, 1–13. New York: Routledge.

Saldaña-Durán, Claudia E., Gerardo Bernache-Pérez, Sara Ojeda-Benitez, and Samantha E. Cruz-Sotelo. 2020. "Environmental Pollution of E-Waste: Generation, Collection, Legislation, and Recycling Practices in Mexico." In *Handbook of Electronic Waste Management: International Best Practices and Case Studies*, edited by Majeti Narasimha Vara Prasad, Meththika Vithanage, and Anwesha Borthakur, 422–442. Oxford: Butterworth-Heinemann.

Sánchez Prado, Ignacio. 2014. *Screening Neoliberalism: Transforming Mexican Cinema 1988–2012*. Nashville, TN: Vanderbilt University Press.

Sandvig, Christian. 2015. "The Internet as the Anti-Television: Distribution Infrastructure as Culture and Power." In *Signal Traffic: Critical Studies of Media Infrastructures*, edited by Lisa Parks and Nicole Starosielski, 225–245. Champaign: University of Illinois Press.

Santillán Vera, Mónica and Ángel de la Vega Navarro. 2018. "Do the Rich Pollute More? Mexican Household Consumption by Income Level and CO_2 Emissions." *International Journal of Energy Sector Management* 13.3: 694–712.

Schiwy, Freya. 2019. *The Open Invitation: Activist Video, Mexico, and the Politics of Affect.* Pittsburgh: University of Pittsburgh Press.

Walker, Janet and Nicole Starosielski. 2016. "Introduction: Sustainable Media." In *Sustainable Media: Critical Approaches to Media and Environment*, edited by Nicole Starosielski and Janet Walker, 1–20. New York: Routledge.

3

ENERGY AND EXHAUSTION IN A COAL MELODRAMA

Kaala Patthar (1979)

Debashree Mukherjee

Kaala Patthar (*Black Rock,* Yash Chopra, 1979) begins with title credits rolling over a bustling colliery shot at night, as coal workers emerge from the depths of the earth and wearily amble toward their meager dwellings. The sky gently changes from dark to light; it is dawn, and we follow a lone coal miner walking with hunched shoulders and exhausted steps. Our hero, barely distinguishable from the mass of tiny coal miner shapes, looms on screen as a shadowy and grimy figure. Depletion clings to his body as he climbs up the wooden stairs to his mining quarters. The camera slowly follows him as he wearily places one foot before the other, dragging himself to his shanty room and collapsing on his cot. A most unusual entry for a Hindi film hero.

Most Hindi film viewers in 1979 would recognize the actor playing this coal miner protagonist—beloved national celebrity, Amitabh Bachchan—whose lanky figure was instantly identifiable whether in silhouette or covered in coal dust. What's most interesting in this opening sequence, however, is the focus on exhaustion as the key register that marks life in a colliery. In this chapter, I explore themes of energy and exhaustion imbricated with the ecological extraction that is the central premise of *Kaala Patthar*. The film, which can be termed a "coal melodrama," helps us examine the entangled materialities of human and nonhuman in sentimental stories about coal. This essay is a foray into energy humanities – a nascent field in South Asian film studies – and one of my arguments is that situated cinematic histories of coal can help us understand current attitudes toward fossil fuels spanning scales of intimacy to governance. As I will show, *Kaala Patthar* offers us glimpses into the simultaneous co-depletion of minerals and humans and thus helps ecomedia scholars revisit the relation between cinema and energy.[1]

DOI: 10.4324/9781003246602-5

In recent years, media studies have taken an accelerated interest in energy as a material resource that supports mediatic functioning. The focus has largely been on energy forms and extractive sites such as oil and coal, electricity, and data centers (Bozak 2012; Cubitt 2017; Starosielski and Walker 2016). What has been less visible is the human itself as a site of energy that can be materially depleted and destroyed. Even as academia grapples with the complex inequalities between humans and their differential stakes in the current ecological crisis, there is an urgent need to think of human and nonhuman as *collectivities* – processual, co-constitutive, and politically necessary. Therefore, rather than treat energy as a discrete resource or something "out there," I describe energy as relational, produced, and activated in encounters between a multiplicity of actors that extend across the worlds of production, circulation, and representation. While histories of modern energy take fossil fuels as their obvious site of inquiry, it is the category of exhaustion that has recently seen interest in both the human and the nonhuman as equally relevant subjects of concern (Gorfinkel 2012; Miller 2021; Schaffner 2016). Still, it is rare to see scholarship that insists on the entangled exhaustions of *both* fossil fuels and the human body. As a concept and a material phenomenon that lies between life and death, exhaustion forces us to think of the relationalities between the living and the nonliving, rather than see them as oppositional ontologies (Mukherjee 2020). Drawing on Kathryn Yusoff's work, I contend that at this juncture in the history of the planet, energy humanities might benefit from a non-binary focus on the "geologic subject" (2015), a category premised on the co-constitution of humans and geology and mindful of the variable scale of what counts as geology and what counts as human, at which point in history, and where.

In this chapter, I examine the 1979 big-budget multi-starrer coal melodrama, *Kaala Patthar*, to trace the connections between filmed bodies, coal ecologies, and mediatized economies of sentiment. *Kaala Patthar* opens up the history of coal (and cinema) as a history of not just energy, but also exhaustion, which is clearly framed in the film as industrial capitalist extraction. The extraction of fossil fuels from the ground is firmly linked to the extraction of labor from the human body and connects up with the sentimental extraction that the melodramatic film affects on the viewer. In highlighting the aesthetic work of film melodrama, I join a growing body of ecomedia scholarship that approaches the ongoing planetary climate emergency as partly a crisis of storytelling (Arnold 2018; Ghosh 2016; Wenzel 2019).

Coal Nationalism & Sentimental Extraction

Many Indians are proudly aware that India is the world's second-largest producer and consumer of coal after China. In 2020 Prime Minister Narendra Modi vowed to make India the world's largest exporter of coal as a policy in energy independence. A "Vision Document" announced that accelerated coal production was imperative to "further the Nation's ambition to be a global economic leader. India is dependent on the import of hydrocarbons to a great extent. However, the country is blessed with abundant coal and renewable energy resources that need to be tapped optimally" (Government of India 2019). The linking of coal production with national security and sovereignty renders coal into a nationalist symbol and effectively makes critiques of governmental coal policies susceptible to charges of "anti-national" sentiment. This is precisely the rationale under which the Modi government has sought to halt the activities of environmental groups such as Greenpeace India (Bidwai 2015). This sentimental mobilization of coal nationalism by the Indian state is not new. In fact, there was a time when, as Ranjani Mazumdar points out, "coal [] occupied an outsized role in Independent India's developmental imagination" (2022, 548). Coal was the material substrate driving postcolonial India's developmental vision, the fuel that powered large-scale projects dear to Prime Minister Jawaharlal Nehru's Five-Year Plans for dams, steel plants, railway infrastructures, and electrification. *Kaala Patthar* was made when the nationalization of coal mines began in earnest under the leadership of Nehru's daughter, Indira Gandhi. It is only in the last few years that the commercial coal mining sector has opened up again to private players (Kohli and Menon 2020). The postcolonial euphoria of the 1960s and 1970s that linked coal to national development, public infrastructure-building, and economic self-reliance has been repurposed today to erase distinctions between ends and means, state and corporate. Circulating coal imaginaries and situated histories of sentimental narratives thus help us chart the fortunes and futures of fossil fuel extraction.

A popular film form such as Hindi melodrama, with its broad-based address and spectacular appeal, is key to tracking the cultural status of coal in the Indian public imagination. The organizers of a recent academic workshop coined the term "sentimental extraction" to name the ideological and aesthetic work done by cultural texts to "stabilize" societies' emotional investment in fossil fuels, marshaling affects such as love, addiction, and nostalgia (Friedrich-Alexander-Universität 2021; LeMenager 2011). *Kaala Patthar*, a disaster movie starring six of the most popular Hindi film stars of the 1970s, can be read as a sentimentally extractive text that mobilizes fandom and melodramatic affect to conflate coal with heroic energy workers. Directed by the acclaimed Yash Chopra, with impassioned dialogues by the superhit writer duo Salim-Javed and song lyrics by the beloved socialist poet Sahir Ludhianvi, the film was destined for cult status. The story revolves around the privately owned Dhanraj Coal Mines and its close-knit mining community. There are three heroes: an ex-naval officer, Vijay (Bachchan), who has turned to mining as expiation for having abandoned a sinking ship under his command; an earnest engineer, Ravi (Shashi Kapoor), who just wants to do the job well; and an escaped convict, Mangal (Shatrughan Sinha), for whom the mining town offers disguise and shelter. The coal mines thus serve as a refuge for some, like Mangal, and purgatory for others like Vijay. All three men are provided with love interests, but though the male friendships in the film cross class divides, their heterosexual couplings stick to class allegiances. The engineer couples with a fashionable journalist (Anita, played by Parveen Babi), the ex-naval officer romances a doctor (Dr. Sudha, by Rakhee), and the convict befriends an itinerant jewelry vendor (Channo, by Neetu Singh). The film mobilizes all the hallmarks of Indian melodrama, from sensational dialogue to song-and-dance sequences, to tell a convoluted story about extractive logics and effects. At the center of the film is a spectacular mine explosion that leads to the flooding of underground tunnels and offers an opportunity for our three heroes to transform into cinematic saviors. When *Kaala Patthar* was first released, critics chided it for its rhetorical excesses (Mohamed 1979). However, it is precisely the hyperbolic and utopian register that allowed it to occupy a national-popular sentimental space.

Melodrama is widely considered a cinematic mode conducive to transitional periods of collective crisis. Scholars of popular Indian cinemas have focused on film melodramas made in the immediate decades after Independence, especially the 1950s when the nation grappled with remaking a national identity while dealing with the traumatic Partition of India and Pakistan (Vasudevan 2011). *Kaala Patthar* speaks to a different era of transition in the life of the postcolonial nation – the 1970s. This period has been framed as "India's crisis decade," a time when "India experienced war, inflation, student and popular protests and, most impactful of all, the Emergency of 1975–77: a twenty-two-month period when Prime Minister Indira Gandhi suspended constitutional rights and democracy and governed in authoritarian mode" ("India's Crisis Decade" 2018). *Kaala Patthar* allows viewers in the twenty-first century to re-enter this crisis decade with the help of the melodramatic mode that is known for voicing crisis by staging sentiment. The film offers a relatively untold shadow history of this decade – one in which coal was both celebrated as a fuel for the nation, and sharply critiqued for the structural extractive violence it unleashed on human bodies and landscapes.

In India, the story of coal seems to have always been the story of coal miners, or rather, the story of the infernal conditions of life as a subterranean laborer. After the late-nineteenth-century coal boom in eastern India, a range of European interests haphazardly converged here, building shaky infrastructures that were prone to collapse and stripping every inch of value from the landscape. For those who toiled in these coalfields, this was a "*patala bhoomi*," or a literal hell on earth, composed of fire and heat and smoke and death (Shutzer 2021, 402). After Independence in 1947, coal was restituted from this narrative of bleakness by those reclaiming it as a newly born nation's primary source of energy, a veritable "black diamond." Kuntala Lahiri-Dutt points out that the "precocious language of coal nationalism was created during the [1950s–1960s] ... to present independent India's response to earlier coal colonialism" (2016, 17). Cinema was actively employed to reinforce this newly reconfigured status of coal. Between 1958 and 1979, the state-run Films Division produced at least ten documentary films that highlighted the significance of coal as a valuable national asset.[2] The developmental story of coal as a critical ally in the march toward national progress was, however, tempered by the much older and ongoing story of coal as a killer of humans. In the early 1960s, a series of mining disasters erupted across India's famous eastern coal belt, driving home the message about the huge human costs of the nation's "black diamond."

In an effort to regulate the mining sector, the Indian government started a process of nationalizing existing coal mines in 1971 drawing on "the belief that a country's mineral wealth is the nation's patrimony" (Lahiri-Dutt 2016, 17). In 1975 Coal India Limited was established, a public-sector holding company that is the world's single-largest producer of coal today. Its brand logo is a black diamond. The government spent large amounts of public funds to advertise this giant company and its many subsidiaries. Advertisements highlighted the centrality of coal to Prime Minister Gandhi's 20-point economic program, which was instituted during the Emergency ostensibly to alleviate poverty. The government claimed to prioritize the health and wellbeing of miners and their families (e.g., Western Coalfield Ltd. advertised images of its hospitals, water supply, and housing schemes for its employees), and highlighted the urgency of pivoting away from oil after the 1973 oil crisis (*Times of India* [*ToI*] Nov 18, 1976a: 6; *ToI* Mar 5, 1977: 1). This public relations exercise was designed to change public perception that coal was an exploitative industry and to reframe the consumption of domestic coal as patriotic duty (*ToI* Jun 29, 1976b: 12). The visual design of these ads (and movie posters for *Kaala Patthar*) drew on the iconicity of the figure of the rugged coal miner with his hard hat and miner's lamp. One design from 1976 renders this image of the coal miner as a collage of euphoric words about nationalized coal printed in multiple Indian languages, to represent the diversity of the more than 600,000 miners reportedly employed by the Indian state in 1976.[3] Many of these designs are conspicuously part of the socialist and developmentalist design aesthetic that circulated between India, Russia, and China in this period. *Kaala Patthar* draws on this heroic-epic imagery and the government's boosterist coal propaganda in its portrayal of heroes and villains (Figure 3.1).

There remained, however, one slight obstacle in the path of Project Black Diamond and the redemption of King Coal as an unqualified good: the continued spectacular violence of mining accidents. On December 27, 1975, there was a blast in the Chasnala coal mines, which unleashed 50 million gallons of water into the tunnels at a rate of 500 km a minute. 375 miners lost their lives, their unrecognizable bodies only retrieved days later. *Kaala Patthar* was directly inspired by this incident. Today, the film is significant not only for its commercial and popular appeal but also for its oddly anachronistic championing of coal

FIGURE 3.1   Heroic figurations of the Indian coalminer, as crafted by public coal companies, made their way into *Kaala Patthar's* publicity design.

nationalization in a period when frequent coal catastrophes were taking place under the state's watch.

Melodrama and Energetic Modernity

Victorian stage melodrama was "a primary genre of energetic modernity," according to Devin Griffiths, "an economic system based on the accelerated extraction of petrofuels that took a recognizably modern shape in the nineteenth century" (2018, 612–613). By the 1970s, and in the Indian context, this assertion would also be valid for film melodramas. Big-budget commercial filmmaking in India was, and remains, heavily dependent on carbon infrastructures that power railways, airplanes, electrical grids, studios, vanity vans, editing suites, exhibition theaters, and computer screens. In this sense, the films of director–producer Yash Chopra were decidedly energy-intensive spectacles. His lavish melodramas were exceedingly resource-intensive, drawing on deep reserves of finance, labor, and the renewed national turn to coal. Chopra's pre-dilection for multiple stars, elaborate costumes and set design, and sumptuous song sequences qualify his films as a form of "conspicuous production" (Adorno and Horkheimer [1947] 2002, 97).

Kaala Patthar was shot on a massive outdoor set, "a replica of a coal mine complete with lifts, railways and ropeways," spread over 20 acres of land in Raj Kapoor's Loni Farm near Pune (Sethna 1979). Intent on adequately exploit-ing the scale of this manufactured set with the use of high-angle wide shots, Chopra transported all film equipment including a large crane from Mumbai, about six hours away. Even as man-made coal mines remake the earth and devastate landscapes, a man-made simulacrum of a coal mine offers a funhouse mirror view of Man's geomorphic ambitions. In Jennifer Fay's words, such cinematic ambition partially describes "how the Anthropocene answers a wish for a human-made and manipulated planet" (2018, 9). The energy-intensive infrastructural basis of Chopra's films is further exemplified in his imaging practices. Chopra's romantic melodramas have a characteristic brightness in their dependence on color and luminosity, and though he described the dark coal mines as the "central character" in *Kaala Patthar*, this film too is brightly lit (Sethna 1979). This film about coal thus served as a display of luminous filmic energy that, in turn, literally drew on significant electrical and coal energy for its production. *Kaala Patthar*'s coal-derived luminosity is best illus-trated through an anti-alias rendering of the film's timeline (Figure 3.2). You will note that the darkest sequence is in the climactic portion of the *diegesis* visualized below.

The energetic brightness in Chopra's films is also a factor of bodies that are exceptionally dynamic. In *Kaala Patthar*, human energy is showcased as a spec-tacle in scenes of violent action and energetic romantic optimism. Here it helps to think of energy as a relational and multi-sited force rather than an inert and extractable fuel. Characters like Ravi Malhotra, the engineer, seem to be burst-ing with vitality, virility, and exuberance. An upper caste Hindu, Ravi belongs to the new generation of technocratic elite who were much favored by Nehru and later Indira Gandhi. His character is what Victor Seow might term a "car-bon technocrat," representative of "a technopolitical system grounded in the idealization of extensive fossil fuel exploitation through mechanical and mana-gerial means" (2021, 8). The film introduces Ravi in an early song sequence as he makes his way from an unnamed city to his new job posting at Dhanraj Coal Mines. He rides his motorbike on a smooth open road, singing about life as a continuous journey. We witness not only the arrogant promise of continuous motion that is central to energetic modernity but also a form of infrastruc-tural nationalism, which showcases India's developmental vision for providing basic infrastructure amenities like roadways with the promise of connecting the remotest parts of a very large and diverse nation. The energetic joy that exudes

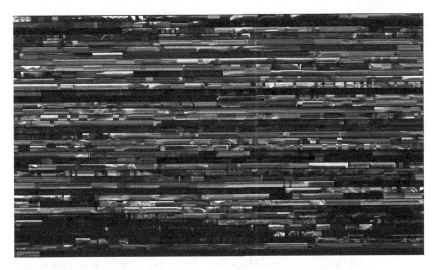

FIGURE 3.2   Lighting design of *Kaala Patthar* as mapped on anti-alias view on www. indiancine.ma.

from Ravi stems from a confidence that all this has been made available to him; the land, the trees, and the rivers are all accessible through infrastructure. However, infrastructural promises can be as unequal as the promise of citizenship itself because they are mediated by caste-class privilege.

During his journey through a fertile and frictionless new India, Ravi encounters several women, exotic cinematic stereotypes of the tribal and the rural woman. Near-naked Adivasis ("first inhabitant" or Indigenous) carrying firewood on their heads beckon and flirt with Ravi. One woman, bathing in a river, sings: "Oh traveler, don't leave these arms, these roads/ Come back and stay a while." The unabashed sexualization of these socially-marginalized figures reflects Ravi's status in this environment as the neocolonial master of all he surveys. The fact that he is a mining engineer responsible for extracting and denuding the geography he is about to enter is compatible with his characterization in this song as a virile, energetic male. The Adivasi woman embodies the fertile, resource-rich land that, under the shadow of nationalism, offers itself to the nation's chosen representatives. Ravi, the emblem of energetic extraction-as-national good, is contrasted with the Adivasi woman, an emblem of all that is extractable, and the song sequence unreflexively visualizes the gulf between India's first citizens and its first inhabitants. What remains unseen and undiscussed in the film is the role of Adivasi labor in the subterranean work of mining itself (Shutzer 2021). If Ravi represents the myth of inexhaustible coal energy in the service of the postcolony, then surely mustn't there be some cinematic space made for those other geologic subjects who represent exhaustibility?

Slow Violence across Geologic Life

One of the continued blindspots in the fields of energy history and environmental humanities is that depletion and extraction are mainly understood in the realm of the nonhuman, the elemental, the geological, and the mineral. We agree that quarries and mineral deposits get depleted, or that oil wells and freshwater fish are exhausted. But can we apply the same terms to the human bodies that work these quarries and rivers? Most recently, Elizabeth Carolyn Miller has persuasively argued that the onset of the industrial revolution, premised on extractive practices such as coal mining in nineteenth-century Britain, must also be seen as the start of the "long exhaustion." Miller looks at literary texts from the nineteenth and twentieth centuries that betray an acute awareness of the fact that subterranean minerals such as gold and coal are defined by their very exhaustibility and finitude. The long exhaustion thus marks a prescient anxiety and understanding that "extraction-based life is a future-depleting system" (2021, 12). Miller acknowledges that "extractive capitalism was premised on the exploitation of [Indigenous and enslaved] workers as on the exploitation of natural environments" (92), but what if we more directly considered the ways in which human and mineral have been historically co-constituted? "Geologic life," a term coined by Kathryn Yusoff, is particularly useful here. Yusoff urges that we "use the Anthropocene as a provocation to begin to understand ourselves as geologic subjects, not only capable of geomorphic acts, but as beings who have something *in common* with the geologic forces that are mobilized and incorporated" in the age of carbon capitalism (2013, 780–781; italics in original). Such an approach has obvious epistemic advantages for a non-binary, non-anthropocentric study of extractivism. More crucially, the idea of geologic life offers a political advantage as it shows us that the geologic, as that which extends across human-mineral, is a form of "differentiated planetary inhabitation and corporeal affiliation" (781). Produced through historical, environmental, and cultural processes of capture and resistance, the geologic subject is multiple and multiply depleted, far exceeding the remit of the limited category of "human." *Kaala Patthar* affords glimpses of how to think the differentiated exhaustion of multiple geologic subjects.

The opening sequence of *Kaala Patthar*, described at the start of this chapter, introduces several aesthetic hierarchies and relations that are germane to both coal and to melodrama: a dramatization of the moral contest between darkness and brightness, and alongside this, a parallel struggle between human and nonhuman. Through its shot division, the sequence develops a grammar of verticality as anonymous energy workers ascend from the depths of the earth and climb upwards into their tenement homes. The coal miner as a historical figure and geological subject was both romanticized at the height of the industrial age as a harbinger of energetic modernity and reviled as an uncanny subterranean hybrid in texts such as HG Wells' 1895 novel *Time Machine* (Dawson 2017, 84). It is precisely this ambivalent status of the coal miner, between the nonhuman and human, that joins his exhaustibility with that of the coal he digs, allowing us to see their co-constitution as geologic subjects.

Exhaustion is not, as is commonly understood, simply the emptying out of a substance or the slow disappearance of human energy. Exhaustion is, as the Hindi poet Mangesh Dabral writes, "what's left in the end" (2008, 117). It is the residue that accrues in the shadow of cultural techniques, often quite literally as the "exhaust" or waste that is expelled from a machine during its operation. Rather than an absence, the exhaust that is discharged from extractive machineries constitutes an active, if life-denying, presence. This form of exhaust quite literally hangs in the air around a coal mine. *Kaala Patthar* picks up this literal point early in the film in a sequence where we are introduced to the arch-villain, the mine owner Mr. Dhanraj (Prem Chopra). He has just arrived in town and is received at a private airfield by the chief engineer, Saxena. As they drive toward the mines, Dhanraj asks to roll up windows and turn on the air-conditioning. "It's a dirty 'atmosphere' around here," he exclaims, and Saxena explains that this is due to the coal particles in the air. Coal dust emissions are a familiar byproduct of mining activities and accumulate during the extraction and transportation of coal. This dust is commonly composed of coarse particles that are black in color and hence quite visible in the form of dust, smog, and grimy layers that settle on surfaces, clothing, and bodies (Ghose and Majee 2020). A routine residue of coal extraction, this "exhaust" material is marked by its polluting presence, rather than absence. This atmospheric presence of coal, which saturates the air and is present in every breath, embodies a form of "slow violence" (Nixon 2011) that gradually scours the surfaces of things and the interiors of human bodies.

In his well-known work, on slow violence, Rob Nixon notes that "different kinds of disaster possess unequal heft," and it is only events of spectacular, immediate, and sensational violence that grab public attention and grip spectatorial imaginations (3). Nixon points out that mainstream assumptions of what counts as violence and disaster are temporally limited and ocular-centric. Thinking about the durational and accretional effects of climate change, he argues that we need to think of a "different kind of violence," a slow violence that "occurs gradually and out of sight, a violence of delayed destruction that is dispersed across time and space, an attritional violence that is not viewed as violence at all" (2). The carbon exhaust of coal dust and ash lines the lungs, brain, liver, kidneys, and intestines of coal miners leading to such notorious ailments as Black Lung Disease, also known as Coal Worker's Pneumoconiosis (CWP). Miners do not die overnight from such ailments; the toxic effects accrue over time. This too is a form of exhaustion where the body is eaten up from inside. Coal dust, then, is a mediating force that joins humans and landscapes in a mutually corrosive bind. Carbon exhaust shows us that human and nonhuman are not only co-constitutive but also *co-depleting*. *Kaala Patthar* gestures toward this co-depletion most pointedly through the story arc of Dr. Sudha. One of the first lessons this idealistic young doctor learns when she is transferred to the mining town is about the futility of primary care medicine in the face of long-term lung disease, chronic fatigue, and frequent accidents. At the same time, *Kaala Patthar* also cautions that the category "human" can obfuscate more than it can reveal. As Dhanraj rolls up his car windows, the film (melo)dramatically illuminates that exposure to exhaust is disproportionately experienced by coal labor and coal landscapes.

The exhaustion of landscapes can be fast or slow, and never wholly available to sight. Landscapes devastated by large-scale opencast mining are familiar to us through innumerable photographs and aerial shots. Images of gray, winding stone, rock hill faces, "spoil heaps," and gaping craters in the ground have become the visible face of the destructive scale of anthropogenic geomorphism. The northeastern coalfields of India, where the Chasnala mines are located, are famous for their unusual geological feature of being coal-rich in the upper layers of the ground, with inferior grades of coal located deeper underground. Smita Gupta points out that

> this natural bounty has proved to be [the region's] ecological undoing since this has meant cheap and quick extraction of quality coal from a spread-out area, covering the entire landscape into a large scarred coal mine, and displacing and impoverishing local people.
>
> *(2019, 70)*

Not all of this scarred landscape is photogenic or available for optical capture. The first mine fire in Jharia was reported in 1916 and by 1972 approximately 70 active fires burned across an area of 100 square miles in abandoned and exhausted mines (Ferris 2015). These fires simmered underground, visible only as irregular plumes of smoke. About 37 million tons of coal have been consumed by the Jharia fires, which have now raged for over a century (Figure 3.3).

Half a million people are estimated to be living on this affected ground and thousands of others have been evicted and displaced. The perverse poetry in this simmering slow burn of a fire that feeds on itself year after year was not lost on the writers of *Kaala Patthar*. Ravi says of Vijay, the guilt-ravaged miner, that "he reminds me of that mine in Dhanbad in which tons of coal have been burning for years. There's something coal-like smoldering in him too." This reference to the Jharia fires highlights the subterranean, unseen, but potent slow violence that is eating up Vijay and the landscape he labors in. Exhaustion as slow burning is an apt metaphor that brings affect, substance, and presence together.

FIGURE 3.3   Underground fires have been burning for over a century in the coal town of Jharia. Photograph by Ronny Sen, c. 2016.

Accident

If energy and its depletion is one key theme in *Kaala Patthar*, the other is the everyday nature of accidents. The film routinizes accidents and renders them familiar and inevitable, right from the opening minutes of the film. As Vijay collapses onto his skinny bed, the film drives home the psychic "long emergencies of slow violence" by taking us into his nightmare world where he is routinely haunted by memories of cowardice and inaction. And almost immediately he is woken up by blaring sirens. There has been an accident. The problem of coal is thus repeatedly underlined in this opening sequence, through visual, gestural, and aural registers, and identified as the problem of precarious labor. From this moment onwards, *Kaala Patthar* seesaws between slow violence and spectacular disaster, especially through the narrative overuse of fight scenes and explosive accidents.

The word "accident" signifies that which takes place abruptly and violently. In his discussion of the technological accident in modernity, Paul Virilio questions this conceptual premise predicated on surprise which serves to deflect attention from systemic causes. Via Aristotle, for whom "the accident reveals the substance," Virilio argues that every technological invention contains within it the future accident, which in turn illustrates something crucial about the invention (2007). Industrial modernity, with its privileging of speed and heavy machinery, thus inherently produced not just commodities but also accidents on a mass scale. Mining accidents can be similarly read as coded into the destructive intents and technologies of fossil fuel extraction. Virilio's technological approach to the industrial accident allows us to question the premise of the accidental – as that which is exceptional. A more *longue duree* and systemic approach to accidents has tremendous purchase for ecomedia and energy studies, as it helps us grasp the ideological trappings behind word-concepts and historical epistemes surrounding terms such as "spill" which serve to deflect causality and culpability (See Juhasz 2017; Mukherjee 2020). However, Virilio's framing carries an inevitability logic that ascribes all agency to the technological invention and the "substance." Miners themselves often internalize this preprogrammed "nature" of extractive labor. In *Burning Stone* (Lokesh Lalvani 1978), a Films Division documentary on the life of coal miners in Bihar, a miner says: "the nature of the work is such that these things [accidents] keep happening, no matter how many precautions you take." And indeed, even today there seems little abatement to the seeming inevitability of mining accidents. Between 2010 and 2021, the Indian government recorded ~120 coal mining accidents with 170 deaths (ENVIS 2022). These statistics are recorded with relative impunity as it is the "nature of the work" that is often held responsible for the accidental. Film mimics life, it seems, and one of the lead actors in *Kaala Patthar*, Shashi Kapoor (Ravi) was reportedly injured during the climactic flooding of the tunnel scene. Reported as a "shooting accident" in the fan magazines of the day, the incident took place when the crew released water at very high pressure into a constructed tunnel set in Mumbai's Film City. The tunnel wall "caved in inexplicably, burying Shashi under it" and it was apparently a stroke of pure luck that he escaped with minor injuries (*Filmfare* 1979).

Melodrama, since the time of the Victorian stage, has thematized both the banality and the shock of industrial accidents. There is something here that exceeds the resigned narrative of inevitability. Building on Ben Singer (2001), Griffiths argues that "the instability of [Victorian stage] melodrama—the sense that violence always lurks in the wings—is a more general feature of energetic modernity," but "melodrama does not simply reflect and reproduce the energy culture." Rather its "thematics, stock characters, situations, and narratives often dramatize the struggle to control the machines and explosive instruments of energetic modernity, and to manage the laborers—miners, factory workers, and soldiers—required to construct, power, and deploy them" (2018, 621). The melodramatic mode par excellence that inherits this nineteenth-century obsession with accidents born of a techno-extractivist and energist modernity is the disaster movie, which became a global genre in the 1970s. Big-budget disaster films are always melodramas – they pit asymmetrical powers against each other and often narrativize social inequalities as spatial forces (Kakoudaki 2002). These disasters are often technological – featuring the nightmare vision of modernity gone rogue – burning trains, sinking ships, crashing cars, and exploding coal mines (Keane 2001). In their pitting of human and nonhuman forces and their suggestion of unequal agonistic battles, disaster melodramas have the capacity to exceed the logic of technological inevitability. Unlike the popular reportage surrounding Kapoor's near-death accident, *Kaala Patthar* refuses to explain away mining accidents as "inexplicable" aberrations or as an intrinsic feature of coal as substance. Instead, the film takes great pains to exhaustively break down the chain of human decision-making and capitalist greed that leads to land subsidence or water flooding. In fact, one central engine of the sprawling plot is the steady drive toward disaster once the dangers of reckless tunneling have been ignored by Dhanraj and his henchmen.

The focus on the accidental as a particular temporality, combined with the commercial logic of the big-budget Hindi melodrama, creates a sentimental arc that ends with a new dawn and a clear savior. Following Griffiths, one might suggest that *Kaala Patthar* asks one central question: who will master energetic modernity, and how? Nationalization is the film's answer; the film's true heroes are a harmonious and hardworking collective of laboring bodies and a benevolent state. With the benefit of hindsight, it is now possible to read *Kaala Patthar* as a tortured product of a postcolonial patriotic vision striving to reconcile coal nationalism with labor rights, melodramatic collectivism with heroic individualism. Salim-Javed's decision to structure the film as a Manichean battle between worker and capitalist, while holding up nationalization as a future panacea, is at once disingenuous and genuinely confused. Produced at a time when it was still too early to tell if the misfortunes of the coal industry were due to governmental malfeasance or a consequence of decades of short-sighted mismanagement by various colonial and neocolonial private interests, *Kaala Patthar* points hopefully toward a governmental solution to the "coal problem."[4] We must also recall that the film was released in August 1979, in the aftermath of the Emergency and during a period of chaotic governmental upheavals, and it might be that the filmmakers sought to evade the political volatilities of the time by turning to a less controversial enemy. However, by obfuscating, anachronistically, the role of the state in the dangerous travails of extractive labor, the film prevaricates.

One last point remains to be made: inspired by the Chasnala mining disaster of 1975 in which 375 miners lost their lives, *Kaala Patthar* cleaves close to the human in its explicit aesthetic address via dialogue and speech-making. The protagonists' rousing activist dialogues focus on capitalist greed and exploitation, and subaltern heroism and sacrifice, but take little cognizance of the environmentalist discourse that was gaining traction in India and across the world in the late 1970s. There are clear contradictions between the film's evocative mise-en-scène which visually maps collective energy and exhaustion, and its use of impassioned speech which speaks only of human loss. This can partly be explained by the historically anthropocentric implications of the "industrial accident" as immediate loss of human life rather than the durational and systemic depletion of human–nonhuman assemblages. The film's uneven approach to the catastrophic thus allows us to parse Indian coal melodrama's potentialities and failings in narrating ecological futures.

Conclusion

Kaala Patthar sensorially maps the sentimental journey of coal, coal mines, and coal miners in an age of national development and economic growth. It mobilizes heightened sentiment, musicality, and action – the three pillars of early melodrama – to generate a romantic-epic myth of the heroic male energy worker, be it a miner or engineer. At the same time, it also dramatizes the counter-temporality of extractive modernity – the slowness of *longue durée* exhaustion that impacts bodies and landscapes alike. The film visibilizes the uneven social relations that are entangled within coal economies, with differential access to energy production, consumption, and accumulation. As such, this sprawling, multi-plot coal melodrama offers modest ways to spatialize questions of labor and extraction across the continuum of human–nonhuman, figure and ground, and brings new geologic subjects into view.

Sentimental cultural narratives centered around fossil fuels play an important role in sustaining popular enthusiasm for, or indifference toward, accelerated carbon extraction. Coal melodramas can help us understand the shadow histories of carbon capitalism and important national narratives that produced fossil fuels as romantic and energy workers as heroic. Looking at this history of cultural production from the Global South allows us to see the ways in which energetic modernity was critical to postcolonial state formation. The developmental drive of the newly-formed Indian nation-state regularly tapped into the affective script of "coal nationalism" to garner popular consent for extractive industrial projects that were once deemed "coal colonialism." As we enter an era wherein coal is once again being repurposed as a nationalist symbol, coal melodramas can give us tools to understand not only how we have come to this pass, but where we can go from here.

Notes

1 Here I'd like to highlight emerging work on mining, minerals, and coal, from film and media scholars such as Brian R. Jacobson, Liam Cole Young, and Priya Jaikumar.
2 Eg. *In the Coal Mines* (1958), *Black Diamond* (1961), *Mining Coal* (1968), *King Coal* (1977), *Coal* (1978), *Burning Stone* (1978), *Coal for the Masses* (1979).

3 Readers with access to the ProQuest Historical Newspapers database can view the ad at this permalink: https://www.proquest.com/hnptimesofindia/docview/501064664/A897D934F53C45A6PQ.
Display Ad #2. Coal India – no title, *Times of India*, Nov 1, 1976: 6. Image ID 501064664.

4 There are indications in the pre-release publicity of the film that initially the film-makers had wanted to depict "the pre- and post-nationalization conditions of a mining village while it tries to tackle the problems of miners." *Screen*, August 17, 1979, image caption on page 20.

Works Cited

Adorno, Theodor and Max Horkheimer. [1947] 2002. "The Culture Industry: Enlightenment as Mass Deception." In *The Dialectic of Enlightenment*. Translated by Edmund Jephcott, 94–136. Redwood City: Stanford University Press.

Arnold, Annika. 2018. *Climate Change and Storytelling: Narratives and Cultural Meaning in Environmental Communication*. Cham: Palgrave Macmillan.

Bidwai, Praful. 2015. "Indian Government Sanctions Greenpeace to Send a Menacing Message." *Ecologist*. April 28, 2015. https://www.tni.org/my/node/14767

Bozak, Nadia. 2012. *The Cinematic Footprint: Lights, Camera, Natural Resources*. New Brunswick: Rutgers University Press.

Cubitt, Sean. 2017. *Finite Media: Environmental Implications of Digital Technologies*. Durham: Duke University Press.

Dabral, Mangalesh. 2008. "Exhaustion." Translated by Robert A. Hueckstedt. *Indian Literature* 52.4: 117–118.

Dawson, Ashley. 2017. "Coal." In *Fueling Culture: 101 Words for Energy and Environment*, edited by Jennifer Wenzel and Patricia Yaeger, 83–86. New York: Fordham University Press.

ENVIS Centre on Environmental Problems of Mining. 2022. "Mining Accidents in India." http://ismenvis.nic.in/Database/Mining_Accidents_in_India_24483.aspx. Accessed March 10, 2022.

Fay, Jennifer. 2018. *Inhospitable World: Cinema in the Time of the Anthropocene*. New York: Oxford University Press.

Ferris, Robert. 2015. "India's Jharia Coal Field Has Been Burning for 100 Years." *CNBC*. December 2, 2015. https://www.cnbc.com/2015/12/02/indias-jharia-coal-field-has-been-burning-for-100-years.html. Accessed March 7, 2022.

Filmfare. 1979. "Buried Alive." January 1–15, 1979: n.p.

Friedrich-Alexander-Universität. 2021. "Global Sentimentality Project." https://www.sentimental.phil.fau.de/

Ghose, M.K. and S.R. Majee. 2020. "Assessment of Dust Generation Due to Opencast Coal Mining – An Indian Case Study." *Environmental Monitoring and Assessment* 61: 257–265.

Ghosh, Amitav. 2016. *The Great Derangement: Climate Change and the Unthinkable*. Chicago and London: University of Chicago Press.

Gorfinkel, Elena. 2012. "Weariness, Waiting: Endurance and Art Cinema's Tired Bodies." *Discourse* 34.2–3: 311–347.

Government of India. 2019. "Five Year Vision Document, 2019–2024. Group III – Resources." https://coal.nic.in/en. Accessed April 15, 2022.

Griffiths, Devin. 2018. "Petrodrama: Melodrama and Energetic Modernity." *Victorian Studies* 60.4: 611–638.

Gupta, Smita. 2019. "Jharia's Century-Old Fire Kept Ablaze by Crime and Politics." In *The Wild East: Criminal Political Economies in South Asia*, edited by Barbara Harriss-White and Lucia Michelutti. London: UCL Press, 68–91.

"India's Crisis Decade: the 1970s and Contemporary Analogies." 2018. Princeton Institute for International and Region Studies panel. Panelists Gyan Prakash and Srinath Raghavan. Moderator Sunil Khilnani. https://piirs.princeton.edu/event/indias-crisis-decade-1970s-and-contemporary-analogies.

Juhasz, Antonia. 2017. "Spill." In *Fueling Culture: 101 Words for Energy and Environment*, edited by Jennifer Wenzel and Patricia Yaeger. New York: Fordham University Press, 318–320.

Kakoudaki, Despina. 2002. "Spectacles of History: Race Relations, Melodrama, and the Science Fiction/Disaster Film." *Camera Obscura* 17.2: 109–153.

Keane, Stephen. 2001. *Disaster Movies: The Cinema of Catastrophe*. London and New York: Wallflower Press.

Kohli, Kanchi and Manju Menon. 2020. "India's U-Turn on 'Clean' Energy is a Bad Move." *Wire*. June 16, 2020. https://thewire.in/environment/coal-washing-environment-ministry-changing-rules

Lahiri-Dutt, Kuntala. 2016. *The Coal Nation: Histories, Ecologies and Politics of Coal in India*. London and New York: Routledge.

LeMenager, Stephanie. 2011. "Petro-Melancholia: The BP Blowout and the Arts of Grief." *Qui Parle: Critical Humanities and Social Sciences* 19.2: 25–55.

Mazumdar, Ranjani. 2022. "Technological Obsolescence and Space in Bombay Cinema." In *A Companion to Indian Cinema*, edited by Neepa Majumdar and Ranjani Mazumdar, 540–568. Hoboken and Chichester: Wiley Blackwell.

Miller, Elizabeth Carolyn. 2021. *Extraction Ecologies and the Literature of the Long Exhaustion*. Princeton and Oxford: Princeton University Press.

Mohamed, Khalid. 1979. "*Kaala Patthar*: Stress on Superficiality." *Times of India*, August 26: 4.

Mukherjee, Debashree. 2020. *Bombay Hustle: Making Movies in a Colonial City*. New York: Columbia University Press.

Nixon, Rob. 2011. *Slow Violence and the Environmentalism of the Poor*. Cambridge and London: Harvard University Press.

Schaffner, Anna Katharina. 2016. *Exhaustion: A History*. New York: Columbia University Press.

Seow, Victor. 2021. *Carbon Technocracy: Energy Regimes in Modern East Asia*. Chicago: University of Chicago Press.

Sethna, Hilla. 1979. "Yash Calls *Kaala Patthar* an Adventure, Not a Disaster Film." *Screen*, August 24, 1979: 24.

Shutzer, Matthew. 2021. "Subterranean Properties: India's Political Ecology of Coal, 1870–1975." *Comparative Studies in Society and History* 63.2: 400–432.

Singer, Ben. 2001. *Melodrama and Modernity: Early Sensational Cinema and its Contexts*. New York: Columbia University Press.

Starosielski, Nicole and Janet Walker, eds. 2016. *Sustainable Media: Critical Approaches to Media and Environment*. New York: Routledge.

Time of India. 1976a. "Caring for One Lakh Coal Miners Is a Big Job." Advertisement. November 18: 6.

———. 1976b. "Today More and More Textile Mills Are Changing to Coal in Preference to Oil." Advertisement. June 29: 12.

————. 1977. "Participative Management Is an Integral Part of the Coal India Philosophy." Advertisement. March 5: 1.

Vasudevan, Ravi. 2011. *The Melodramatic Public: Film Form and Spectatorship in Indian Cinema*. New York: Palgrave Macmillan.

Virilio, Paul. 2007. *The Original Accident*. Translated by Julie Rose. Cambridge: Polity.

Wenzel, Jennifer. 2019. *The Disposition of Nature: Environmental Crisis and World Literature*. New York: Fordham University Press.

Yusoff, Kathryn. 2013. "Geologic Life: Prehistory, Climate, Futures in the Anthropocene." *Environment and Planning: Society and Space* 31: 779–795.

————. 2015. "Geologic Subjects: Nonhuman Origins, Geomorphic Aesthetics and the Art of Becoming Inhuman." *Cultural Geographies* 22.3: 383–407.

4

THE SUSTAINABLE AUDIOVISUAL INDUSTRY IN CATALONIA SEEN THROUGH THE GREEN SHOOTING INITIATIVE

Marta Lopera-Mármol and Manel Jiménez-Morales

Introduction

Globalization has undoubtedly caused diverse challenges. It has entailed rapid and complex environmental stewardship and raised questions about social inequality, progress, and inclusion, as well as economic and demographic changes (Pattberg 2007, 1–2). Consequently, to manage these consequences and effects, institutions, businesses, and administrations worldwide are encouraging actions and discourses that align with a commitment to sustainable development. In fact, the European Union and the United Nations are partnering in efforts to achieve, within the implementation of the 2030 Agenda framework, a practical, multilateral approach and a rules-based international order in which Sustainable Development Goals (SDGs) act as a valuable vehicle for projecting the EU's values and objectives on a global scale, as well as facilitating a shared framework for forging international partnerships (United Nations 2015). These actions have implications for global political stability in their effort to meet the diverse socioeconomic and environmental needs of different communities.

Unquestionably, mass media echoes this sustainability phenomenon, placing discourses within sustainability's three major components – economic, social, and environmental – on the public agenda and in audiences' social imaginary (Berglez 2008). Hence, mass media's *agenda-setting* (Berglez and Olausson 2014, 54) presents a public discourse cross-media on the subject of sustainable development. For scholars, "there has never been a greater need for analyzing and understanding the roles of media and communication in the politics of the environment" (Hansen 2019, 1), which they attend to along with attention to media's societal and economic interrelationships (Hansen 2019; Hickel 2020; Hornsey et al. 2016; Starosielski 2016). In this

DOI: 10.4324/9781003246602-6

junction between societal action, economic context, and mass media impact, a great deal of communication research focuses on how the media covers and reports socioeconomic and environmental issues (Hansen 2019, 106). Nevertheless, less attention has focused on how the UN "pillars and SDGs seem to have forgotten one main goal: culture and its industry" (Lopera-Mármol and Jiménez-Morales 2021, 1). Media culture not only allows us to create environmental imagery but also a social agenda that could lead to changes in other SDGs. The media industry needs to scan and rethink its *raison d'être*, its practices, the institutions that finance its products publicly, and whether they are local, national, European, or global.

Current data about the lack of sustainability measures throughout all sectors is worrying, and media culture is not isolated from that reality. Research has shown that, unfortunately, media industries, particularly film and television, have many negative impacts on sustainability. In this setting, the European Union launched a proposal in 2017 titled "Green Screen," with a five-year development plan and a budget of 2.2 million euros, which attempted to apply, at the regional level, environmental European policies to reduce the carbon footprint and enhance the best practices of the audiovisual industry (Sáez 2019). In addition, the Technology and Innovation department of the European Broadcasting Union (EBU-Tech) has launched a section dedicated to sustainable media workshops, reports, news, events, and publications (European Broadcasting Union 2022).

In this context, the concept of Green Shooting is conceived to describe "a countercultural concept linked to the financial, health, social, professional and educational concerns of the audiovisual field and its sustainable well-being" (Lopera-Mármol and Jiménez-Morales 2021, 4). Green Shooting attempts to define and disseminate collective sustainable practices from the preproduction to consumption phases of the audiovisual field and aims to foster sustainable awareness among newer generations of professionals and scholars. Green Shooting was chosen as it evokes the idea of "green" as a synonym for "sustainable," "ecological," "equitable" and "social," among others – and also appeals to and aligns with the European Union's Green Deal, "an ambitious package of measures ranging from ambitiously cutting greenhouse gas emissions, to investing in cutting-edge research and innovation, to preserving Europe's natural environment" (European Commission 2020). Thus, the concept takes on sustainable practices beyond an ecological imaginary. Green Shooting also deals with "social sustainability" and "brings us to the real heart of a post-capitalist economy ending planned obsolescence, capping resource issues, shortening the working week, reducing inequality, and expanding public goods. These are all essential steps to reducing energy demand," as Hickel has pointed out (2020, 232). In other words, Green Shooting is framed on the premise that to achieve degrowth and environmental balance, social and economic players need to be accounted for. There is a need for highly specialized, integrated bottom-up approaches and associated experts to achieve transformative results. Nonetheless, due to the audiovisual industry's heterogeneous nature, there is no one-size-fits-all solution when it comes to addressing its impact. The audiovisual sector is a multifaceted arena in which many profiles and several production practices hamper the creation of clear policies on Green Shooting.

Unsurprisingly, policies and practices of Green Shooting have been approached differently depending on the EU country where these audiovisual productions have been produced. Sustainable measures are timidly but nonetheless rapidly reaching Hollywood and European screen culture. Many countries have already implemented and systematized these practices, such as Belgium with entities including the Flanders Audiovisual Fund (VAF) and CineEuro; the United Kingdom, with the industry-wide BAFTA Albert Consortium that includes the British Broadcasting Corporation (BBC), the non-profit group Julie's Bicycle, and others; and the Nordic countries with such initiatives as the Nordic Eco Media Alliance (NEMA) (Kääpä 2018). Norway has the Northern Norway Film Commission and Sweden has a collaboration between Film I Väst, Filmpool Nord, and the Öresund Film Commission that launched, thanks to regional funds, a sustainable digital tool titled Hållbar Film that tries to improve the working conditions for the production companies while at the same time tracking and documenting the industry's impact. In Denmark, Sustainable Film and TV Production is an alliance that strikes for media sustainability initiated by Vision Denmark.

These sustainability practices across Europe are mainly enacted by a conscious and involved niche of individual professionals, and rarely through institutional policies. Unfortunately, this situation shows that the environmental sustainability movement is still a subculture within the entertainment industry, challenging the implementation of Green Shooting effectively. First, public detachment and cognitive dissonance tend to push threats such as socioeconomic inequality and climate change into the background. Climate researchers are "urging us to wake up and act right now, but at the same time, they imply that the trauma is not yet fully here, that there is still time to avert a disaster" (Hickel 2020, 17). These threats, more often than not, seem to be distant or not linked to people's everyday personal worries, or to an understanding of how their own actions, including those of media production and consumption impact the environment (Hornsey et al. 2016). Second, despite the EU's Green Screen funding, there is a general lack of academic studies, specific policies, institutional aid, and funds devoted to promoting sustainable media practices. This provokes a paucity of incitements to improve practices. Sustainability should be regarded as a non-negotiable axis, and not as a complementary or added value as it has been so far.

Furthermore, there is an avoidable yet prevalent confusion about the concept of sustainability, which is often understood as solely focused on the environment, but in fact, merges within cultural and socioeconomic discourses and considers policies oriented to values like equity, social democracy, and prosperity, as theories like the Triple Bottom Line (TBL) propose.

Despite these challenges, as mentioned, the sector is changing its roots and philosophy. This chapter attempts to provide a diagnosis of the current situation of the Catalan cinematographic sector, identify the centers of action, and detect some individual phenomena that have recently emerged in the industry of this Spanish region. By attending to Catalan cinema as ecocinema, this chapter contributes to research on the current state of this national industry while underlining some necessary practices and aiming to inspire new policies.

The Current Status of Catalan Cinema

"Catalan cinema," although difficult to define accurately, typically relates to productions produced and/or acted by Catalonians or dealing with Catalan issues. In the 1990s, certain individual films or filmmakers became known and led to what we know today as Catalan cinema (Allum 2016). In the 2000s, Catalan cinema began to be framed internationally as a particular industry due to the rise of co-productions, which boosted its presence beyond Spain's borders. The foundation of the *Acadèmia del Cinema Català*[1] (ACC) in 2008, a non-profit cinematography association created to bring together the entire Catalan film sector within a solvent and prestigious entity, was another step in the consolidation of the Catalan cultural and creative industry. Also, the Catalan language plays an important role (Jiménez-Morales and Balló 2020), despite the fact that Catalan film doesn't have the requirement that it should be spoken in the Catalan language. Catalan cinema "cuts across regional, national and international borders" (Allum 2016); it can also refer to multilingual productions, as with films such as *La vida secreta de las palabras* (Isabel Coixet 2005), *El cant dels ocells* (Albert Serra 2008), *Pa negre* (Agustí Villaronga 2010) *Les amigues de l'Àgata* (Laia Alabart, Alba Cros, Laura Rius and Marta Verheyen 2015) and *Júlia ist* (Elena Martín 2017).

Catalonia cinema is currently one of Spain's two most dynamic audiovisual industries (alongside Madrid) and has become highly competitive in Europe. However, the main challenge Catalan cinema now faces is the lack of investment, as Judith Colell, president of the ACC, explained in a recent interview with *Crónica Global* (Colás 2022). This lack of investment leaves Green Shooting policies on the back burner. In fact, it was not until 2017 that the Institut Català de les Empreses Culturals[2] (ICEC) began to show interest in sustainable practices. From 2019, it began to consider ecology or the environment (though leaving aside economic and social axes of sustainability) as an evaluation criterion for the purpose of subsidies, but not as a requirement. The Catalan cinema and cultural industry often present the confusion over sustainability as solely an ecological issue, as CreArsa (a consultant company specialized in Audiovisual Social Responsibility) points out, Catalan cinema features many policies and lists of good practices, although scarce compared with other countries, provided by institutions or businesses, and mainly focused on environmental aspects. Moreover, they mistakenly use some of the tools and resources to present their social responsibility as a marketing value when other countries are already one step ahead. For instance, there seems to be competition over which carbon footprint calculator needs to be used, since some businesses require payment to use them, an issue the United Kingdom, for example, has already addressed (Calawerts 2022).

Cultural industries in Catalonia present a lack of specific policies, aid, and knowledge about sustainability for both audiences and practitioners. In fact, the *Consell Nacional de la Cultura i de les Arts*[3] (CoNCA), which acts as an adviser to the Catalan Government on cultural policies, recognizes that the cultural, media, artistic, and cultural community in Catalonia has room for improvement and that it requires procedures to better embody a sustainable transition and to promote mechanisms, models and tools to meet current sustainable challenges (CoNCA 2020). Green Shooting is a niche market, primarily because while sustainable media measures are well-received, the misconception still exists that applying them makes productions more expensive (Lopera-Mármol and Jiménez-Morales 2021). A small number of businesses and particular production companies have started work on Green Shooting policies and applied them to their audiovisual products. For example, *Jurassic World: Fallen Kingdom* (2018), can be considered an example of sustainable filming (Calawerts 2022) within the Spanish film industry if we take into account the nationality of the film's director (Antonio Bayona), coproducer (Belén Atienza), and several crew members (including cinematographer Óscar Faura and editor Bernat Vilaplana), although it is generally considered a Hollywood production.

To improve the present situation, there is a need for institutions to support Green Shooting policies to promote greater cooperation at the national and international levels, rather than opting for internal competition. In this context, European projects such as the above-mentioned Agenda 2030 play a considerable role. Moreover, it is fundamental that, both at an enterprise and an institutional level, the industry should consider cultural and social rights that protect gender, diversity, and minorities in the sustainability framework (in other words, create regulations that benefit people both in and outside the audiovisual industry) because the cultural and creative sector has the capacity and, up to a certain point, the responsibility to help citizens understand the challenges facing humanity (CoNCA 2020).

The focus of this chapter is the cinema industry, but other current Catalan proposals exist in other sectors that link sustainability to other creative and cultural industries. Many exciting ideas are being advanced by publishers, video gamers, and in the scenic arts and at festivals, among others. For example, Pol·len Editions promotes the concept of eco-publishing, the management of environmentally sound publications, which consists of an analysis of the book's life cycle, its ecological backpack space, eco-designs, and monthly activities that revolve around issues of contemporary thought. La Central del Circ – which offers a creative space for experimentation, research, and creation among professionals in the field of the live performing arts – holds days for reflection featuring workshops and joint laboratories to help many companies improve their contribution to environmental responsibility. Centris, a promoter of music festivals, attempts to convey values that will be useful throughout life, such as recycling. Finally, Herobeat Studios, through its game *Endling*, presents an eco-aware adventure narrative.

Green Shooting: Steps toward a Sustainable Catalan Film Industry

The current artistic paradigm of sustainability, although far from being an example to follow, does welcome change because artistic procedures and creativity can be the key to innovation. In these areas, Catalan universities and other higher education institutions are starting to lead some of the research on media sustainability regionally, through attention to the work that researchers such as Seán Cubitt, Toby Miller, Anders Hansen, Stephen Rust, Nicole Starosielski, and Janet Walker, to name just a few, have been working on for 15 or 20 years. Catalonia's universities can promote collaborations and build on prior works by devoting more resources to education on environmental and sustainable materials and procedures, investing in research in all the various fields and sectors that play a role in the cinema industry, and promoting the development of sustainable technologies that meet the sector's needs and sanction poor practices. To do this, Universities such as Pompeu Fabra (UPF) and the University of Barcelona (UB) are applying certain results of this research to particular subjects in their curricula, with the awareness that they are training the future professionals of the industry.

Specifically, from 2020 to the present, an educational initiative titled "Green Shooting: Sustainable Culture," from which the concept previously mentioned was conceived, has been promoted by UPF under the "Planetary Wellbeing" framework. The latter term corresponds to an institutional proposal to ensure that sustainability is applied to all disciplines across the university. The initiative considers the established idea of planetary health, as proposed by the Rockefeller-*Lancet* initiative. Thus, the extension was deliberate since it corresponds to an amalgamation of more concepts aligned with the three pillars of sustainability and the 17 SDG. Hence, "Planetary Wellbeing" is a normative concept; it sets a regulative ideal for all of humanity and the planet. "Securing the complete wellbeing of every living being is unattainable but is a guiding aspiration" (Antó et al. 2021, 5). The aim of this institutional proposal, which was clearly inspired by international initiatives committed to a sustainable culture in economic, social, and environmental terms, is envisaged as "an overarching concept, providing institutional impetus and top-down support for an integrated understanding of the unprecedented challenges that our planet faces concerning the Anthropocene and the climate crisis" (Antó et al. 2021, 9). As this initiative shows, while a great deal of international research has been done, sustainability is still a niche of academics and policymakers, which is worrying since information and communications technologies (ICTs) and their developments and impacts are increasingly palpable. There is still a lack of mandatory implementation by the Spanish Ministry of Education to establish a long-term strategy in the public media sector.

It is also important to note that filmmaking practices, typically those of regional cinemas and specific genres like documentaries, due to their already small scale and low budget, already adopt measures that are somewhat sustainable. For instance, documentaries, often tend to consider how to tackle socioeconomic and environmental issues or themes in their ideation. However, although they tend to fall under a de-growth model necessary for cinema as a global industry, they still need measures and guidelines to better inform and help them adopt more sustainable filmmaking practices. The Green Shooting project enabled us to analyze the current status of the audiovisual industry in Catalonia and the steps the industry should take to move toward a sustainable future, which we outline below.

Incentives to Promote Green Shooting, such as Funds or Valuable Recognition for the Productions That Apply to Funds

As we have seen, there is a need for clear regulations that genuinely inform the current situation and the actual measures of action that can be taken. In addition, an incentive or public aid plan could be developed to encourage sustainability in all the cultural industries in the Catalonia region (CoNCA 2020). Although understandings exist of the different framings and cultural packages as to how to tackle these issues, they do not solve the root problem. Unfortunately, instead of pushing forward socioeconomic and environmental change, many enterprises and public/private organizations are mistakenly falling for the well-known phenomena of greenwashing, purplewashing, redwashing, etc. Behind these terms lurk extremely complex issues that require a great deal of engagement – scientific, philosophical, ethical, moral, and economic. In the case of the film industry, many studios fall for the fallacy that they are being sustainable by switching their scripts from paper to digital, hiring women in managerial roles, opting for a flexitarian diet, etc. However, the truth is that a transparent investigation needs to be carried out to confirm whether such changes are making an impact, real or not, at a structural and systematic level.

Promotion and Dissemination of the Notion of Green Shooting

In the Catalan film industry, there is still a long way to go in terms of political leadership, budgets, and strategy for investment in sustainability that would significantly impact the field, despite the efforts that have been devoted to this goal. Hopefully, practitioners who attended the workshops will continue to create networks by sharing experiences, knowledge, and tools to encourage others to join them in the challenge to build a sustainable cinema, as in the cases of *Fresco Films, Promálaga, PAC, CFFF,* etc. However, this training, advice, and assistance should be offered and provided by the funding institutions of Catalan cinema, which are primarily public.

Visibilization of Green Shooting Practices

Audiences draw most of their knowledge on scientific and sustainable issues from mediated communication, and consequently, this acts as a primary source of information (Hansen 2019, xviii). Hence, portrayals of media sustainability on- and off-screen significantly influence policy discourse at the national and international levels (Anderson 2011). The influence of artists and the community must play a key role in fostering a change of mindset. In this context, celebrities play a significant part, particularly actors/actresses, athletes, influencers, musicians, and artists. In recent decades, they have become claim-makers and advocates for sustainable issues and discourses ranging from the #MeToo Movement to the climate change debate. In fact, in the last ten years, "special attention is paid to the *celebrification* of climate change as research indicates that it is of growing significance and constitutes a newly-emerging area of academic interest" (Boykoff and Goodman 2009). Celebrity possesses a certain cultural power and acts at a symbolic level. Celebrities can provide a human-interest angle to themes that would otherwise be perceived as remote from audiences' everyday lives. Consequently, stars can offer greater visibility, grab the attention of the public, and reach out to people thanks to their high-profile status and persuasive power. By doing so, they can shine a light on specific sustainability issues for the purpose of agenda-setting and help to shape public opinion. However, celebrities can function as a double-edged sword. On the one hand, they can act as a valuable means for sustainable groups – both at a state or NGO level – to mobilize and promote a particular discourse in the public arena. On the other hand, as Weiskel argues, "celebrity politics is a deception that distracts people from dealing with fundamental issues concerning democracy and social change" (2005, 397). Hence, their involvement in sustainable politics can be perceived as either a democratization process or a distraction. Consequently, while NGOs can benefit from a celebrity spokesperson, due to their excellent public relations function, the message they are providing and its legitimacy may eventually be questioned. Even so, the audiovisual industry should commit to fostering a content that is sustainable, restorative, inclusive, equitable, intersectional, and circular. Many authors and creators maintain that "the forces of supply and demand should be freed from interventions by regulation authorities"' (Hornsey et al. 2016, 2).

In the case of Catalan cinema, there is a lack of celebrification, though female directors have been taking a bigger role in the last 20 years, thereby allowing a different kind of sensitivity and gaze to emerge, but still far from the promotion and dissemination of other Green Shooting policies that go beyond intersectional gender initiatives. The fact that the Catalan star system clearly intersects with the Spanish one makes it difficult to see if the celebrification strategies target specifically Catalan audiences or a broader spectrum. At the same time, the Catalan industry is well-known for the greater multimedia activity of its artists, and their media impact chiefly depends on the impact of the production they are working for, not on their own charisma.

Guidelines for Applying Green Shooting

Catalan cinematographic and media institutions need to draw up a catalog of comprehensive measures related to sustainable production with which actors in the sector must comply to access the corresponding grants. Current guidelines launched by different enterprises and businesses already exist, but they are simplified and outdated in comparison to the measures that other countries have already devised and applied such as *The Green Production Guide*. There are two main shortcomings in this regard: first, sustainable measures need to be applied from the very start, and that includes the creative, storytelling, and narrative processes. Second, the absence of the figure of eco-consultant/eco-assistant/eco-supervisor.

The inclusion of these measures as a requirement to obtain specific, competitive funds from public institutions to develop audiovisual productions can make a difference from the point of view of promoting the Green Shooting culture. At this moment, the ICEC is in charge of the regional aid for the Catalan audiovisual projects. Among the requirements for any production applying for an ICEC-funded grant, there are no explicit allusions to anything related to sustainable production, probably because the attribution of these funds is mainly content-driven and because Green Shooting policies are still a pending issue. The progressive inclusion of certain requirements for promoting socially and environmentally responsible productions can help to foster a more effective public policy.

Institutionalization of the Figure of the Eco-Consultant

An eco-consultant, also known as eco-assistant is a representative or go-to person responsible for the sustainability of film production. They educate and assist production staff and employees on everything from pre-production conceptualization to on-set practicalities, as well as contributing to the final strategy of distributing and exhibiting the film according to the principles of sustainability. They can act on their own or, if the production is big enough, the eco-consultant can have an eco-supervisor/eco-manager responsible for monitoring and reducing the film's carbon footprint. This role is well-established in specific productions, mainly in the United States, but it has not yet become an established figure like that of director, art director, screenwriter, etc. This role needs to be institutionalized to guarantee a smooth transition to sustainability policies and Green Shooting practices.

In the specific case of the Catalan industry, it's not just that there is a lack of institutionalization of this particular role, the problem is that there are not, at present, enough professionals capable of taking it on. It is indeed an emerging profession and needs to be recognized, made visible, and promoted in terms of training and education. The inclusion of this figure in professional unions could also help to promote this role. Again, from the perspective of the higher education industries, full training should be offered for these specific profiles.

Awards and Prizes for Green Shooting Perspectives

Currently, the Catalan Cinema has no recognition in the form of awards or prizes for productions that have applied a strong Green Shooting policy or social minority representation (gender, race, LGBT+, etc.) (Lopera-Mármol and Jiménez-Morales 2021, 3). This is particularly significant when we consider that the Catalan context depends on public finance. Catalonia has at least 25 festivals and screenings of film and audiovisual creations using different approaches and genres. None of them take this issue into account. The two main festivals, the D'A film festival and Sitges Festival, have not created such an award category, nor does it feature among the categories of the ACC's *Premis Gaudí*. Nonetheless, it is important to note that there are international festivals, such as *Suncine Fest*, devoted exclusively to Green Shooting practices and content, though unfortunately their viewer numbers are less significant than those of other festivals, partly due to the ways in which local government promotes these different kinds of festivals, but also because theme-focused festivals have tended to be less popular than their generalist counterparts.

Education for Future Professionals, Current Professionals, and Audiences (Inclusion in Media Literacy Practices)

Finally, the Green Shooting initiative encompassed within the Planetary Well-being framework at Pompeu Fabra University aims to create a solid, expandable program about sustainable productions in which undergraduate and graduate students come to grasp the importance of this crucial issue and understand how to demand it as an audience by fundraising and raising awareness campaigns and how to apply it as future filmmakers, no matter what role they are playing in a production. The educational program currently seeks to link the academic practice to industrial agents to establish a connection with the real concerns of the Catalan industry. For example, the project facilitates a conceptual scientific, social, and educational dissemination of media sustainability through face-to-face workshops aimed at 20 UPF students and ten professionals from the media industry. The curriculum includes an introductory explanation of Green Political Thinking followed by case studies that detailed planning and communication of the sustainability strategy from pre-production topics such as logbook of meetings, inclusion, and diversity in the cast and the crew, production topics such as strategic waste management, the introduction of an eco-consultant (who advises production companies at all stages of a film's production) as a permanent crew member on set, to post-production topics such as promotion. Finally, an exercise invites participants to evaluate their own impact and that of their productions and to create a rough action plan for additional feedback.

Researchers need to identify the best spheres of commitment, in the absence of any educational consensus, while documenting the practices and developments that favor sustainable spaces and practices. Educational research in Green Shooting should range from short-term policy and local challenges to long-term visions of sustainable societies since, as Ralph and Stubbs point out "research and community involvement can produce long-lasting environmental effects and societal change" (2013, 71).

Conclusions

Research shows that Green Shooting in the Catalan film industry is regarded as a subculture community of involved practitioners who are applying its measures in a *modus operandi* that has not yet been systemized. Therefore, the need exists to create and support a pedagogy based on sustainable literacy, in which universities and public institutions should be at the center of its conceptualization and research, thus creating a school of thought. The amateur movement in the Catalan industry and the emergence of new forms of communication mediated through audiovisual tools require the promotion of new training policies and the dissemination of a culture of respect for Green Shooting practices that go beyond the professional industry. In addition, as we have analyzed throughout this chapter, the Catalan audiovisual industry needs to catch up with some of the fascinatingly skillful ways that other sectors, industries, and claim-makers (large corporations, governments, and public institutions) have managed, thanks to enlarged resources, to influence audiences on sustainability. For instance, the Catalan industry could make use of the advantages afforded by the digital media landscape or use well-researched and open access guidelines that have been applied successfully in previous media texts around the world with similar scales and budgets.

Sustainability policies in the film industry need to be tackled as a joint, coherent strategy that adopts standardized measurement tools, because while some individual institutional measures do help and their continuation is essential for the foreseeable future, education plays a significant role in the shift of attitudes and behavior toward a sustainable future in the media industry, as well as being an effective microphone for criticizing malpractice. Media plays a huge role in highlighting the wrongdoings of other industries, such as those of food and fashion as seen in documentaries like *Cowspiracy: The Sustainability Secret* (Kip Andersen and Keegan Kuhn 2014), climate change as seen in series such as those of David Attenborough, and socioeconomic issues including films and TV series such as *Dear White People* (Netflix 2017–21), *Get Out* (Jordan Peele 2017), *On the Basis of Sex* (Mimi Leder 2018), *The Bold Type* (Universal Television 2017–), and others. So, while we are not saying that these media texts should not continue to be produced (quite the opposite), we do need to recognize the material impacts the film industry plays on our planetary well-being. The industry must examine more in-depth its socioeconomic and environmental impact and rectify its current shortcomings. For this reason, universities and film schools should undertake the transformational changes necessary to embed environmental sustainability into all areas (theoretical, research, and practice) and into the general policies of the institution in question. Furthermore, educating and building sustainability awareness for future generations will prove crucial for a successful social citizenship strategy, since they will be tomorrow's leaders and advocates of sustainability. The aim of this strategy is to move the industry forward, thanks to the emerging talent and the new professionals who, little by little, will become incorporated into more established companies, teams, and crews.

In conclusion, if Catalan cinema wants to carry out a comprehensive, updated transformation of its sector, it should place sustainable recovery at its epicenter and champion the promotion of Green Shooting practices; systematic and well-prepared guidelines that are currently available and examples of other countries or regions to the media industry can serve as inspirational guidance for a very specific and effective application, awards that acknowledge these type of initiatives to funds that incentivize the adoption of green practices, and the development of pedagogical tools like the Planetary Wellbeing initiative to train future filmmakers. In addition, the actions of other creative and cultural industries that operate in similar ways could help the Catalan media sector find a way to implement these changes. A responsible cultural ecosystem should be fostered, and, above all, new practices elsewhere should be communicated and highlighted as an exemplary source of inspiration. By doing so, there might be a chance that an effective paradigm shift can be achieved, however, the industry first requires intelligent, strategic planning, with a solid and determined motivational system based on fiscal incentives.

Notes

1 English Translation: Catalan Film Academy.
2 English Translation: Catalan Institute of Culture Enterprises.
3 English Translation: The National Council of Culture and the Arts

Works Cited

Allum, Stephanie. 2016. "The New Catalan Cinema: Regional/National Film Production in a Globalized Context." PhD diss., Northumbria University Newcastle.
Anderson, Alison. 2011. "Sources, Media, and Modes of Climate Change Communication: The Role of Celebrities." *WIREs Climate Change* 2: 535–546. https://doi.org/10.1002/wcc.119.
Antó, Josep Maria, et al. 2021. "The Planetary Wellbeing Initiative: Pursuing the Sustainable Development Goals in Higher Education." *Sustainability* 13.6: 3372. https://doi.org/10.3390/su13063372.
Berglez, Peter. 2008. What Is Global Journalism? *Journalism Studies* 9.6: 845–858. https://doi.org/10.1080/14616700802337727.
Berglez, Peter and Ulrika Olausson. 2014. "The Post-Political Condition of Climate Change: An Ideology Approach." *Capitalism Nature Socialism* 25.1: 54–71. https://doi.org/10.1080/10455752.2013.845588.
Boykoff, Max and Michael Goodman. 2009. "Conspicuous Redemption: Promises and Perils of Celebrity Involvement in Climate Change." *Geoforum* 40: 395–406.
Calawerts, Georgia. 2022. "The Impact of Emerging Sustainable Practices in the Film Industry." *Arts Management and Technology Laboratory*, March 1, 2022. https://amt-lab.org/blog/2021/12/what-does-sustainability-look-like-in-the-film-industry.
Colás, Joan. 2022. "Judith Colell: La salud del cine catalán es mala, no por talento, sino por la falta de inversión." *Crónica Global*, January 9, 2022. https://cronicaglobal.elespanol.com/creacion/judith-colell-salud-cine-catalan-mala-talento-falta-inversion_586630_102.html.
CoNCA. 2020. "Lideratge mediambiental en el sector cultural i creatiu català." Accessed January 14, 2022. https://conca.gencat.cat/ca/detall/publicacio/sostenibilitat-00001
European Broadcasting Union. 2022. "EBU Technology & Innovation." Accessed May 7 2022. https://tech.ebu.ch/groups/spsm
European Commission. 2020. "European Green Deal." Accessed January 14, 2022. https://ec.europa.eu/clima/eu-action/european-green-deal_en.
Hansen, Anders. 2019. *Environment, Media and Communication*. Abingdon & New York: Routledge.
Hickel, Jason. 2020. *Less Is More: How Degrowth Will Save the World*. London: Windmill Books.
Hornsey, Matthew, Emily Harris, Paul Bain, and Kelly Fielding. 2016. "Meta-Analyses of the Determinants and Outcomes of Belief in Climate Change." *Nature Climate Change* 6: 622–626. doi.org/10.1038/nclimate2943.

Jiménez-Morales, Manel and Jordi Balló. 2022. "The Real and the Spoken: How the Use of Language in Catalan Films Contributed to the Construction of a Sense of Reality." *Journal of Catalan Studies* 1.23: 171–186.

Kääpä, Pietari. 2018. *Environmental Management of the Media*. London: Routledge.

Lopera-Mármol, Marta and Manel Jiménez-Morales. 2021. "Green Shooting: Media Sustainability, A New Trend." *Sustainability* 13.6: 3001. https://doi.org/10.3390/su13063001

Pattberg, Philipp. 2007. "Conquest, Domination and Control: Europe's Mastery of Nature in Historic Perspective." *Journal of Political Ecology* 14.1: 1–9. https://doi.org/10.2458/v14i1.21681.

Ralph, Meredith and Wendy Stubbs. 2013. "Integrating Environmental Sustainability into Universities." *Higher Education* 67: 71–90.

Sáez, Cristina. 2019. "Eco-Friendly Practices in the Film Industry." *CCCB Lab*, January 28, 2019. https://lab.cccb.org/en/eco-friendly-practices-in-the-film-industry/.

Starosielski, Nicole. 2016. "Pipeline Ecologies." In *Sustainable Media: Critical Approaches to Media and Environment*, edited by Nicole Starosielski and Janet Walker, 38–55. New York: Routledge.

United Nations. 2015. "Transforming Our World: The 2030 Agenda for Sustainable Development." Accessed January 14, 2022. https://www.un.org/ga/search/view_doc.asp?symbol=A/RES/70/1&Lang=E.

Weiskel, Timothy C. 2005. "From Sidekick to Sideshow—Celebrity, Entertainment, and the Politics of Distraction: Why Americans Are 'Sleepwalking Toward the End of the Earth.'" *American Behavioral Scientist* 49.3: 393–409. https://doi.org/10.1177/0002764205280203.

PART II
Ecocinema Discourses

5

EXTRACTION AND WILD CINEMA IN AFRICA

Cajetan Iheka

African film has always been twined with ecology. Africans were presented in colonial films as aspects of the landscape, as part of nature, nonhuman or lesser-human. They were excluded from filmic scenes to portray an idyllic Africa devoid of people and ready for colonization. When they appeared, it was as creatures in their natural state, with little interiority (Barlet 2000). With African filmmakers behind the camera at the height of decolonization struggles in the mid-twentieth century, film became a tool for enunciating African subjectivities (Diawara 1992). In these early celluloid films, Africans were positioned in relation to the land that they tilled for subsistence. The camera thwarts human mastery by lingering on the nonhuman world and positioning humans within their expansive landscape, showing their interconnection with ecologies. Safi Faye's film *Kaddu Beykat* (1975)—the first film by an African woman to gain critical acclaim—for instance, features numerous scenes of women working the land; this is also the case in Ethiopian filmmaker Haile Gerima's *Harvest: Three Thousand Years* (1975), where men and women are pictured tilling the land. The drought in Faye's film brings ecological problems to the forefront, foregrounding human dependence on land and elements. Gerima's film critiques Ethiopia's feudal system of land dispossession within a Third Cinema revolutionary register, but at its core makes an ecological argument. In both films, as in others from the period, the environment is not a mere backdrop. It is in constant relation with humans.

Ecology continues to be a theme today in African cinema as evident in both contemporary feature films and documentary films. I do not distinguish between commercial and independent or between fictional and documentary films in my understanding of African ecocinema. Following David Ingram in adopting a "pluralistic eco-aesthetic" (2013), I suggest that analyzing fictional

DOI: 10.4324/9781003246602-8

and documentary filmmaking can help us understand how African ecocinema is attentive to critiquing and ameliorating (neo)colonial extractive practices on the continent. African ecocinema encompasses blockbuster movies such as Neill Blomkamp's *District 9* (2009) and Chiwetel Ejiofor's *The Boy Who Harnessed the Wind* (2019), documentaries including Idrissou Mora-Kpai's *Arlit, deuxième Paris* (2004), Sarita Siegel and Gregg Mitman's *The Land Beneath Our Feet* (2016), and Julia Dahr's *Thank You for the Rain* (2017), as well as classical celluloid films such as Faye's and Gerima's.

While I briefly gesture to Gerima's *Harvest* to provide a historical analog, I limit my primary analysis here to Blomkamp's *District 9*, a commercial science fiction film about land contestation and bio-extraction in South Africa, and Siegel and Mitman's *The Land Beneath Our Feet*, a documentary focused on land concessions in Liberia. By paying attention to the technologies of filmmaking, we can see how both films reveal a preoccupation with extraction and exploitation. This preoccupation with depletion—of land, human labor, and nonhuman life—in *District 9* and *The Land* is significant. Even more, however, is each film's insistence on the possibility of repair: in Blomkamp's film, through renewable creative energy from waste; in Siegel and Mitman's film, via a proposal for an alternative wild cinema. "Wild cinema" should not be mistaken for the wildlife film that characteristically repeats the colonial stereotype of Africa as devoid of humans and peopled by animals and forests. As Jack Halberstam reminds us: "Colonial notions of the wild ... are all too familiar, but they do not exhaust the meaning of wildness" (2020, 9). As in Halberstam's *Wild Things*, wildness, in my usage, brims with potential; the wild refers to the "space beyond the home but also as a challenge to an assumed order of things from, by, and on behalf of things that refuse and resist order itself" (3). Bucking convention toward the open commons, wild cinema names a process—from production through distribution to consumption—that is attentive to a variegated social ecology, attuned to the land, and generative of community relations. As I demonstrate in the following pages, wild cinema incarnates both cinematic and ecological freedom.

Ecological Precedent in African Celluloid Film: The Example of Gerima's *Harvest*

Early African celluloid works such as Gerima's *Harvest* offer eco-social precedence to contemporary films. The film's opening scenes accentuate an ecology of interspecies connection. A peasant family wakes to nonhuman sounds—cocks crow, goats bleat, and cows moo—before beginning their arduous tasks. Nonhuman sounds enable logistical and ecological productivity. The film's "crowded acoustic field" accentuates the logistical value of the nonhumans, whose sounds orient the workers' day (Mattern 2021, 76). The film's protagonist, the revolutionary Kebebe, renders an ode to nature's free gifts: refreshing air, plant life, and water, "our friend." Long takes, aerial shots, and camera movement in Gerima's film foreground the earth even as close-up shots of human hands tending the soil show the mixing of human and nonhuman, of sweat and soil. Landscape shots foreground the hills and valleys. Animals are depicted using close-ups that emphasize their subjectivity and their labor in the feudal system, where they are joined by peasants as members of the exploited class. Within the Marxist theory of alienation that inspires Third Cinema, depicting human labor alongside animals can speak to dehumanization (Gabriel 1982). In this framing, the problem would be reducing the human to the status of animal within the feudalistic system of oppression. However, an ecocritical lens invites a different reading of human-animal interconnection. In equating human and animal exploitation, Gerima's film disrupts hierarchies and allows us to visualize their shared victimhood. The film's conflict is the tragedy of dispossession that extracts labor from people and land for the benefit of a few elites.

Besides their investment in ecological themes, the making of African films such as Gerima's also follows ecological principles. Operating with a limited budget, African filmmakers maximize film stock to save costs. They depend on natural light to shoot films, with scenes mostly shot outdoors on location. *Harvest* was shot using 16 mm with a small crew during the transition from Haile Selasie's rule to the regime of the Provisional Military Administrative Council in 1974. Using equipment borrowed from UCLA where Gerima was a film student, the crew maintained a 1/1 shooting ratio during the two weeks that they worked in Ethiopia. Gerima is not unique in practicing what he calls "guerilla-style" filmmaking (Willeman 1978, 33). The Senegalese filmmaker Ousmane Sembène made films from leftover film strips discarded by other filmmakers. Samba Gadjigo mentions, in his acclaimed biographical film *Sembène!*, how filmmakers from abroad would send leftover stocks after shooting their projects. Sembène describes this improvisational and ecologically conscious practice as *mégotage*, that is, filmmaking as akin to making cigarettes from the bits of tobacco left in the butts one collects off the street (Sugnet 2010).

Like the endangered animals and ecosystems they depict, many of these celluloid films themselves are at risk of disappearing due to the fragility of the medium and neglect. These films are inaccessible to Africans because the few existing copies are in libraries of Western and select African universities/institutes and 35 mm projection facilities are even rarer on the continent. These libraries/institutes approximate the zoos holding captive animals in Africa. It can be argued, as proponents for zoos and other animal enclosures do, that the libraries protect the films. However, such enclosures restrict access and freedom for both animals and films. Moreover, like some of the enclosed animals, surviving VHS tapes often suffer from neglect. African film and animals are in their own ways each threatened by extinction. To be sure, digitality has expanded the range of what constitutes African film and has increased access to

African materials just as it has brought animals closer to humans (Lippit 2000; Bousé 2003; Iheka 2021). Digitization has rescued African celluloid films from disappearing and made it easier to access them. African filmmakers have also embraced collaborations with major media platforms such as Netflix to produce and distribute African films. Yet the earlier celluloid films do not enjoy the wide accessibility that the video and digital revolutions have afforded contemporary filmmakers in Nollywood and elsewhere, including Blomkamp, whose *District 9* I turn to next.

But How Can We Go Back? Energy Extraction and Posthuman Collaborations in *District 9*

"But how can we go back?" asks Tania, Wikus van de Merve's wife in *District 9*, as her husband gradually transitions into an alien. He is sitting on the floor in District 9, the temporary camp of the aliens or "prawns," as they are pejoratively called. With tentacles in place of human hand, the distraught Wikus holds the phone to his ear as he denies false allegations of a sexual liaison with an alien.

Tania's poignant question serves as the film's verbal "punctum": that "element which rises from the scene, shoots out of it like an arrow, and pierces me," as Roland Barthes describes it (1981, 26). Wikus and viewers are invited to ponder what going "back" means. The close-up shot of Wikus invites a contemplation of the nature of return for the protagonist and his wife and for the aliens whose plan to return home was disrupted by the Multi-National United (MNU) invasion that Wikus leads. The film's conflict centers on the aliens' refusal to relocate to a new camp outside Johannesburg and Wikus' effort to regain his humanity after a gradual transformation into an alien. As soon as Wikus' transformation begins, following contact with alien technology, he is forcefully recruited as an experimental subject for biomedical research. Like the aliens, he becomes disposable and harvestable for energy yield. Wikus' life loses its human value. *District 9* problematizes the commodifying logic of energy extraction that undergirds the treatment of Wikus and the aliens even as it occasions the possibility of interspecies collaboration for renewable creativity.

District 9's poster features a mother ship suspended over the city of Johannesburg; the same shot appears in the film's opening sequence. Underneath the ship is written No Humans Allowed, which orients us to more-than-human presences, the alien occupants of the suspended ship, before we have even seen the film. Stuck and unable to go home, they constitute common enemies for the diverse humans of Johannesburg. Historically, Johannesburg's human population has been divided primarily along racial lines because of the colonial expropriation of land from black people and the segregation of the Apartheid policy that discriminated against non-whites including black South Africans. During Apartheid, black South Africans were forced into reserves known as

Bantustans, with passes required to access white areas. In the film, however, which was shot in Soweto (one of Johannesburg's townships), blacks and whites put away their differences to confront a common enemy: the aliens (Moses et al. 2010).

Like contemporary migrants from other African countries resident in South Africa, the film's aliens—foreigners—are accused of crime and disrupting the social climate. A plan is hatched by MNU to move them out of sight—200 kilometers outside of Johannesburg, to a concentration camp. Echoing the spatial segregation of Black Africans during apartheid, relocation here is a violent act of expulsion that the aliens resist. Wikus and his MNU colleagues arrive to offer the required 24-hour notice of eviction, which the aliens reject. As the officials search the aliens' homes, they discover weapons and sophisticated technological contraptions, including one that contains the fluid that begins Wikus' alien transformation when it accidentally spills on his body.

The choice of Johannesburg—Africa's world city—is significant for an ecological analysis of *District 9*. The city's (and South Africa's) economic status is a product of exploiting black lives lowered into the earth to excavate gold, beginning in the nineteenth century. Gold mining generates ecological destruction—from caved mines to dust and other waste—from the complex technical process. The gold miners are expendable bodies, disposable to the extent that the capitalist extractive process works smoothly (Mbembe and Nuttall 2004).

A similar logic of expendability undergirds *District 9*. After the alien camp is breached, many of the aliens are killed and others are taken away for biomedical research. Wikus is not spared as his transformation begins. He is forced to the lab where his body is subjected to the whims of scientists and the police force. He loses his name and human identity, as men in suits (including his own father-in-law) speak around him, indifferent to his presence and suffering. He is described as a specimen whose organs are to be harvested. He is not alone in this harvesting scene, however. Linked to him are other alien bodies decapitated for medical experiments. One poignant scene demonstrates their interconnected exploitation. Here, Wikus is forced to shoot an alien with one of the weapons recovered from raiding District 9. As the weapon can only be effectively operated by an alien, Wikus' transformed alien hand becomes especially useful for the experiment. When he initially refuses out of concern for the alien, his hand is mechanically forced to shoot the alien in a process that also hurts Wikus. As in Gerima's work, the hand returns as a rhetorical figure of extraction. With the peasants in *Harvest*, it is alienated labor working the landlord's land. With Wikus, it is an alienated body part, not just because it is turning "alien" but also because its agency is extracted from him. As the camera pans from Wikus to the alien and back to him as the alien is destroyed, the film concretizes their shared vulnerability. Rejected by humans as he gradually loses his human form, Wikus becomes a posthuman assemblage who must collaborate with nonhumans—aliens, machines, and the wild—to survive.

It is significant that Wikus finds refuge in the wild—in the grassland—as he escapes the lab. Hunted with helicopters and military officers in vehicles and on foot, he swerves from the urban and urbane into the wild. His yellow skin is camouflaged by the withering yellow grasses, which protect him even as they figure Wikus's own deterioration and assimilation into the nonhuman realm. As significant as Wikus' "collaboration" with plant life is, however, it is not the most transformative version of interspecies relationship in the film; that would be his work with the alien Christopher Johnson.

Initially conceived as a predatory relationship as Wikus tries to evict the aliens, the relationship between the two changes as both realize they need each other—Christopher for the fuel that Wikus confiscates to restart the mother ship while Wikus for the cure to recover his human corporeality. Working together, Wikus and Christopher storm the lab where they retrieve the fluid container. The lab is an instance of Elizabeth A. Povinelli's "architectures of geontological governance" (2016), which over-determine the status of life and nonlife in late liberalism. The lab is where "industrial capital depends on and, along with states, vigorously polices the separations between forms of existence so that certain kinds of existents can be subjected to different kinds of extractions" (16). As Wikus' initial capture enlightens him to the degree of exploitation happening in the lab, Christopher too learns of the predatory behavior of humans toward his own kind. The camera lingers as he stays with the remains of a dead alien—a victim of human extractive practices. This moment resonates for its emotional depth. Christopher's silence and his bowed head orient viewers away from the shine of the lab. The thing on the table once had life, the lingering camera seems to be telling us, but has now taken on new life as a prized specimen, as a commodity. Christopher's and the cadaver's silence speak volumes. They testify to human violence against others, which is further established with sounds from the exchange of gunfire between Wikus and the military chasing them. The acoustic ecology of this scene accentuates human violence even as it deepens the cross-species relationship between the human and nonhuman.

Escaping the lab, Christopher and Wikus return to Christopher's dwelling. Hidden beneath the dwelling is the infrastructure needed to revive the ship. The underground spaces of the film suggest an informal economy of exchange and resistance within the film. A vibrant informal "underground" commerce between aliens and humans (Nigerians) flows beneath the radar of the state, hiding an elaborate trade in bodies, weapons, and food. The xenophobic representation of Nigerians has been detailed elsewhere (Moses et al. 2010). But the supposedly barbarous Nigerian humans are not dissimilar from the South Africans; they also speak South African languages and prize alien flesh for its potency. As the South African state (represented by MNU and the military) intensifies its search for Wikus, given the value of his becoming-alien-body, the head of the Nigerian gang is also desirous to find him. Both groups plot to capture him alive: both want Wikus for his energy. Activating a form of capitalist fetishism, scientific medicine and traditional medicine cojoin uneasily in the quest for power. Alien technology ultimately rescues Wikus from the bloodthirsty South Africans and Nigerians.

District 9's alien technologies indicate a complex energy regime. When he first visits Christopher's workspace, Wikus is shocked to find a networked system of computers and, further underground, the ship infrastructure along with the recovered fuel. This scene, like Imre Szeman and Dominic Boyer's work in *Energy Humanities* "shed[s] light on the fuel apparatus of modernity, which is all too often invisible or subterranean" (2017, 9). This moment displaces the energy unconscious as it lays bare the "energy-intensive" nature of technological modernity (Chakrabarty 2009). The wires connecting the computers make apparent the flow of electric current just as the struggle for the fuel—Christopher accumulated the fuel for 20 years—indicates its powerful potential. In this underground scene, *District 9* also appears to be commenting self-reflexively on its own energy expenditure. In fact, the conglomeration of computers, cameras, ship components, lighting, and fuel closely resembles a robust film set. To use the title of Nadia Bozak's illuminating work on film's carbon expenditure, the underground—set off from the rest of the environment like the conventional film set is condoned off from the real world—represents much of *District 9's* "cinematic footprint" (2012).

The underground scene in *District 9* as a zone of energy radiation offers a way to rethink the form and function of other components of that space: Wikus and the aliens (Christopher and his son). Ultimately, "humanalien" and aliens are potential energy producers. We can reread the lab as an energy station, as the site for harvesting nonrenewable energy at an exorbitant and unsustainable cost. In this energy regime, Wikus is extremely valuable; however, his value derives less from his human qualities. In fact, he is incompetent. Wikus is special because of his nonhuman currents. He is a prized energy currency for MNU operatives and for the gang leader who covets his exceptional nonhuman power.

Wikus is rescued, in the end, by aliens who attack and kill his nemesis, MNU operative Koobus, therefore strengthening the interspecies solidarity in the film. In the last shot, we see Wikus fully transformed into alien. Refusing to be harvested or harnessed for his energy power, Wikus goes off-the-grid at the film's conclusion. As he loses touch with his human form, his cell phone becomes waste. The phone is matter out of place—as Mary Douglas would say (1966, 44); junk human technology, to put it differently. The cellular device becomes an indistinguishable part of the waste ecology (Maxwell and Miller 2012; Cubitt 2017).

Off-grid, outside human social circuits, with "the passage across the border," as Kenneth Harrow might describe it (2013, 62), Wikus models a form of energy creation, from waste. In message, Blomkamp's film joins the African films that Harrow analyzes for their waste potentiality. In *District 9*, posthuman Wikus crosses the border of the human into the posthuman category. Shunned by humans, he actualizes the productive renewal of trash. The film provides an affective economy as viewers see him among a heap of waste, making a flower-like object that he leaves on his (ex-)wife's doorstep. Posthuman Wikus "embraces" dirt, thinks with it, and marks it as symbolic of futurity (Lioi 2007; Sullivan 2012; Past 2019). The production of this artifact—an artificial flower—offers a model for the regenerative potential of waste. The final scene accentuates the creative potential of nonhuman assemblages.

We must return to Tania's haunting question: but how can we go back? The verbal punctum strikes again. Like Barthes' mother, whose picture is absent in *Camera Lucida*, Tania is nonvisible when she utters these memorable words. She is offscreen mediated by the cell phone on which her husband communicates with her. Yet her words, like Barthes' description of his mother's photograph, are striking and deserve reflection as the film ends. There is no "back" to which Wikus can return, because of human greed and disdain for the Other. Humans in *District 9* are not only incompetent; they are dirty, deceptive, and dangerous. The film's central message might be that humans have become unsustainable because of their extractive compulsions. *District 9* asks us, in the end, to stay with the posthuman as an aesthetic and ethical imperative.

Before turning to *The Land Beneath Our Feet*, it is worth considering the significance of the film's use of mockumentary techniques, including interviews and archival footage, for its ecological claims. A claim to truth and empirical reality underpins documentaries, which seek to render the film event close to historical reality through interviews and witness accounts. Blomkamp's film utilizes mock interviews throughout the film, including at the beginning where interviews with Wikus' parents and wife foreshadow his difficult experience. Interviews also include expert witnesses that heighten the film's aura of the real. Incorporating archival footage into the film aesthetic underscores its reality effect and extends recycling and reuse from *District 9*'s trash heap to its composition and editing. We can return to Wikus in the trash heap as figuration of filmmaking from discarded objects. The making of the artificial flower into its shape and color approximates film design into a particular narrative and visual style. Wikus in the dump even evokes resonances that go further back to the history of African filmmaking: Sembène's use of *mégotage*, that is, producing cigarettes from discarded butts, to explain the making of his film from recycled filmstock. The mockumentary impulse of the film points to its own constructedness as an aesthetic object, but it is best analyzed for its ecological relevance. The documentary impulse discourages viewers from being numbed by the science fiction spectacle, to refrain from seeing this film as mere big screen entertainment. The film's strategy nudges viewers to take the film's social message seriously: that is, to take seriously the extractivist orientation of human capitalism that has resulted in the absolute commodification of everything.

Liberia's Storied Landscape and Wild Cinema in
The Land Beneath Our Feet

On the surface, Blomkamp's film appears to have nothing in common with Siegel and Mitman's. *District 9* is a blockbuster science fiction film about an alien encounter in Johannesburg, while *The Land Beneath Our Feet* (hereafter, *The Land*) is a social documentary focused on land rights in Liberia. However, they share formal and thematic features: both films utilize the documentary techniques of interviews and archival footage and, most importantly, they critique land displacement and an extractivist disposition toward the earth. In one of the rallies for the legal enshrinement of land rights—the subject animating *The Land*—a woman carries a placard affirming that the earth belongs to the people. The poetics of land as commonwealth is negated in practice in the documentary—as it is in *District 9*. Both films propose wildness as an antidote to extraction. Ultimately, *The Land* instantiates as ecocinema through the film's preoccupation with land, its role as conservation technology, and for modeling an ecological cinematic process.

As an example of African ecocinema, Siegel and Mitman's co-directed documentary foregrounds the perspectives of the Liberians themselves as they tell their stories, unlike in the archival footage shown in the film where the Africans are seen but rarely heard. The archival footage is from the Harvard expedition to Liberia in 1926, an expedition supported by the Firestone Corporation. Mitman, who encountered the footage when he was invited to serve as a consultant on another film project, is the link to the film protagonist, Emmanuel Urey, who at the time was a graduate student at the University of Wisconsin Madison where Mitman is a professor of environmental history. *The Land* follows Emmanuel, who returns to Liberia with his degree and the archival footage. Mitman also wrote a book detailing Firestone's extractive practices in Liberia, *Empire of Rubber: Firestone's Scramble for Land and Power in Liberia* (2021). *The Land* must be understood within the context of ongoing contestation over land rights in Africa, from Angola to Zimbabwe.

Liberia, a country that attained independence in 1847, offers an insight into the land struggle in Africa because of both its history of land concession to corporations such as Firestone and of cohabitation and territorial counterclaims between the Indigenous ethnic groups and the freed Africans who settled there on their return from the Americas. This settlement involved a land purchase by the American Colonization Society in the nineteenth century and transformed land tenure in Liberia. As the film's interviewees clarify, land claims are traditionally communal. The individual or family takes custody of land on behalf of the real owners: the community. The nineteenth-century purchase, therefore, complicated the customary understanding of land as commonwealth while anticipating the historical dispossession that land concessions portended in Liberia, where successive conflicts rendered the government vulnerable to the lure of foreign investment for developmental purposes (Burrowes 2016).

Rapidly growing scholarship on land in Africa presents the problem as if predatory concessions and land grabs are recent developments on the continent. *The Land* challenges this presentist discourse through its attention to the 1926 Firestone concession that forcibly removed people from their land (literally removing the land from "beneath their feet"). The film's opening presents archival footage from the expedition showing the clearing of land and Africans working to build roads and rowing boats across water. Newspaper headlines also mark the Harvard biomedical expedition in Liberia, supported by Firestone, between July 7 and November 21, 1926 (Strong 1930). One prophetic newspaper headline displayed in the film reads: "Firestone declares door is open in Liberia." That the company—not the people or government of Liberia—is the agent here, registers the dispossession of the people. The people's agency is denied in this forceful door-opening but also as they are conscripted to build roads and displaced from their communities to grant a concession to Firestone. Mitman's book further details the ecological devastation resulting from Firestone's activities: "the felling, clearing, and burning operations that displaced people and denuded hilltops" (2021, 164). Humans and nonhumans in Liberia also became experimental subjects for medical research that supported Firestone's activities and furthered scientific advancement (Barber, Rice, and Brown 1932).

Part of the film's visual style is its use of parallel editing to demonstrate the continuation of that dispossession in contemporary concessions to foreign corporations. As the film cuts from archival footage to the present and back, it establishes a long history of extractive practices detrimental to the earth— conceived as an assemblage of humans and nonhumans. In this "cine-ecology" to borrow Debashree Mukherjee's term, "differential human depletion" coexists simultaneously with "planetary exhaustion" (2020, 14). The documentary suggests that the improvement of the video quality notwithstanding, there has been no substantial improvement in the conditions of the ecological beings in Liberia. Put differently, the people and the land remain rightless subjects.

Siegel and Mitman's film offers a cautionary note to attempts to separate land and water, as is often theorized in Western scholarship. In one telling scene, we learn from Emmanuel that boundaries in Liberia traditionally are marked by trees, footpaths, and creeks, all connected to communal stories of becoming and being. The land is a dense interconnected web of complex relations in this mode of being and seeing, encompassing the human people who live on it, their ancestors buried beneath it, and the other nonhuman beings it holds. Terrestrial and aquatic boundaries break down here, too, as the water is part of the land and vice versa. There is no land without the rivers and creeks and the stories of their interlinkage. This imbrication becomes especially apparent in a series of scenes focused on West Point, a township of the capital Monrovia, and one of the city's most populous areas. West Point is also the area most affected by environmental change since it is located on a peninsula and consistently experiences ocean erosion.

The West Point scenes in *The Land* reckon with the same issues as Ian Baucom's work on the Black Atlantic and climate change. In a telling scene showing the demolition of houses erected on the ocean shore in West Point, one evictee invites the camera crew to witness their dispossession by the state even as the water steadily encroaches on their homes. The film vision here aligns with Baucom's suggestion that we supplement the historical Black Atlantic analytic with awareness of "forcings of climate change" (2020, 5). With the return of former enslaved people to Liberia pivotal to land contestation in the West African country, the Black Atlantic model fits this West Point example. Relatedly, the encroaching ocean highlights climate change. Added to the pressures of climate change is the particular force of the postcolonial state. Climate change and the Black Atlantic may be residual features of this scene, but the dominant force of state violence is enshrined in the visual ecology of the scene and testimonies from those impacted by the event.

While mock archival footage bears witness to violence in *District 9*, actual archival material from the 1926 Harvard African Expedition provides the impetus for Siegel and Mitman's film, enabling a reckoning with the past and providing valuable insights for land reform policy in Liberia. Emmanuel, for instance, describes viewing the footage as the first opportunity to confront the Liberian past in visual terms. His feelings are not unique. When Emmanuel shows the footage as he travels around Liberia, the resonance is strong. People have limited knowledge of this history, so the footage becomes a pedagogical tool and a purveyor of the public sphere. As Emmanuel travels around showing the footage on phone and computer screens, the young people expand their historical knowledge of their country. The footage actualizes a participatory culture of engagement among citizens and presents an opportunity for the young to query the older generation about their experiences. Emmanuel, for instance, asks his father about the older man's participation in forced labor for road construction. In this scene, with the camera centered on him in close-up, Pa Taylor becomes the focus of knowledge production.

The archival material, and *The Land*, more broadly, serves as a technology of conservation. Siegel and Mitman's film positions the older generation as a repository of oral history and secures the (uncomfortable) memory of past ecology for the present and future. This conservationist role matters as the camera turns to Pa Taylor's grave at the end. With his passing, he cannot provide answers to Emmanuel's questions anymore. Emmanuel and the generation to come will now rely on the sound and images from *The Land* and from the archival material. Pa Taylor and his peers interviewed for *The Land* produce an alternative epistemology that will be preserved on film. Their histories trouble and supplement materials in the existing colonial and postcolonial libraries.

The ecological and epistemological import of *The Land* as message and as production practice becomes apparent in a scene that takes place, appropriately, outside of a library. On the wall behind Joseph Saye Guannu, the interviewee, is the name of the longest serving president of Liberia, for whom the library is named: W. V. S. Tubman. Land privatization in the form of concessions expanded significantly under the leadership of Tubman, a planter who served as president from 1944 to 1971 (Van der Kraaij 1983). In shooting outside the Tubman library, the film appears to be rejecting his privatization logic for the idea of the commons. Within a context of destroyed archives from the Liberian civil wars (1989–1997; 1999–2003), *The Land* produces a living knowledge generated against the formal structures of colonialism and the postcolonial state. At the same time, shooting outside returns film to the natural element. The environment provides natural light and ventilation for human participants and film apparatus. Renewable sources—sun and wind—power film machinery while trees protect against heat. Filmmaking, in this scene, becomes an organic process that reduces its dependence on carbon expenditure. Siegel and Mitman thus model the production, distribution, and consumption of what I call wild cinema—both the message and production minimize capitalist production.

Moreover, while some early African films remain captive in the library, as I posit early in the chapter, *The Land* proposes an alternative cinema with its guerilla distribution for the 1926 footage. As Emmanuel travels from village to village, and from town to town, sharing the archival material with Liberians on computers and cell phones, film becomes a free ecological artifact linking people and places. Emmanuel takes cinema on the road in a move that echoes Alessandro Jedlowski's notion of "small screen cinema" in Nigeria (2012). Small screen culture promotes wide distribution of pirated copies through flash drives, phone, and computer transfers, but they also enable official viewing using television, internet streaming, and mobile downloads (2012, 439). Emmanuel's circulation of the 1926 footage shares some of the features of small screen culture. The mobile and communal mode of exhibition especially links the footage to the Yoruba traveling theater that preceded Nollywood. Whereas the development of film in Africa (including video film, popularized by Nigerian Nollywood), displaced the traveling theater, *The Land* combines the attributes of both film and traveling theater (Haynes 2016). Audience participation—central to traveling theater—animates and extends the film footage (Barber 2000, 204–239). The melding of film and theater combines the attributes of western technology and Indigenous performance to produce national culture.

In the screening of the footage, cinema is not a solitary act of individual consumption or a passive, personal experience in a theater. Rather, viewing happens in groups with the congregants commenting on the footage at the same time. The space for film viewing and commentary is the outdoors, often in rural areas. Wild cinema discourages the unidirectional consumption of film in theaters and other private arenas, preferring instead a dialogic process of inter-action between film and audience, among the audience, and between audience and the land. In its theory and practice of a wild cinema, *The Land* concretizes its status as decolonial ecocinema.

The film highlights its dynamic open-endedness as it announces that citizens supplemented the footage with their stories, a rhetorical move that refers to the making of *The Land* itself. Joseph's interview outside the library, for instance, underscores the ethnic groups' customary relations to land before the settlers' arrival, thereby foregrounding a rich culture prior to settlement. *The Land* presents a nomadic epistemology that is rootless and mobile, like the moving image. As the film adds to the 1926 footage, it remains unruly, without a conclusion. The passage of the Land Rights Act in 2018 (two years after the film's release) notwithstanding, the land struggle continues in Liberia. Ultimately, *The Land* invites the present generation and the future to continue the story in pursuit of a proper ecological relationship with the land.

For the fruit of the struggle to be realized, though, the 1926 documentary and the 2016 metadocumentary must become archival documents readily available and accessible to Liberians in the present and future. Unlike Nollywood films that circulate on, often pirated, cheap VCD and DVD, television, and streaming platforms (Adejunmobi 2019), older celluloid African films and even recent independent art cinema remain largely inaccessible to Africans. Some of the celluloid films are unavailable anywhere, others are endangered with few copies existing on degrading VHS tapes owned by libraries, while the more readily available ones in digital forms require subscriptions unaffordable to many Africans. African libraries, like the Tubman Library in Liberia, rarely hold such films. As such, filming outside the library in *The Land*, in the open commons, and Emmanuel's nomadic dissemination of the archival footage model an accessible and ecological model of distribution for *The Land* and for ecocinema more broadly. Will ecofilms follow such a model or will they require the private viewing that I did courtesy of Mitman's generous provision of a Vimeo link and by renting *District 9* from Amazon Prime? This question matters because the ecocinematic potential of films such as Siegel and Mitman's can only be fully realized if they remain widely and wildly accessible.

Conclusion

African ecocinema accentuates the roles of institutions such as colonizing countries, nonstate actors such as Harvard and Firestone, and the postcolonial state in the plundering of land and other resources in Africa. The 1926 Harvard expedition was designed for biomedical research into tropical diseases and to collect specimens for classification and knowledge production about this region of the world. Enjoying Firestone's support, the expedition yielded the capture of Africans and their ecologies on camera, as well as the physical looting of ecological resources including plants and animals. Whether it is in *The Land Beneath Our Feet*, where viewers bear witness to the land being opened for exploitation during the Harvard expedition or in *District 9*, where aliens are dismembered so that their specimen can serve biomedical research, the notion of specimen serves as a cover for ecological violence. African ecocinema and wild cinema challenge viewers and readers to refocus attention on the violence of the never-ended expedition to Africa with a view toward never going back. The survival of the earth depends on the ethical claims of African ecocinema.

Works Cited

Adejunmobi, Moradewun. 2019. "Streaming Quality, Streaming Cinema." In *A Companion to African Cinema*, edited by Kenneth W. Harrow and Carmela Garritano, 219–243. Hoboken: John Wiley & Sons.

Barber, Karin. 2000. *The Generation of Plays: Yorùbá Popular Life in Theater*. Bloomington: Indiana University Press.

Barber, Marshall A., Justice B. Rice, and James Y. Brown. 1932. "Malaria Studies on the Firestone Rubber Plantation in Liberia, West Africa." *American Journal of Hygiene* 15.3: 601–633.

Barlet, Olivier. 2000. *Decolonizing the Gaze*. London: Zed Books.

Barthes, Roland. 1981. *Camera Lucida: Reflections on Photography*. Translated by Richard Howard. New York: Hill and Wang.

Baucom, Ian. 2020. *History 4° Celsius: Search for a Method in the Age of the Anthropocene*. Durham: Duke University Press.

Blomkamp, Neill, dir. 2009. *District 9*. 2009. QED International, Wingnut Films, and Tristar Pictures. 112 min.

Bousé, Derek. 2003. "False Intimacy: Close-Ups and Viewer Involvement in Wildlife Films." *Visual Studies* 18.2: 123–132.

Bozak, Nadia. 2012. *The Cinematic Footprint: Lights, Camera, Natural Resources*. New Brunswick: Rutgers University Press.

Burrowes, Patrick. 2016. *Between the Kola Forest and the Salty Sea: A History of Liberian People before 1800*. Bomi County, Liberia: Know Your Self Press.

Chakrabarty, Dipesh. 2009. "The Climate of History: Four Theses." *Critical Inquiry* 35.2: 197–222.

Cubitt, Sean. 2017. *Finite Media: Environmental Implications of Digital Technologies*. Durham: Duke University Press.

Dahr, Julia, dir. 2017. *Thank You for the Rain*. Banyak Films and Differ Media. 87 min.

Diawara, Manthia. 1992. *African Cinema: Politics & Culture*. Bloomington: Indiana University Press.

Douglas, Mary. 1966. *Purity and Danger*. New York: Routledge.

Ejiofor, Chiwetel, dir. 2019. *The Boy Who Harnessed the Wind*. Participant Media, BBC Films, and Potboiler Productions. 113 min.

Faye, Safi, dir. 1975. *Kaddu Beykat* (Letter from My Village). Safi Faye. 98 min.

Gabriel, Teshome H. 1982. *Third Cinema in the Third World: The Aesthetics of Liberation*. Ann Arbor: UMI Research Press.

Gadjigo, Samba and Jason Silverman, dir. 2015. *Sembène!* Galle Ceddo Projects. 88 min.

Gerima, Haile, dir. 1975. *Mirt Sost Shi Amit (Harvest: 3,000 Years)*. Haile Gerima. 150 min.

Halberstam, Jack. 2020. *Wild Things: The Disorder of Desire*. Durham: Duke University Press.

Harrow, Kenneth W. 2013. *Trash: African Cinema from Below*. Bloomington: Indiana University Press.

Haynes, Jonathan. 2016. *The Creation of Nigerian Film Genres*. Chicago: University of Chicago Press.

Iheka, Cajetan. 2021. *African Ecomedia: Network Forms, Planetary Politics*. Durham: Duke University Press.

Ingram, David. 2013. "The Aesthetics and Ethics of Eco-Film Criticism." In *Ecocinema: Theory and Practice*, edited by Stephen Rust, Salma Monani, and Sean Cubitt, 43–61. New York: Routledge.

Jedlowski, Alessandro. 2012. "Small Screen Cinema: Informality and Remediation in Nollywood." *Television & New Media* 13.55: 431–446.

Lioi, Anthony. 2007. "Of Swamp Dragons: Mud, Megalopolis, and a Future for Eco-criticism." In *Coming into Contact: Explorations in Ecocritical Theory and Practice*, edited by Annie Merrill Ingram, Ian Marshall, Daniel J. Philippon, and Adam W. Sweeting, 17–38. Athens: University of Georgia Press.

Lippit, Akira Mizuta. 2000. *Electric Animal: Toward a Rhetoric of Wildlife*. Minneapolis: University of Minnesota Press.

Mattern, Shannon. 2021. "The Pulse of Global Passage: Listening to Logistics." In *Assembly Codes: The Logistics of Media*, edited by Matthew Hockenberry, Nicole Starosielski, and Susan Zieger, 75–90. Durham: Duke University Press.

Maxwell, Richard and Toby Miller. 2012. *Greening the Media*. Oxford: Oxford University Press.

Mbembe, Achille and Sarah Nuttall. 2004. "Writing the World from an African Metropolis." *Public Culture* 16.33: 347–372.

Mitman, Gregg. 2021. *Empire of Rubber: Firestone's Scramble for Land and Power in Liberia*. New York: The New Press.

Mora-Kpai, Idrissou, dir. 2004. *Arlit, deuxième Paris* (Arlit, the Second Paris). Idrissou Mora-Kpai. 75 min.

Moses, Michael Valdez, Lucy Valerie Graham, John Marx, Gerald Gaylard, Ralph Goodman, and Stefan Helgesson. 2010. "*District 9*: A Roundtable." *Safundi: The Journal of South African and American Studies* 11.1–2: 155–175.

Mukherjee, Debashree. 2020. *Bombay Hustle: Making Movies in a Colonial City*. New York: Columbia University Press.

Past, Elena. 2019. *Italian Ecocinema: Beyond the Human*. Bloomington: Indiana University Press.

Povinelli, Elizabeth A. 2016. *Geontologies: A Requiem to Late Liberalism*. Durham: Duke University Press.

Siegel, Sarita and Gregg Mitman, dir. 2016. *The Land Beneath Our Feet*. Alchemy Films. 60 min.

Strong, Richard P., ed. 1930. *The African Republic of Liberia and the Belgian Congo, Based on the Observations Made and Materials Collected During the Harvard African Expedition, 1926–1927*, 2 volumes. Cambridge: Harvard University Press.

Sugnet, Charles. 2010. "Ousmane Sembène: A Silenced Continent Speaks." *Walker Reader*. October 6, 2010. https://walkerart.org/magazine/ousmane-sembene-a-silenced-continent-speaks.

Sullivan, Heather I. 2012. "Dirt Theory and Material Ecocriticism." *Interdisciplinary Studies in Literature and Environment* 19.3: 515–531.

Szeman, Imre and Dominic Boyer. 2017. "Introduction: On the Energy Humanities." In *Energy Humanities: An Anthology*, edited by Imre Szeman and Dominic Boyer. Baltimore: Johns Hopkins University Press.

Van der Kraaij, Fred P. M. 1983. *The Open Door Policy of Liberia: An Economic History of Modern Liberia*. Bremen: Selbstverlag des Museums.

Willeman, Paul. 1978. "Interview with Haile Gerima on *Harvest: 3000 Years*." *Framework* 7/8: 31–35.

6

POLYTEMPORALITY IN THE SLOW ECOCINEMA OF LAV DIAZ

An Installation in a Trauma Field

Elio Garcia

In this chapter, I offer a theory of ecocritical spectatorship called polytemporality and illustrate its two theoretical dimensions—aesthetics on the one hand and alterity on the other—by reading *Mga Anak ng Unos, Unang Aklat* (*Storm Children, Book One*, 2014), an observational documentary by Lav Diaz released after super typhoon Haiyan hit Tacloban, the Philippines in 2013. With sequences shot a few months apart, the 143-minute film shows the dismal situation of people ravaged by the storm with an undertow of accusation on the Philippine government for its glaring neglect of the survivors. *Storm Children* joins Diaz's growing body of ecocritical cinema, namely, *Kadaganan sa Banwaan Ning mga Engkanto* (*Death in the Land of the Encantos*, 2007), *Ang Araw Bago ang Wakas* (*The Day Before the End*, 2016), *Ang Hupa* (*The Halt*, 2019), *Genus, Pan* (2020), and *When the Waves are Gone* (2022). I chose *Storm Children* as a representative Diaz film for analysis because of its capacity to evoke climate catastrophe and simulate an installation artwork where the nation is re-worlded into a trauma field through the aesthetics of the "long take."

Recent scholarship on the cinematic "long take" focuses on its functions and effects such as 'sustained looking' and precision of mise-en-scene (Gibbs and Pye 2017, 20 and 30), and the creation of the wondrous looker (Koepnick 2017, 1) in which "wonder is looking without obstructions and being aware of the audience's own seeing" (Garcia 2021, 132). While the long take and single camera techniques are not exclusive to non-mainstream cinema, they often provide aesthetics in independent films such as Diaz's that can be read as radical and politically insightful. For example, I have elsewhere argued that Diaz's long take is isomorphic to the postcolonial nation-form, through an understanding of how he uses it to engage space, duration, and bodies (2021, 128).

DOI: 10.4324/9781003246602-9

This chapter expands my formulation of the long-take by showing how it transcends the nation-form—the latter breaks due to climate catastrophe and transforms into a trauma field where new subjectivities emerge. Furthermore, this chapter describes how the radical aesthetics of the extreme long take and single-camera technique construct the cinematic experience similar to an art installation in which the spectator is captured and co-textualized. As often happens with installation art, whose spaces a viewer must physically negotiate, I maintain that the film's "radical aesthetics" place not only spectator's conscious-ness but also their body in an ethical and critical encounter, which I describe as *polytemporality*. Polytemporality—a state of being made actively aware of our own bodies experiencing the flow of time, in relation to that of other bod-ies experiencing streams of time in other spaces, i.e., as a time matrix—is a cinematic process that Diaz masterfully constructs. *Storm Children* invites the spectator to be bodily transfixed within the new coordinates of post-national climate catastrophe. To make my case, I draw on Brechtian theory to outline my framework of polytemporality as a fundamental characteristic of cinema's long take. I then illuminate how it expands on ecocinema studies' current discussions of slow cinema, before turning to the particulars of *Storm Children*.

Polytemporality through Brechtian Lenses

While the Anthropocene, our human-impacted climatic era, shapes the vulner-ability of our current planetary worlds, cinema engages in aesthetic worlding with the intention to simulate the world. As Jennifer Fay argues, the Anthro-pocene and cinema are parallel in their worlding processes:

> [N]ot only is cinema like the Anthropocene in its uncanny aesthetic effects, but also, insofar as cinema has encouraged the production of artificial worlds and simulated, wholly anthropogenic weather, it is the aesthetic practice of the Anthropocene. Or, to put it more forcefully, cinema helps us to see and experience the Anthropocene as an aesthetic practice.
>
> *(2018, 4)*

Diaz's *Storm Children* presents the Anthropocene as a worlding force manifested in new geographical coordinates of a trauma field of displacement, confusion, and unfamiliarity. In theorizing how thought and criticality emerge in this film and in how radical aesthetics install the spectator's body in the cinematic expe-rience, I go back to Bertolt Brecht's anti-Aristotelian framework, which posits that radical aesthetics can destroy audience identification by deliberately shat-tering the illusion of dramatic coherence. Through such dissonance created by performance, the spectator is invited to adopt "critical positions in relation to the dramatic spectacle, so as to interrupt and puncture its illusionism as based on aesthetic unity" (Chow 2012, 6). This dissonance results in a dis-identification meant to deliberately foreground the alterity or otherness between the observer and the observed. Radical aesthetics makes estrangement possible and enables the spectator to notice things that are otherwise unnoticeable, thus, inviting them to "re-world" their understandings of the world.

Alienation or estrangement, or in the vocabulary of Viktor Shlovsky, *ostranenie* or defamiliarization (Crawford 1984), is crucial in the process of re-worlding as a cognitive experience. Brecht theorizes that alienation "make[s] the spectator adopt an attitude of inquiry and criticism in his approach to the incident" (Brecht qtd. in Chow 2012, 15). For Brecht, in theater, coherent suture is destroyed through the mode of montage, which ruptures the spectator's process of affective identification (Chow 2012, 16). However, in film, montage, once considered radical in early films of Sergei Eisenstein, has become the hegemonic form mainstream cinema utilizes. Montage, as an affective structure that works to establish continuity of space, time, and narrative in mainstream cinema has become too familiar and thus serves to enforce identification. Used much less frequently, the long take, in contrast, tends to have the effect of alienating and defamiliarizing its audiences by offering an alternative, dissonant temporal cinematic experience. In doing so, it presents radical aesthetics because it confronts the mainstream aesthetics of montage cuts that condition our *not* seeing. Through the long take, the *things* overlooked or not seen otherwise require deliberate attention from the spectator and may open possibilities to new images, meanings, and re-worldings.

Re-worlding becomes possible through reflexivity, where we become aware of our own active processes of thinking, "a conscious form of staging" (Chow 2012, 18). In Diaz's case, where the extreme long take is regularly used, duration requires the spectator to pay attention to time slowly unfolding on screen, which in turn makes the spectator aware of their own presence outside the screen. Instead of being simply absorbed or immersed in the story, they notice themselves observing time. Caught in a realization of the objectification-subjectification process between spectator and spectacle, the spectator enters a time matrix of cinematic experience as opposed to what most mainstream cinema works to ensure, which is a unitary linear temporality in which we are so absorbed that we lose our sense of time *outside* the screen. This time matrix, which I call polytemporality, creates a textured experience of time on the body.

Polytemporality incorporates screen time *and* the flow of time experienced by spectators becoming aware of their own bodies' engagement in the process of watching time unfold. This network of times is translatably an embodied means of reminding the spectator of being networked into the act of looking, which is also a network of power relations. Trin T. Minh-ha analyzes this act of looking too long as a surrender of power:

> to pause and look more closely than is required, to look at what one is
> not supposed to look at ...upsets the established order in all its forms, to

the degree that the very duration or intensity of the gaze is controlled by society...The image is subversive, not through violence and aggression, but through duration and intensity.

(1991, 114–115)

Being aware of how viewers' bodies are implicated in a network of *looking* at bodies on screen—and realizing the film medium itself as a "body" on which bodies are projected—is a *difference* mainstream cinema seeks to efface.

When the spectator is immersed in mainstream entertainment and suspends the act of critique, they are invited to forget about the passing of non-screen time. If such time is recognized, then the film is considered a waste of time or money since homogenous time is measured against productive human labor (Schoonover 2012, 65, 74). This form of mainstream cinema is developed by capital:

> though the meanings of cinema are found in language, its significance is not language; its significance is in the symbolic known as capital. In principle, all of the possibilities, affects, and experiences available in the cinema are capable of being symbolized as capital—in other words, converted to exchange-value at some earlier or later stage of social production.
>
> *(Beller 1995, 188)*

Movie making, moviegoing, the modes of viewing, the capture of audiences—everything is organized via the logic of capitalism (Beller 1995, 198). Beller refines this theory in *The Cinematic Mode of Production* which argues that

> cinema and its succeeding (if still simultaneous) formations, particularly television, video, computers, and the internet, are deterritorialized factories in which spectators work, that is, in which we perform value-productive labor.
>
> *(2006, 2)*

If the spectator's attention is diverted to the excess screen time, they become conscious of the hidden labor of spectating. If the spectator is wholly absorbed *in* cinematic time, then they feel as if they have had their money's worth because watching no longer feels like laboring.

Diaz's cinema throws mainstream cinema's temporal formulation of attention economy into crisis because it provides no entertainment, and his long take is an aesthetics based on an alternative logic. The long take as a form of staging is a paradox of wholeness and brokenness—the wholeness of the long take is due to the duration of "dead time" that is "normally" otherwise edited out and the brokenness is because the long take breaks the illusion of narrative continuity that the spectator is used to experiencing in mainstream cinema.

As a result, when watching Diaz's films, as the spectator becomes aware of cinematic time slowing down, their attention drifts to awareness of their own bodies—the body begins to experience cinema as conscious labor. Cinema in this sense becomes an "assemblage" where disparate objects, politics involved in the spectacle, and different ways of perceiving are triggered by the film text but are not immanent in it. The spectator participates in the process of piecing aspects of the screen and their own material worlds together, even as they become part of it (as is often the case when encountering and interpreting installation art). This process has important ecological ramifications.

Polytemporality as Radical Eco-Aesthetics

Ecocinema scholars have problematized how the radical aesthetics of slow cinema's long take advance the ecological consciousness of the spectator through reflexivity and criticality. Scott MacDonald, in the first volume of *Ecocinema Theory and Practice*, looks to avant-garde cinema to define ecocinema as a filmmaking practice that offers viewers a "cinematic experience that models patience and mindfulness—qualities of consciousness crucial for a deep appreciation of and an ongoing commitment to the natural environment...inverse of the fundamentally hysterical approach of commercial media" (2013, 19). In this formulation, aesthetics is key to train perception anew. Silke Panse, reading the films of James Benning, expounds on the concept of eco-aesthetics as a quality that indirectly connects ecology and image by evoking what is imperceptible (2013, 37). Panse further explains that

> the immanence of the world to the work and the artist is an ethical and ecological issue. Images are not just visual. The image and the filmmaker are parts of 'the environment' that is not only around us, but goes through us.
>
> *(44)*

Panse points to how the films involve radical aesthetics that the spectator may materially experience within the media's environmental world.

Such formulations on radical eco-aesthetics originate from the Global North, and they take on a different polytemporal character in the Global South because slow films more deliberately critique colonialism and simulate the multiple temporalities of subaltern and Indigenous communities in their contact and negotiations with modernity. For example, the work of May Ingawanij on the films and installations of Apichatpong suggests a richness of experience through what she calls, via Adrian Martin, the cinematic dispositif, which, rather than suturing "various elements into a coherent fictional world," serves as a "'catalog' of references, citations and allusions" (2013, 92). Ingawanij notes that the fragments in the aesthetics of Apichatpong are productive referential sites that allude to political and historical events in Thailand. Among Apichat-pong's ecocritical films are *Uncle Bonmee Who Can Recall His Past Lives* (2010) and *Cemetery of Splendor* (2015) which are not only slow but also masterfully play with multiple temporalities of history, modernity, and myth. The poly-temporal aesthetics of such films are not only an artistic choice but also a political-cultural *necessity* to expand the consciousness of spectators regarding the uneven enactment of the destructive powers of the Anthropocene.

Global South slow cinema's radical aesthetics get to the core of what it means to transcend the privileged Self in relation to its Other. Polytemporality with its "time matrix" of relations invites one to consider how if the "other" is configured alongside the self and vice versa, *other* time can become a critique of homogenous self-time. Adapting knowledge of multiple temporalities into an ethics of time forwards a moral gravitas on our attitude to and with time which, to McGowan, is also our attitude toward the Other. "Someone who uses time or views it as a means to be exploited for profit will take up this same attitude toward the other," McGowen explains (2011, 4). He expands that such exploitation is the very core of capitalism as it

> treats time as an entity that can be broken up into discrete parts in order that it might be bought, sold, and used. Time becomes a quantity rather than a qualitative experience in the process of reification. Reification transforms the temporality (and the labor) of the production process into the spatial form of a commodity.
>
> *(21)*

In contrast, if someone is able to experience slow cinema's polytemporal time-matrix as an invitation to be aware of one's own body, of the other, of the film as (using phenomenologist Vivian Sobchack's phrase) an "irreducible ensemble" of inter-objectivity (2004), then these temporal entanglements can help disintegrate the boundaries between self and other, creating a circulation "like a series of skin contacts that leave mutual traces" (Marks 1995, xii). The collapsing of such boundaries is one way to experience a sense of re-worlding, which in the case of films from the Global South make visible power relations such as racism and colonialism, even as they work to transcend these relations.

I turn to *Storm Children* to demonstrate how it implicates the spectator in these power relations. With its non-narrative structure and long takes that lin-ger on "uneventfulness," it promises no clear affective direction but instead constructs assemblages of subjects borne out of the storm, a post-national phenomenon that challenges a national discourse. *Storm Children's* radical aes-thetics of the long take are an invitation to polytemporality—the film refuses nation-forming narratives to shift spectators from a solely geographical dimen-sion of otherness to a temporal dimension of relations.

Polytemporality and the (a)historicality of Climate Trauma

What is the relationship between uneventfulness and ahistoricality? Historicity is the narrative apparatus of modernity where an event is not arbitrary but conditioned and shaped by power. Modernity hinges on colonialism, which brought catastrophic destruction of cultures and environments in the Global South to make development and progress possible in the Global North. Non-event, non-teleology, being outside history, is the end of modernity. Though colonialism has been bookended by history, its lingering effects make possible the creation of spaces of vulnerabilities for postcolonial subjects. Modernity, in this context the Anthropocene, has impacted the climate, which in turn has created trauma fields as people respond to new and devastating weather conditions—storms, heat, etc.—and their aftermath. As *Storm Children* reminds us, such trauma fields begin to feel like non-events because they describe catastrophes from long colonialism compounded by the devastation from climate change; in other words, time becomes unmoored from a unitary and forward momentum of Modernity's belief in progress.

The scalar threat of climate catastrophe calls for a temporal understanding of trauma not only in its pastness but also in its futurity. E. Ann Kaplan, in *Climate Trauma*, proposes the concept of pre-trauma in which "people suffer from an immobilizing anticipatory anxiety about the future...in fear of a future terrifying event" (2015, xix), as evidenced in climate dystopian film and fiction. Michael Richardson expands Kaplan's thinking by arguing that "affects of climate catastrophe are traumatically affecting without necessarily being traumatizing: they are jarring, rupturing, disjunctive experiences of future crisis in the now" (2018, 1). The stance of Kaplan and Richardson reading Western film and literature is undergirded by privilege and is racially blind as it places the impact of climate change at a temporal distance–the future. In the Global South the reality of climate impacts has already been and is also now; it is not just "traumatically affecting," it is traumatic in its material toll as well. While it is helpful to establish how affects emanating from threats in the future can create anxiety among subjects in the present, such an estimation of the temporal dimension of trauma is narrow.

I do not intend to diminish the fears and affects of subjects regarding climate threat but wish to emphasize that affects have different intensities from one subject to another. Climate catastrophes are already experienced by many communities made vulnerable through colonialist and capitalist mechanics both in spectacular and glacial time. In other words, channeling Rob Nixon's concept of slow violence (2011), in mainstream cinema of the Global North apprehensions of violence are rendered visually eventful—needfully evidenced by spectacle—in order to be recognizable; in *Storm Children*, however, such violence is rendered visually uneventful through an aesthetics of simulation that exposes the long, slow violent processes of suffering, the ill effects of exploitation, and vulnerability that collectives experience without end. Populations who are climate victims primarily do not exist in fear of threat but live trying to survive with catastrophe. Conceptualizing the impacts of Anthropocene as a pre-trauma denotes a power differential and temporal disjuncture, liquidating the present time of the climate subaltern while intensifying the anticipation of future threats for the privileged. Pre-trauma is inseparable from privilege. The fear of losing does not equal losing and having lost.

In *Storm Children*, the uneventfulness, or excess of time in each take, requires the spectator to witness a drifting image of traumatized subjects who are aimlessly moving in the trauma field. The camera details the lived experiences of its subjects and calls the spectator into an act of witnessing. In Diaz's filmic world, there is no color, only a binary of black and white which has an effect of blurring time. Even when it is day, it seems that it is always afternoon in this village after the storm, an uncannily homogenous order. Space and people seem to be outside time or contained in a time of their own. As an effect, the non-progression of non-events reverts the world to, and simulates the spectator's cinematic experience of, a time that is cyclic in its homogeneity. In this loss of telos and power, the spectator is destabilized, re-textualized, ahistoricized.

The feeling that one is experiencing an art installation is accomplished through the single camera mapping, which decides where the observer is in the field with each coordinate rendered in extreme duration. By placing the single camera in different geographical coordinates around a focal space, a post-national space of trauma is established, and the spectator is emplaced in every coordinate, not simultaneously but one painstaking long take at a time, effectively situating the spectator within what we might understand as a "cinematic installation". Unlike an art installation, the absence of camera movement in this cinematic installation clashes with human freedom to survey the spatial diegetic elements or turn around or gaze somewhere else (Arnheim 1957, 16). The viewing experience disciplines the spectator's body to cognitively map out the filmic world and its characters. When the camera does not move, the human eye inspects and finds objects within the frame and creates connections; meaning is the fruition of slow time. A transfixed spectator cannot help but look extensively at the images flowing in actual duration in *Storm Children* and notice contingencies and minute details which are often elided in mainstream cinema. As each sequence deepens, it becomes apparent that the subject of the documentary is the climate-trauma field and its post-national subjects, the storm children. Each shot or sequence has no sense of resolution, only a logic of piling up time in which subjects are idle or doing aimless labor, moving to scaffold a life permanently changed by the storm.

Storm Children opens with a long establishing shot of a city inundated by flood and rain. The next shot is of an overflowing river with tall buildings as background, hinting at the age-old problem of flooding in the metro. Next is a close-up of floating debris and then a shot of children playing in the flood. The camera does not move but the subjects move within the flooded world. The camera is distant and unintrusive; it stands and waits and there are no close-ups of children's faces. In the background is graffiti "Tuta ng Kano" which translates as "America's lapdog," obviously commenting on the colonial, neocolonial, and neoliberal relations between the Philippines and the United States. While the city floods, it pulsates with life; a reflection of a motorcycle running on a flooded street becomes surreal—revealing a vitality flowing even in this traumatized space.

The first sequence establishes *Storm Children* as a film about space, a field where the traumatized subjects, the children, play, work, and wander about. The cut between the shot of the river and the shot of children in the flood contains the master code regarding the temporality of climate trauma: the storm gives birth to new subjects, the children of the storm. To present the re-worlding of the Anthropocene through typhoon Haiyan in 2013, Diaz films the ship *Eva Jocelyn* and makes it appear imposing in the sunlight. Parked beside the highway, people live within and around *Eva Jocelyn*. It functions as a wall, a house, and because of its size, an epicenter of a community thriving around it. *Eva Jocelyn* has become a semiotically rich object of climate catastrophe, the organizing principle of a village reconfigured by a storm into a trauma field (Figure 6.1). Pushed inland by giant waves during the storm surge, *Eva Jocelyn* and other ships bulldozed the littoral dwellings of people in Tacloban and killed half its population. Although destroyed, the village is reorganized into a world where life thrives after a chaotic and deadly worlding process. In many moments in the film, people's movements in the trauma field are punctuated by the rain, emphasizing how nature and climate function as the temporal logic of human activity. In another sequence, a water-fetching child is seen in different coordinates. The camera does not follow the child's movement but analyses his emplacement always in relation to where the camera/spectator is. Each shot comments that anywhere you look, it is all the same. In a sense, the film presents a new kind of homogeneity that is more pronounced than the hypothetical homogeneity of the nation-state. The mapping and reference to previous coordinates are done through deep focus.

In an early sequence, two children play and scavenge along the bridge. The single camera is placed on their right, then to their left, then behind them— the geographical coordinates that function as the perimeter of the scavenging-space. Occasionally, a raindrop falls on the camera lens and the subjects look at the camera, which punctures the viewing experience by breaking the fourth wall. The frame juxtaposes vitality and ruins in what Rahul Mukherjee may refer to as *ruination* which "encapsulates the widespread feeling of being amidst slow (and sometimes accelerating) environmental decay, depletion, and exhaustion... the working conditions and/or lived worlds of people who are inhabiting the ruins-in-the-making" (2017, 290). The flood gathers the garbage into a

FIGURE 6.1 The ship *Eva Jocelyn* in *Storm Children* (2014) by Lav Diaz.

heap—accumulating images of debris, which is a symptom of the density piling of capitalism (Canlas 2011, 324).

In another sequence where two children are constantly digging, the spectator is made to witness their random act of excavating in the ruins. The children do not talk and there is no way for the spectator to know their story, their background, their identity, and their motivation. After a while, the unproductive digging appears like a desperate act of recovery of what might have been lost or still has the chance to be saved. At first, the digging gestures are small but they later on intensify into big gestures. Are they looking for dead bodies? Are they brothers? Are they orphans? Every extreme long take agonizes the spectator until a sense of the subjects' helplessness invites an air of despair.

For the first half of the film, the spectator's sense of movement is restrained. In the second half, as the camera, handheld, follows the children roaming around the village, the spectator gets a reconnaissance of the village as a trauma field over time through an aggregate of film sequences. Finally, the subjects speak of the catastrophe, and we finally learn that the younger boy lost his mother, grandmother, and siblings when their house was hit by one of the ships. The storm metaphorically gave birth to these children by taking away the children's family. At this point, the viewer becomes not just a spectator, but a witness of climate trauma. As Kaplan explains:

> Art that invites us to bear witness to injustice goes beyond moving us to identify with and help a specific individual, and prepares us to take responsibility for preventing future occurrence. "Witnessing" thus involves a stance that has public meaning or importance and transcends individual empathic or vicarious suffering to produce community.
>
> *(2005, 23)*

Diaz secures the texture and character of the trauma field by restraining the viewer's sense of movement and denying them the ability to identify with the characters in the first half of the film. This structure effectively triggers many questions and thought constellations for the spectator who is installed and yet alienated at the same time. The camera mobility and speech that follow in the second half of the film heighten the stasis and silence of the first half. The spectator, as witness, is let in more fully into the trauma field as the subjects are humanized by being able to put the trauma that changed their lives into language, by tracing their network of relationships in the community, and by the film acknowledging the traumatized environment not merely as a space of pain but also of survival, play, work, friendships.

Life thriving in the village, however, does not change the film's tone nor glorify resiliency. *Storm Children* presents things as they are: bleak, destroyed, heart-rending, aimless. In the film's rather endearing final sequence, Diaz captures the exhilaration of children playing in the sea. The play is a cycle of jumping from the ship and climbing to its highest level, screaming and oblivious of the rain (Figure 6.2). Nadin Mai speaks of the final sequence as

> rather hopeful, and perhaps the most hopeful ending I have ever come across in Diaz's work. In a long shot, we see children using the big ships as an opportunity for diving. They make the best out of the situation, as children always do. Only much later will they realise what has actually happened to them. … Despite the gravity of the situation, there are small glimpses of hope and joy, leaving the viewer with mixed feelings.
>
> *(2014)*

Describing the children as "making the best out of the situation" and in the state of unknowing regarding the recent tragedy of their lives risks romanticizing resilience, which has often been utilized by the Philippine government for several decades to cover up their inefficiency in addressing survivors of climate catastrophes, and disregarding the children's knowledge of the intensity and depth of the event. Yet, consider why Diaz would render this sequence in slow motion and without sound. The slow motion and silence starkly contrast with

FIGURE 6.2   Play/struggle in slow motion in *Storm Children* (2014) by Lav Diaz.

"small glimpses of hope and joy;" thus the final shot looks like a simulation of what may have transpired during the storm and what the children needed to do to survive rather than a hopeful Hollywood ending.

The children's act of swimming, pulling on ropes, climbing, and jumping while the camera records them from afar exudes an energy of struggle and desperation in the midst of a life-threatening catastrophe. Muting deletes the play's laughter and makes it disturbing. Time is decomposed via slow motion which, in the words of Cortade, situates "a tension between movement and immobility, giving rise to a 'tragedy' of duration, and also imbues the image with transparency, revealing the hidden movements of reality which would otherwise remain invisible to the naked eye, thus making slow motion a "microscope of time" (Cortade 2012, 162).

Conclusion

By using slow motion in the final shot of *Storm Children*, Diaz magnifies action but ironically this shot is faster than the rest because it punctures the uniform slow pacing of long durations. The difference is unique and sharp such that the slow motion is an exception to dead time, and rather a moment of semiotic vitality. The slow motion reminds me of Epstein's concept of the photogénie, "a flicker of an expression that seems to contain all the meaning in a scene" (Ivins 2017). According to Germane Dulac, tics, change in movement, and sound are intensified by slow motion (Cortade 2012, 163). By putting together stillness and movement, the spectator perceives time uniquely, becoming aware not only of objects on screen but also of the space between screen and spectator

(164). According to Bazin, "the function of slow motion does not lie in demonstrating the power of the technique, but rather in capturing and organically revealing the ambiguous stages of the deployment of movement as duration" (quoted in Cortade 2012, 173). Through *Storm Children's* polytemporality, its complex time matrix, Lav Diaz reveals the temporal dimension of the climate tragedy as an effect of slowing down motion—traumatized subjects move on with their lives, but motion is not to be regarded as an absolution of the collective responsibility of exploitative empires, despotic regimes, and the main actors in the racial geometry of the Anthropocene to answer for the environmental injustice that has decimated the habitats and vulnerable populations in the Global South. In Diaz, radical aesthetics is politics—the long take, deep focus, and single camera that prompt viewers to experience polytemporality are necessary to not only represent what it means to survive in the trauma field but also to construct and simulate for the spectator the long exhaustion of the climate subalterns and emphasize the urgency to change the course of the Anthropocene from creating unlivable worlds.

Works Cited

Arnheim, Rudolf. 1957. *Film as Art.* Berkeley and Los Angeles: University of California Press.

Beller, Jonathan. 2006. *The Cinematic Mode of Production: Attention Economy and the Society of the Spectacle.* Hanover: Dartmouth College Press.

———. 1995. "The Spectatorship of the Proletariat." *boundary 2* 22.3: 171–228. https://doi.org/10.2307/303727.

Canlas, Ryan. 2011. "The Time of Poverty and the Image of Real." *Positions* 19.2: 307–334. muse.jhu.edu/article/453328.

Chow, Rey. 2012. *Entanglements, or Transmedial Thinking about Capture.* Durham: Duke University Press.

Cortade, Ludovic. 2012. "The 'Microscope of Time': Slow Motion in Jean Epstein's Writings." In *Jean Epstein: Critical Essays and New Translations,* edited by Sarah Keller and Jason Paul, 161–176. Amsterdam: Amsterdam University Press.

Crawford, Lawrence. 1984. "Viktor Shklovskij: Différance in Defamiliarization." *Comparative Literature* 36.3: 209–219. doi:10.2307/1770260.

Diaz, Lav, director. 2016. *Ang Araw Bago ang Wakas (The Day Before the End).* Philippines: Sine Olivia Pilipinas. https://video-alexanderstreet-com.libproxy.uoregon.edu/watch/the-day-before-the-end.

———. 2019. *Ang Hupa (The Halt).* Philippines: Sine Olivia Pilipinas, Spring Films. https://mubi.com/films/the-halt.

———. 2020. *Genus, Pan.* Philippines: Sine Olivia Pilipinas. https://mubi.com/films/genus-pan.

———. 2007. *Kadaganan sa Banwaan Ning mga Engkanto (Death in the Land of the Encantos).* Philippines: Sine Olivia. https://mubi.com/films/death-in-the-land-of-encantos.

———. 2014. *Mga Anak ng Unos, Unang Aklat (Storm Children, Book One).* Philippines: DMZ Docs and Sine Olivia Pilipinas. https://uoregon.kanopy.com/video/storm-children.

————. 2014. *Mula sa Kung Ano ang Noon (From What is Before)*. 2014; Philippines: Sine Olivia Pilipinas.https://www.kanopy.com/en/uoregon/video/4825406.

————. 2022. *When the Waves Are Gone*. Manila: Epicmedia Production and Berlin: Films Boutique. https://mubi.com/films/when-the-waves-are-gone.

Fay, Jennifer. 2018. *Inhospitable Worlds: Cinema in the Time of the Anthropocene*. Oxford: Oxford University Press.

Garcia, Elio. 2021. "Beyond Aesthetics: The Long Take as the Nation-Form in the Cinema of Lav Diaz." *Asian Cinema* 32.2: 127–143. https://doi.org/10.1386/ac_00038_1.

Gibbs, John and Douglas Pye, eds. 2017. *The Long Take: Critical Approaches*. London: Palgrave Macmillan.

Ingawanij, May Adadol. 2013. "Animism and the Performative Realist Cinema of Apichatpong Weerasethakul." In *Screening Nature: Cinema Beyond the Human*, edited by Anat Pick and Guinevere Narraway, 91–109. New York: Berghahn Books.

Ivins, Laura. 2017. "What Is Photogénie?" July 20, 2017. http://blogs.iu.edu/aplaceforfilm/2017/07/20/what-is-photogenie/.

Kaplan, E. Ann. 2015. *Climate Trauma: Foreseeing the Future in Dystopian Film and Fiction*. New Brunswick: Rutgers University Press.

————. 2005. *Trauma Culture: The Politics of Terror and Loss in Media and Literature*. New Brunswick: Rutgers University Press.

Koepnick, Lutz P. 2017. *The Long Take: Art Cinema and the Wondrous*. Minneapolis: University of Minnesota Press.

MacDonald, Scott. 2013. "The Ecocinema Experience." In *Ecocinema Theory and Practice*, edited by Stephen Rust, Salma Monani, and Sean Cubitt, 17–41. New York and London: Routledge.

Mai, Nadin. 2014. "Storm Children, Book One—Lav Diaz (2014)." http:theartsofslow-cinema.com/2014/11/04/storm-children-book-onelavdiaz-2014/.

Marks, Laura. 1995. *The Skin of the Film: Intercultural Cinema, Embodiment, and the Senses*. Durham: Duke University Press.

McGowan, Todd. 2011. *Out of Time: Desire in Atemporal Cinema*. Minneapolis: University of Minnesota Press.

Minh-ha, Trinh T. 1991. *When the Moon Waxes Red: Representation, Gender, and Cultural Politics*. New York and London: Routledge.

Mukherjee, Rahul. 2017. "Anticipating Ruinations: Ecologies of 'Make Do' and 'Left With'." *Journal of Visual Culture* 16.3: 287–309. https://doi.org/10.1177/1470412917740884.

Nixon, Rob. 2011. *Slow Violence and the Environmentalism of the Poor*. Cambridge: Harvard University Press.

Panse, Silke. 2013. "*Ten Skies, 13 Lakes*, 15 Pools—Structure, Immanence and Ecoaesthetics in *The Swimmer* and James Benning's Land Films." In *Screening Nature: Cinema Beyond the Human*, edited by Anat Pick and Guinevere Narraway, 37–59. New York: Berghahn Books.

Richardson, Michael. 2018. "Climate Trauma, or the Affects of the Catastrophe to Come." *Environmental Humanities* 10.1: 1–19. https://doi.org/10.1215/22011919-4385444.

Schoonover, Karl. 2012. "Wastrels of Time: Slow Cinema's Laboring Body, the Political Spectator, and the Queer." *Framework* 53.1: 65–78. https://www.jstor.org/stable/41552300.

Sobchack, Vivian. 2004. *Carnal Thoughts: Embodiment and Moving Image Culture*. Berkeley and Los Angeles: University of California Press.

Weerasethakul, Apichatpong, director. 2015. *Cemetery of Splendor*. Bangkok: Kick the Machine Films. https://www.sbs.com.au/ondemand/movie/cemetery-of-splendor/1595779139582.

———. 2010. *Uncle Bonmee Who Can Recall His Past Lives*. Bangkok: Kick the Machine Films. https://www.amazon.com/Uncle-Boonmee-Recall-Past-Lives/dp/B008XCZ43A.

7

EXPLORING SF ECOCINEMA

Ideologies of Gender, Infrastructure, and US/China Dynamics in *Interstellar* and *The Wandering Earth*

Andrew Hageman and Regina Kanyu Wang

Our chapter features a collaboratively forged ecocinema ideology critique. We designed the process and product to transcend the limits of individual analysis. As an ideology critique, identifying and analyzing core contradictions in each of the two films we explore drives our work. One of our aims is to develop and extend the practice of ecocinema ideology critique articulated by Andrew in "Ecocinema and Ideology: Do Ecocritics Dream of a Clockwork Green," in the original volume of *Ecocinema Theory and Practice* (Hageman 2013). To that end, we wrote this chapter through a series of collective discussions, drafts, and revisions to produce arguments that account for the distinct surprises, questions, confusions, and hypotheses that arose from our respective Chinese (Regina) and American (Andrew) ideological perceptions of one Chinese and one American speculative fiction (SF) blockbuster film in conversation. The key insights that emerge point to intersections of ecological futures with patriarchal structures and tensions between collectivities and individualisms.

The primary films in focus are Christopher Nolan's *Interstellar* (2014) and Frant Gwo's *The Wandering Earth* (2019). *Interstellar* imagines a near-future Earth ravaged by climate change combined with widespread agricultural blights and crop failures. The National Aeronautics and Space Administration of the United States (NASA), which now must work covertly, exploits a wormhole to seek out alternative planets and develops the technologies to transplant humanity once a suitable Earth-analog is found. *The Wandering Earth* imagines the Earth under threat as the sun is about to go red giant. A United Earth Government (UEG) is formed, and China takes the lead in engineering and constructing a set of Earth Engines to push the planet out of the solar system to seek a safe new system.

DOI: 10.4324/9781003246602-10

We chose *Interstellar* and *The Wandering Earth* because this pair of films is ready-made for ecocinema studies critical and transnational comparative dialogue. Both are massive budget SF blockbusters released within just five years of each other. Their plots are driven by planetary ecological crises and techno-scientific approaches to interstellar space travel to ensure a future for the human species. The protagonists are three-generation families dominated by grandfathers and fathers, with the conspicuous absence of mothers who died in circumstances connected to the ecological crises. All told, this pair of films shares many common variables in the dramatic SF eco-thought experiments they present, yet there are many disparate variables as well.

Interstellar comes out of Hollywood while *The Wandering Earth* comes out of China, so each film is marked by its own national film industry practices and its distinct appeals to domestic and international markets. Nolan's film embraces a narrative of leaving Earth behind as the cradle of humanity, while Gwo's film promotes a deep commitment to Earth but with a complicated treatment of the planet as a resource stockpile. Suggestively, Liu Cixin, the author of the short story/novelette which the latter film adapted, has commented on *Interstellar* that "it uses the kind of science fiction ideas more common in science fiction literature, but not common in science fiction films, such as black holes, so it is not very innovative" (*Dalian Evening Post* 2014) while praising Gwo's *The Wandering Earth* because it "uses a very rare idea in science fiction: push the Earth away as a spacecraft. This kind of idea would never be adopted in Hollywood" (Du and Dong 2019). The differences in genre conventions and originality that Liu emphasizes further establish the ideological dialogue this pair of films can spark within an ecocritical agenda.

In addition to the blend of shared and disparate variables, the critical responses to both films underscore the value in thinking through them in conversation. Comparing the critical literature available in English on both films,[1] it's apparent how *The Wandering Earth* is taken to be propaganda for China's government and geopolitics while *Interstellar* is treated as Nolan's auteurism and exemplary scientific realism. Articles on *The Wandering Earth* tend either to endorse or chastise its depiction of China's geopolitical strategies and tactics, from Amir Khan's and Weihua He's positive reads of the film's collectivity and cosmopolitanism to Molly Silk's critique of *The Wandering Earth* as soft power propaganda for the current "regime" in China and Ping Zhu's comment that the film "reinforces the authority of the Father and the nation-state" (Khan 2020, 20–37; He 2020, 530–540; Silk 2020; Zhu 2020, 94). By contrast, articles on *Interstellar* follow the film's own marketing moves by delving into the accuracy of its wormhole and/or black hole physics and imagery. Dr. Kip Thorne, a theoretical physicist now retired from the California Institute of Technology (CalTech), was an executive producer of and science advisor to the film. Thorne's book, *The Science of Interstellar* (2014), intensified attention to the scientific accuracy of the film in place of its ideological signals. A key exception is Timothy Morton's exploration of love and openness when he writes of the film, with a powerful focus on the robot TARS, in *Humankind: Solidarity with Nonhuman People* (2017, 145–162). In our merging of the two films, we disrupt the smooth flow of these critical receptions to forge our planetary ecocinema analysis and imagine collective ecological futures.

Our approach to ecocinema ideology critique in this chapter modifies the method Andrew originally adapted from the work of Slavoj Žižek by distinguishing each film's *constituted* and *constitutive* ideological textures. The constituted ideology is what the film appears to promote explicitly, and seemingly intentionally. These are the values the films wear on their sleeves. The constitutive ideology is what the film actually seems to promote implicitly, and seemingly unconsciously. These are the values the films rehearse whether knowingly or not and whether or not their makers would disavow such values. By homing in on where the constituted and constitutive ideological textures contradict each other, we pinpoint the limits to imagining ecological futures that must be engaged and overcome. While Andrew demonstrated this method in the original *Ecocinema Theory and Practice* volume, our chapter radically advances this work by featuring two scholars with backgrounds in disparate national-ideological contexts collaborating to produce a shared analysis of the constituted and constitutive ideologies of each film from both national-ideological contexts.

Our analysis of the constituted and constitutive messages of both films is divided into two sections. First, we delve into the ideological gestures and contradictions in both films' uses of educational settings with a special emphasis on how these scenes establish the principle of young women characters Murphy Cooper and Han Duoduo. Both young women are the educated and the repressed in the system, silenced and purportedly protected when large crises take place. They appear assertive, confident, and intelligent but without real agency. From an ecofeminist perspective, Murphy and Duoduo's roles parallel those of planet Earth, which is forced to provide the last crops of grain in *Interstellar* and be saved from the solar doomsday in *The Wandering Earth*. The planet and the women appear to be loved and valued as the key to the future of humanity yet are figured ultimately as weak objects for male heroism. Furthermore, representations of schools and pedagogies feature frequently in SF cinema as part of its world-building imaginings, and a recent turn in ecocriticism, illustrated by Sarah Jaquette Ray's *A Field Guide to Climate Anxiety* (2020) and Chris Schaberg's *Pedagogy of the Depressed* (2021), is theorizing and redesigning education for this era of anxiety and depression about impending futures near and far. Schools are ideology replication factories, so they are key to ecocinema ideology critique. Second, from the ideological fabrics of education, we pivot to those that inform the food systems and practices both films depict within their eco-crisis futures. Food production has played a fundamental role in producing the Anthropocene and must be a core part of surviving and ameliorating warmer planet futures. These films can reveal through ecocinema ideology critique the unsustainable extent to which agriculture is currently dictated by global capitalism and the ways to potential alternatives.

For a final introductory note, as we revised our first draft of this chapter in October 2021, two unique space travel events unfolded within a three-day span. Billionaire Jeff Bezos sent former *Star Trek* star William Shatner briefly into space aboard a privately owned rocket and China sent three taikonauts, including female pilot Wang Yaping, to the space station it recently completed as part of its long-range plan to establish a moon base to support further missions into space. Ideology critique of SF ecocinema looks to the future, yes, but also helps us find the meanings in yesterday's news.

Education and Ideology

Classrooms and campuses provide productive sites for anticipating which technical acumen, as well as forms of control, both ideological and repressive, might be called for by future conditions of political economy and planetary ecology. School sequences appear early in *The Wandering Earth* and *Interstellar* and perform two interrelated functions. First, these sequences establish the characters of Han Duoduo and Murphy Cooper, the young women protagonists who play important roles in solving their respective planetary crises. Second, the pedagogies deployed in both schools are shaped by the particular ideological responses to planetary ecological catastrophe that each film projects in its constituted and constitutive textures. Educational philosophies and practices, as well as characters' reactions to these, comprise constituted ideologies as they overtly articulate values. Our analysis focuses on contradictions in a combination of individual and social elements in these sequences to identify the constitutive ecocinema ideologies at work in each film. In the process, we leverage the China/US dynamic to critique these imaginations of education at the end of the world.

Han Duoduo's first appearance in *The Wandering Earth* portrays her as a disaffected and rebellious individual, too cool for the academic agenda in this school. The sequence opens with a medium close-up shot of her hand flipping her pen in a style well-known in Chinese classrooms. Juxtaposed with this visual is the collective voice of the students reciting a text about spring, planning, and hope from a famous text, "Spring" by Zhu Ziqing. In actual Chinese education, recitation of this text serves largely to familiarize students with excellent writing. Reframed by the ecological context of the film, "Spring" gains the added power of equipping young people to confront the anxieties and depression of people and the planet in peril. This short scene plants a Humanities education seed that blossoms later in the film as a counterpart to the Technical education behind the Chinese engineers' Earth Engines.

The camera cuts to a medium shot of Duoduo chewing gum with her mouth closed in subtle resistance to the recitation work and then dropping her pen on the floor out of sheer boredom and/or to reject this indoctrination of hope. The next cut moves out to reframe Duoduo from the side, a shot that spatially emphasizes the many symmetrical rows of desks filled by uniform-clad teenagers. Her rebellious spirit is set off by Duoduo's classmates attentively performing for the teacher, who then calls on the class monitor, a top student designated as a classroom model/supervisor, to define hope. While the monitor stands and rehearses a poetic line about how precious hope is in this time of planetary crisis, Duoduo slouches further and delivers an audacious eye roll that does not escape the teacher's notice. Moments later, Duoduo sneaks out of the classroom during a diversion created by Liu Qi, her older brother by adoption.

Through content and form, this sequence characterizes Duoduo as a strong-willed individual and Chinese educational pedagogy as a superficial program for producing compliant cogs to maintain the social machine. For US spectators in particular, Duoduo may act as an individualistic point of identification within this unfamiliar educational scenario that is grounded in collectivity and prescribed programming of what to think and believe. Yet, this initial constituted ideology of force and agency is undermined across much of the film in favor of a constitutive patriarchal approach to ecological crisis.

As the plot of *The Wandering Earth* unfolds, Duoduo plays a surprisingly low-impact role in light of her initial in-school persona. When confronting challenges during the mission to help save Earth, Duoduo almost always appears fearful and ineffectual, whimpering for help from men: her brother, grandfather, and other male members of the rescue team. From an ecofeminist perspective, this lack of imagination in her character arc and development is as unsurprising as it is significant. Duoduo's weaknesses of character imply a failure on the part of the filmmakers, and in social ideologies at large, to imagine what women with strong senses of agency might produce to address planetary ecological catastrophes. Sure, she can chafe against the school and the ideology it perpetuates, but for the majority of the film, the ruling order of patriarchy remains undisturbed.

Even Duoduo's original act of rebellion, the cornerstone of her character, is recontained by her eventual contribution to saving Earth and humanity. When Liu Peiqiang, Liu Qi's biological father and Duoduo's adoptive uncle who left the family years ago to serve on the space station orbiting the wandering Earth, asks the UEG to order remaining units to assist in a last-hope endeavor, he's rejected. The UEG replies that this leadership body will not demand that people set aside their individually chosen ways to meet doom to pursue a low-probability effort at collective species survival. In response to this liberal humanist surrender, Duoduo acts. She delivers an inspiring speech to humanity via a universal public-announcement system – a medium of collective ideology dissemination conventionally familiar in China but coded as dystopian in the United States as a tool of totalitarianism. Specifically, Duoduo rehearses the phrases taught and internalized in that first classroom scene. Duoduo takes up the same role as the teacher she disrespected. True, Duoduo's experiences endow her words with the power of practice beyond theory alone. However, the superficial appearance of elevating Duoduo actually recontains her role, and that of women more broadly, as mere support to a male agenda, which is also true of medical rescue team Lieutenant Zhou Qian. In preserving the patriarchal hierarchy, the film undermines its utopian element of the people of Earth astoundingly forging transnational solidarity and moving the planet out of the solar system. In this way, the constitutive gender ideology of Duoduo appearing strong and savvy while reinforcing a misogynistic status quo works against the constituted ideological vision of a collective ecological future on the far side of its imminent crisis. After all, structural exploitation and extraction of people based on gender as well as race, religion, and more go hand in hand with the exploitation and extraction of nonhuman beings and objects. As Chelsea Mikael Frazier asserts in "Black Feminist Ecological Thought: A Manifesto," ecocriticism must develop, not by adding approaches but by fundamentally changing its "committ[ment] to understanding the intersections of gender, race, and class and bringing those commitments into a larger discussion of eco-critical approaches to literature, art, and culture" (2020).

All told, the depiction of education in *The Wandering Earth* is marked by the core contradiction of paving the way to a human collectivity forceful enough to save the planet and species yet unable to achieve escape velocity from struc-tural patriarchy. This mix of productive aspects and problematic baggage in speculative education approaches is rendered especially visible through this process of ecocinema studies collaborators applying ideology critique to a mix of films from different nations. This is a way toward challenging the national-istic, patriarchal, and other conservative forces that we have all inherited and that prohibit planetary thought and practice.

With the ideology critique underway, we now add the two-film dialec-tic by turning to education in *Interstellar*. Patriarchal ideology dominates the education sequence that provides Murphy's initial characterization. Unlike Duoduo's introduction, the *Interstellar* analog features Murphy's father, teacher, and school administrator discussing her academic performance and disruptive rebellion in a parent-teacher conference while she waits in the family truck outside the school. Ideologically speaking, the narrative choice reinforces the father as the keeper of agency, knowledge, and perspective. Similar to Duoduo, Murphy rebels against an education she considers facile, in this case, because she believes the history textbook's account of the Apollo moon landing to be fraudulent. The textbook claims the landing was faked. Murphy's rebellion against this educational manipulation is grounded in the knowledge her father has provided. Cooper appears dumbstruck when he first hears why Murphy acted out, and he quickly disabuses the educators of interpreting his response as disappointment in his daughter's disobedience. Instead, Cooper supports his daughter's assessment of the textbook's lie and launches into a thematic diatribe that captures the essence of *Interstellar*'s ideology.

你不相信我们登上过月球
You don't believe we went to the moon?

FIGURE 7.1 Cooper attending a parent-teacher conference in *Interstellar*.

Cooper, and by proxy, Murphy, significantly attacks only the veracity of the Apollo moon landing itself and not an education board's decision to disseminate this revisionist history, which frames past US space exploration as a move to bankrupt the former Union of Soviet Socialist Republics. By glossing over the pedagogical choices that shaped the textbook and the broader ideological programming it supports, Cooper implicitly focuses his resistance on the politicization of national space programs. The constituted ideological focus asserts that Cold War politics did not play a role in the Apollo moon landings and should not diminish that great techno-scientific achievement. As such, a sequence ostensibly about Murphy's savvy and rebellious spunk is actually about a privileged white man angrily asserting that space exploration and the planetary ecological crisis are apolitical, ahistorical demonstrations of a universal human call to explore. In short, an ideology with more than a whiff of Musk (Elon, that is). Murphy is thereby introduced as an echo of her father and the fantasy of patriarchy free from history, politics, and ideology that he believes he embodies.

Not only does *Interstellar* twist this education scene away from the young woman supposedly at its center, but it seeds subsequent messaging on morally-warranted control of public narratives. While Cooper chafes at the textbook, he isn't concerned about the false narrative disseminated to the nation about NASA's covertly-continued budgeting and research toward an end for which they believe the public has no will. This instance of a powerful white man, Dr. John Brand, essentially controlling and concealing a public-funded agency doesn't ruffle Cooper's feathers. On the contrary, this patriarchal lie is exactly what lets Cooper do the aeronautical piloting that he's talented at and thereby leave behind the agricultural work he despises. In many ways, the constituted ideology of *Interstellar* perpetually forgets about Murphy, and Earth, as the driving narrative force is Cooper's second chance to realize his colonial, masculine-coded adventures. Recall the joke near the end of the film when Cooper assumes that the station to assist Earth was named after him, but he's informed that it was, in fact, named after Murphy. This brief comic relief moment just before the aged Murphy nudges her father along once more to venture forth and settle the new frontier planet can be read as a return of the repressed in the film's constitutive ideology. Cooper cannot imagine Murphy as a central agent, and the constituted ideological texture itself obscures that role for her in favor of light humor that endorses the continuation of colonial, patriarchal impulses.

More importantly, behind the big lie about NASA having been dismantled is the still more massive one of Dr. John Brand pretending to have nearly solved the gravity issue of transporting the human population off of Earth. In the end, Murphy solves for gravity, but her achievement is made possible by white men's lies while secretly using public works funding, and by her education only after it was removed from a public system that engages political economy and placed in the hands of a paternalistic white male mentor. The fact that NASA is now in the abandoned North American Aerospace Defense Command (NORAD) facility acts as one more return of the repressed. At the surface, the location seems intended to signal the need for post-political thought and transnational work to solve planetary ecological crises. But upon closer inspection, this location can remind audiences that these ecological crises emerged from political and economic conditions. What was the Cold War about if not intensifying global capitalism and its attendant carbon emissions, climate change, and deep wealth inequalities that unevenly distribute the impacts of ecological crises?

The Wandering Earth and *Interstellar* generate insightful ideological frisson in their representations of women in school. Both leverage their young women protagonists in sites of education as points of identification for the audience. Both minimize these women's roles in their narratives so that space programs and exploration, as well as the agency to save Earth and its human inhabitants, are the domains of men. Yet, on one side of this eco-patriarchal coin, *The Wandering Earth* aims to supersede capitalist individualism with the collective political, a concept Xi Jinping has coined "Community with a Shared Future for Mankind." The concept of "Community" here originates from French philosopher Jean-Jacques Rousseau, which refers to the Social Contract in which each individual resigns all their rights to the collective union of the people (Zhao 2017, 28–31). Xi innovatively expands this political idea to articulate "Community with a Shared Future for Mankind" as a central strategy and value in China's approach to politics, economy, culture, security, ecology, and space exploration. The theme film of the Chinese Pavilion at the Expo 2020 Dubai was entitled *Space Dream*, for example, and, like *The Wandering Earth*, it featured a group of culturally and racially diverse astronauts.

On the reverse side of the eco-patriarchal coin, *Interstellar* rejects the political, especially collectivity, to double down on the purported power of individualism to solve problems. True, *Interstellar* is willing to embrace the role of a benevolent authoritarian, but only in the form of a paternalistic white man rather than a committee driven by expertise and/or common values. While *The Wandering Earth* questions and then re-embraces a pedagogy of benevolent propaganda, *Interstellar* takes a more libertarian approach to pedagogy as a tool best kept out of public oversight and implementation. We see it as telling that the former approach is tied to a story about sticking with the troubled Earth, while the latter is tied to a spirit of colonial expansionism that gladly leaves the ruined Earth to molder in its cascade of extinction.

Food and Ideology

In this section, we dive into the food acquisition and allocation in both films. The global ecological crises are depicted as bringing about severe scarcity that ripples through individual, family, national, and species levels. This shared central concern leads to distinct models of food plans and/or practices in *Interstellar* and *The Wandering Earth*. The former portrays a food structure and system that continues the current practice of individual farmers cultivating large single-crop farms geared toward capitalist industrial production of corn products. The latter film imagines a collective food structure and system that plans and distributes nutritional foods at the city level. Such distinctions hint at the different ideologies manifested through foods in the United States and China, and which are rendered clearly through the emergency conditions of planetary catastrophe.

Interstellar begins with a focus on farming and famine. An elderly woman, talking in the style of a documentary interview, delivers the first line of dialogue, "My dad was a farmer, like everybody else back then. Of course, he didn't start that way." Then the shot cuts to a corn field in a burnt yellow hue and then to a flashback of Cooper's air crash nightmare. The memoir-like narration of the elderly woman continues on how an entire wheat crop had died because of blight and they only had acres of corn and lots of dust. Once more, the camera switches to the corn field but this time with a sandstorm blowing and the crops at the brink of devastation. The beginning scenes set the tone with a strong concern for food and farming at the individual and family level.

As the film proceeds, we observe Cooper and his son responding to varieties of crop blights and failures that are especially devastating when agriculture appears to still be organized by corporate interests rather than genetic diversity. The visual and narrative impacts of these scenes at the constituted ideological level work through a kind of ecohorror aesthetic: if the species is going to starve to death on Earth, all the more reason to move to Planet B, so the film suggests. But dig into the constitutive ideology, and what's missing from the narrative are any considerations of what Timothy Morton has called agrilogistics in *Dark Ecology* (2016). Although Cooper stays ahead of his neighbors by using his engineering capacities to bolster his farm practices, the farm remains massive monoculture fields.

A provocative contrast with the role of corn in *Interstellar* is the short film *The 6th World* (2012) written and directed by Nanobah Becker. Instead of attempting apolitical shots of sprawling monoculture fields of corn, *The 6th World* hinges on antagonism between some Omnicorn Corp scientists who use corn by stripping it away from its planty plenitude and political-economic history and Navajo Nation scientists who engage corn from an Indigenous perspective that regards its whole being. Salma Monani has argued about the compelling ecological interconnectedness in this film with cultural and political economic history (2017). Corn plays a similar decolonizing role in techno-ecological futures in Alex Rivera's film *Sleep Dealer* (2008), which features a utopian conclusion to what Andrew and Sharada Balachandran-Orihuela call a "neo-milpa" elsewhere (2011). These and other films help triangulate the ideological fabric of *Interstellar* that the film itself obscures, if not outright ignores, which helps us to further understand the issue behind the monospecies-dependent food industry in America.

The corn-focused food theme continues as Cooper and his children head to the education scene we explored above. When a large autonomous drone passes low and loudly overhead, Cooper diverts their trip so he can capture and repurpose the device. The following action-sequence revels in the cinematic spectacle of a speeding pickup truck plowing through a sprawling cornfield. On a micro-level, the drone chase illustrates the carelessness toward food that's at the film's core, a long way from the traditional Chinese saying that "Every grain of rice is a drop of sweat from a farmer's brow." On a macro-level, the scene is an easy, cheesy way to characterize Cooper as beating swords (a former military drone) into plowshares. The peacefully productive drone is destined only to patch over the structural failure of capitalist-organized agrilogistics embodied in these monoculture fields. After all, these fields are not tied to feeding the starving human population. Vast swathes of corn like those in the film are destined to be processed into high fructose corn syrup, livestock feed for climate-devastating meat industries, and so on, which is not explicitly featured in the film, but reasonable to assume.

A bit later in the plot, Cooper talks with his son, Tom, about choosing his future path – a fake choice due to lack of real alternatives. Confronted by the ecological catastrophes, capitalism seems to have collapsed, and many of the "glorious" professions have vanished, like NASA piloting. He (and later his son) run the private farm as part of an effort at feeding the human population. The film doesn't disclose much about what the US government has done to feed their people, but we can extrapolate that the pre-catastrophe agrilogistics have not shifted much, if at all. The patriarchal logic continues in the family-based survival mode. The food sections of *Interstellar* feature mostly, if not exclusively, strong-willed, middle-aged white men as the central pillar of the family. They are responsible for daily farming as well as family decisions. When Tom reaches middle age, the issue of dust and blight has worsened. However, he refuses to leave the farm and even resists having his son, who is suffering severe respiratory problems, see a doctor. The connection to the farm and the role of the food provider is key to Tom's authority in the family and his patriarchal control. Thus, he represses the will of his wife and son, risking their health to maintain their farm life, even though the farm itself is dying. As such, patriarchal structures not only continue to work but are strengthened by dire food scarcity.

A final and complicated engagement with agriculture in *Interstellar* appears toward the very end of the film. After returning from the black hole and reuniting with Murphy, Cooper sits on the porch of a re-creation of the homestead where the film began. Cooper's body language conveys discomfort, perhaps dismay, in this revenant place. Throughout the film, Cooper consistently denigrates the work of farming. Therefore, an obvious reading would be that he remains an explorer at heart, which fits neatly into his decision to appropriate a ship and fly to Dr. Amelia Brand. Such an interpretation comes bundled with the ideological baggage of individualistic white male privilege as the closing tone of the film celebrates his unilateral resource grab to jump the queue in transplanting to humanity's new home planet. That said, there's also the constitutive ideological messaging of Cooper's reaction to this pseudo-farm in space. Not only does the homestead miss what he personally aspired to, but it embodies a failure of imagination as humanity pivots away from Earth. In this decisive leap forward, the shackles of agrilogistics shaped by global capitalism are not shaken off and left behind. The eerie echo of the early twentieth-century American Dust Bowl in the documentary video recordings at the start of the film suggests a desire to learn from history, yet the recreated homestead reveals the difficulty in realizing that desire. Cooper and the small, privileged sector of the humans who utilize the data from the black hole show little to no sign of imagining their way out of unsustainable food systems. Ecocinema ideology critique of food thus pulls our attention back from the romantically-inclined next chapter for humanity leaving Earth behind so we can wonder harder about what escape velocity from ecologically-devastating ideologies and practices might be and do.

While *Interstellar* locates the food focus in the nuclear family home and farm, *The Wandering Earth* takes a very different approach to representing post-disaster food scarcity. A voiceover near the start of the film states, "At first, nobody cared about this disaster – just another wildfire, another drought, another extinction, another vanishing city – until everyone is entwined with this disaster" while news footage of catastrophes in various languages scrolls across the screen. This sequence delivers vital narrative exposition even as it establishes the tone of collectivist ideology that permeates the entire film. The UEG rises to act as central governor for the survival of all humankind. Ten thousand Earth Engines are built to push the planet away from the sun and an underground city is built under each Earth Engine to accommodate humans who can no longer live in the aboveground climate. The administration of these underground cities appears to be modeled on Chinese cities today, relying on micro-level administration and commodity economy regulated by macro-level central governance. This type of social structure is depicted as maintaining a certain level of food/nutritional diversity despite the scarcity.

Shortly after the opening sequence, we see our protagonists Liu Qi and Han Duoduo planning an escape from the underground city of Beijing. It is during the Lunar New Year and Duoduo is tempted to leave after eating *jiaozi* distributed by the neighborhood committee. *Jiaozi*, small dumplings filled with mixtures of minced meat, greens, or herbs, is a signature food in China. It is both a feature of festivals in northern China and a daily food that every family can make on their own. Although it is quite common in China for local micro-level social units to give out food at festivals as a kind of welfare and care, the fact that Duoduo doesn't want to give up the *jiaozi* distributed by the neighborhood committee hints that it cannot be easily made or acquired daily in that era. To Chinese audiences, these *jiaozi* symbolize the severity of food scarcity and the commitment of a benevolent government to maintain core pieces of identity and ideology beyond mere survival. The scene is a contrasting parallel to Donald, Cooper's father-in-law, waxing nostalgic over hotdogs at baseball games in *Interstellar*.

Shortly after the dumpling scene, the implications of food shortage are further signaled by Duoduo's interest in durian-flavored dried earthworms, and, later on, her grandpa Han Ziang's attempt to bribe prison guards with aged-dried earthworms to let Liu Qi and Duoduo go. Both moments show that earthworms have become a staple food source in this speculative future. In an added scene in *The Wandering Earth: Beyond 2020 Special Edition,* a director's cut of the movie with an extra 11 minutes, Duoduo and Liu Qi sit in a restaurant, but the "two large juices" they order are served in small test tubes, and the "earthworm skewers" are in fact "tiny mini." According to the "Brief Introduction to the 'Worldbuilding' in *The Wandering Earth*," we learn that "Food, water, costumes, and other necessities are regularly distributed by the government…but everyone can pay extra credit points (the currency in the film world) to buy more resources" (Yan and Yang 2019, 270). Based on the conversation between the protagonists and the restaurant owner, they are regular customers and have dined there before, but the food served to them this time is lower in quantity and quality compared with before, which implies that the alternative food resource cannot fully dispel the clouds of intensifying environmental degradation during the planet's trip away. However, various cooking methods and flavors of earthworm-based cuisine reflect the flexible attitude

FIGURE 7.2 "Two large juices" are served in two small test tubes in *The Wandering Earth*.

toward this new protein source: it can be a daily staple, a fun snack, the precious gift, and a small luxury at a restaurant.

These comestible earthworms send a multivalent signal that can endorse and undercut planetary politics with Chinese characteristics in the film. At the constituted level of ideology in which the film promotes Chinese geopolitics, the worms as food work in two positive ways. First, in turning to worms for food, China demonstrates its flexibility when facing a planetary ecological crisis. Just as the Chinese government and general populace outside the film proved ready, distinct from swathes of the US government and general populace, to accept the scientific consensus that climate change is a phenomenon and is caused by human activities, the Chinese government and citizens of its underground cities inside the film prove adept at adapting to the actually existing conditions. Again, contrast this with Donald's remark at the baseball game in *Interstellar*: "Popcorn at a ballgame is unnatural. I want a hot dog." The hotdogs in that instance, a chewy tubular counterpart to the earthworms, are an index of the rigidity bundled with American exceptionalism and nationalism. Confronted with planetary ecological collapse within his grandchildren's lifetime, Donald laments the loss of highly processed foods produced by the profit-driven monoculture food systems that contribute to the collapse and are linked to systemic health crises in the United States. As metonymy of the American food attitude in *Interstellar*, Donald provides an ecological analog to the America-first version of globalization in Roland Emmerich's *Independence Day* (1996). To be sure, *The Wandering Earth* lays out an Earth future with Chinese characteristics, yet with flexibility and adaptability rather than a re-entrenchment in practices causing the catastrophe. The worms are pulled into traditional flavors and food preparation ways to model cultural malleability for the common future of humanity on Earth.

The second positive valence of the worms is that they connect the film diegesis to current trends outside the text of pivoting toward alternate sources of protein and reducing the carbon emissions tied to beef, hogs, and other large-animal husbandries. *The Wandering Earth* skips over the pivot process unfolding outside the films. Even as the film portrays China's food flexibility as laudable, the consumption of worms may trigger hostile ideological responses in audiences outside of China and/or those who are committed to opposing the nation's approach to political economy and geopolitics. The dominant theory of the COVID-19 pandemic places patient zero at a Chinese wet market. The virus transmission from nonhuman to human in that market is tied to trade in animals not typical in Western food systems. However, many of the animals featured in such wet markets are in fact at the extreme margins of mainstream Chinese cuisine, a point often omitted or downplayed in Western journalism.

For one more twist of the worms and ecological ideologies, these beings connect with the fact that humanity has now relocated underneath the Earth's surface. People are becoming like worms. This is a powerful counterbalance to the techno-scientific power of the Earth Engines. Instead of framing the engineering feat to avoid total ecological catastrophe as total domination of nature, this innovation must be meshed with the humbling act of going underground. And this implication of people and worms in parallel can shape readings of many scenes throughout *The Wandering Earth* featuring large-scale mining to maintain life and the engines. Although such scenes may at first strike spectators as deeply unecological in their ready treatment of the planet as a stockpile of exploitable resources, the worms help connect this digging directly to the collective future, quite distinct from actual large-scale mining that serves the interests of a handful of global corporations.

Both films feature food shortages and scarcities caused by planetary ecological crises and how characters respond to them within the quotidian acts of daily life in their climate-changing contexts. In *Interstellar*, food production is highly dependent on the farming activity of each individual family, which ensures the patriarchal control of the male as the major labor force in the family over other members. In *The Wandering Earth*, a collective social system is maintained on the underground city level, where the centralized government provides food and shelter to its citizens (no matter their gender, age, or race) in return for loyalty and service to the common good. The desires for hotdogs in *Interstellar* and *jiaozi* in *The Wandering Earth* imply nostalgia and homesickness for the old days, whether it's the United States or China, the baseball game, or the Spring Festival. However, the former falls into agrilogistics by sticking to the old way of farming crops even when human beings step outside of Earth, while the latter embodies flexibility in dietary structure by adapting to the new underground environment.

Conclusion

We have examined the divergent education and food systems in *Interstellar* and *The Wandering Earth* as people adapt to similarly planet-scaled ecological catastrophes. What remains undiscussed is the matter of who got access to these fundamental resources of nourishment and knowledge. Both films are grounded in the idea that scarcity necessitates sacrificing part of the population – human and nonhuman alike – for the survival of humankind. The protagonists in both films have already survived the initial disaster shocks, ecological, social, political, and economic. In *Interstellar*, there's a key piece of information you could readily miss: the US government tried to make NASA "drop bombs from the stratosphere onto starving people," intending essentially to sacrifice the poor for the survival of the rich. Additionally, there is only one Black person with a name in the film, no Indigenous or other people of color, and no explanation of why the team behind such an important mission is so deeply white. An ideology of eugenics where race and wealth intersect underpins the narrative, yet the characters involved either don't seem to notice this or simply capitulate to the logic as necessary under the emergency conditions.

In *The Wandering Earth*, the UEG conducts a lottery to decide who will be admitted into the underground cities. This method seems fairer and more democratic but no less violent since vast numbers of fellow human beings are to be dehumanized. In both films, the mothers in the central protagonist' families are absent, leaving adult males as the sole supports. While the mother in *Interstellar* died as a result of healthcare technology being deprioritized in favor of governmental investment in agriculture, the mother in *The Wandering Earth* was chosen to die by her husband Liu Peiqiang. A preexisting health condition meant she had a limited time to live, and her sacrifice would be the only way to have both her father Han Ziang and her son Liu Qi gain entrance to the Underground City while her husband served on the space station. Women, people of color, poor folks, and people with illnesses are abandoned for the ostensible benefit of the family and entire species. Neither film can shake loose this hierarchical ideology of domination, this narrative of current emergency demanding an intensification of gender, racial, and class privilege in the guise of a rising tide that will eventually float all boats. But in the Anthropocene, the death and devastation of rising tides will be asymmetrical, within humanity and without.

Both *Interstellar* and *The Wandering Earth* contain inspirational seeds for ecological futures and the ideological entanglements that threaten to distort or destroy these seeds. Our collaborative ideological ecocinema critique that transcends individual minds and national-cultural perspectives is a practice of locating the seeds to cultivate and the ideologies to weed. These processes are complex, continual, open-ended, and urgent at the same time. We share it in the spirit of building collective futures on Earth through the power of cinema narrative and critique as one piece of the work.

Note

1 There is a large body of scholarship on *The Wandering Earth* film in Chinese, ranging from humanities perspectives to law or science analysis in the film. A significant part of this focus on the science fiction film industry/production in China, and the domestic as well as international reception of the Chinese value and esthetics represented in the film. On the other hand, papers on the science in *Interstellar* dominate the research on this film in Chinese, standing out from other approaches such as narration, sound, and ecological analysis. There have been a few comparative analyses of both films, from the perspective of value difference and hometown consciousness in China and the West, and the different approach of techno-mythic narration and catastrophe narration in the two films. See Wang Xinyu's "Jiyu *Liulangdiqiu* he *Xingjichuanyue* qianxi zhongxifang jiazhiguan de yitong" [An analysis of the similarities and differences between Chinese and Western values based on *The Wandering Earth* and *Interstellar*] (2020); Zhou Qingping's "Kehuan dianying zhongde jishushenhua xushi: *Liulangdiqiu* yu *Xingjichuanyue* de bijiaoyuedu" [Techno-Mythic narratives in science fiction films: A comparative reading of *The Wandering Earth* and *Interstellar*] (2019); Li Xianyou's "Kehuan dianying zhongde zaibian xushi: yi *Xingjichuanyue* he *Liulangdiqiu* weili" [Catastrophe narratives in science fiction films: *Interstellar* and *The Wandering Earth* as examples] (2021); Cao Litao's "Dongxifang jiayuanyishi zai dianying zhognde chayihua biaoxian: yi yingpian *Liulangdiqiu* he *Xingjichuanyue* weili" [The differentiation of Eastern and Western homeland consciousness in films: An example of the films *The Wandering Earth* and *Interstellar*] (2020).

Works Cited

Balachandran-Orihuela, Sharada and Andrew Hageman. 2011. "The Virtual Realities of US/Mexico Border Ecologies in *Maquilapolis* and *Sleep Dealer*." *Environmental Communication* 5.2: 166–186.

Dalian Evening Post. 2014. "*Santi* zuozhe tan *Xingjichuanyue*: chuangyi bugou xinying" [The Author of *The Three-Body Problem* Talks about *Interstellar*: The Idea Is Not Innovative Enough.] *Dalian Evening Post*, November 23, 2014. Accessed October 1, 2021. http://www.chinanews.com/yl/2014/11-23/6805288.shtml

Du, Wei and Xingsheng Dong. 2019. "Liu Cixin: Liulangdiqiu de maoxian chenggongle, dan zhongguo kehuan dianying bukeneng meici maoxian dou chenggong..." [Liu Cixin: The Adventure of *The Wandering Earth* Has Succeeded, But the Adventures of Chinese Science Fiction Film Cannot Succeed Every Time.] *National Business Daily*, November 22, 2019. Accessed October 1, 2021. http://www.nbd.com.cn/articles/2019-11-22/1388336.html

Frazier, Chelsea Mikael. 2020. "Black Feminist Ecological Thought: A Manifesto." *Atmos*, October 1, 2020. Accessed October 1, 2021. https://atmos.earth/black-feminist-ecological-thought-essay

Hageman, Andrew. 2013. "Ecocinema and Ideology: Do Ecocritics Dream of a Clockwork Green?" In *Ecocinema Theory and Practice*, edited by Stephen Rust, Salma Monani, and Sean Cubitt, 63–86. New York: Routledge.

He, Weihua. 2020. "*The Wandering Earth* and China's Construction of an Alternative Cosmopolitanism." *Comparative Literature Studies* 57.3: 530–540.

Khan, Amir. 2020. "Technology Fetishism in *The Wandering Earth*." *Inter-Asia Cultural Studies* 21.1: 20–37.

Monani, Salma. 2017. "Science Fiction, Westerns, and the Vital Cosmo-Ethics of *The 6th World*." *Ecocriticism and Indigenous Studies: Conversations from Earth to Cosmos*, edited by Salma Monani and Joni Adamson, 44–61. New York: Routledge.

Morton, Timothy. 2016. *Dark Ecology: For a Logic of Future Coexistence*. New York: Columbia University Press.

———. 2017. *Humankind: Solidarity with Nonhuman People*. London: Verso.

Ray, Sarah Jaquette. 2020. *A Field Guide to Climate Anxiety: How to Keep Your Cool on a Warming Planet*. Berkeley: University of California Press.

Schaberg, Christopher. 2021. *Pedagogy of the Depressed*. London: Bloomsbury.

Silk, Molly. 2020. "*The Wandering Earth*: A Device for the Propagation of the Chinese Regime's Desired Space Narratives?" *SFRA Review* 50.2–50.3. Accessed on October 30, 2021. https://sfrareview.org/2020/09/04/50-2-a13silk/

Space Dream. 2020. China Pavilion of the Expo 2020 Dubai. Accessed on October 30, 2021. https://mp.weixin.qq.com/s/UN_r5jJFGXFCGWBKImx_cg

Thorne, Kip. 2014. *The Science of Interstellar*. New York: Norton.

Yan, Dongxu and Zhixue Yang. 2019. "Dianying *liulangdiqiu* shijieguan gaishu" ["Brief Introduction to the 'Worldbuilding' in *The Wandering Earth*."] In Liulangdiqiu *dianying zhizuo shouji* [*The Making of The Wandering Earth: A Film Production Handbook*], edited by Shuo Fang et al., 261–284. Beijing: Renmin Jiaotong Chubanshe Youxiangongsi [China Communications Press Co., Ltd.].

Zhao, Kejin. 2017. "Renlei mingyun gongtongti sixiang de fengfu neihan yu lilun jiazhi" [The Abundant Meaning and Theoretical Value of the Concept of "Community of a Shared Future for Mankind"]. *Qianxian* [Frontier] 5: 28–31.

Zhu, Ping. 2020. "From Patricide to Patrilineality: Adapting *The Wandering Earth* for the Big Screen." *Arts* 9.3: 94. https://doi.org/10.3390/arts9030094

8
KEATON'S CHIMERA, OR THE COMIC ASSEMBLAGE OF MOUNTAINS

Christian Quendler

In Henri Bergson's "Essay on the Meaning of the Comic," landscape and laughter engage in a paradoxical relationship.[1] Arguing that the comic resides exclusively in a human domain, Bergson contends that "[a] landscape may be beautiful, charming and sublime, or insignificant and ugly; it will never be laughable" (1914, 3). Surprisingly, his first example to illustrate the incongruent logic of the comic is the alpine landscape found in Alphonse Daudet's novel *Tartarin sur les Alpes* (*Tartarin On the Alps*, 1885). In this novel, the eponymous hero is the victim of a tall tale that claims that the Swiss Alps with their wonderful glaciers and waterfalls are really just an artificial show produced by an enormous theatrical apparatus located in a massive basement. "In 'a nature that is mechanically tampered with,'" Bergson argues, "we possess a thoroughly comic theme, on which fancy will be able to play ever so many variations with the certainty of successfully provoking the heartiest hilarity" (43). Bergson's paradoxical claims result from relating landscape to two sets of opposites: human vs. non-human and organic vs. mechanical. Accordingly, landscape only becomes a laughing matter when it is first made human and subsequently turned mechanical. Anthropomorphizing and mechanizing nature are preconditions for locating landscape between elasticity and mechanicalness, which are for Bergson conceptual coordinates that define the comic as "a certain *mechanical inelasticity*, just where one would expect to find the wideawake adaptability and the living pliableness of a human being" (10, italics in the original). Even if we disagree with Bergson's underlying premise[2] his reflections on landscape and laughter draw attention to the complex and layered ways in which landscape is mediated and to the instrumental role humor plays in revealing the multidimensional realities of natural environments.

DOI: 10.4324/9781003246602-11

Almost 50 years after the publication of *Tartarin sur les Alpes*, Siegfried Kracauer, intrigued by the topicality of this novel, penned a film scenario that poked fun at the *Bergfilm*, which had become an immensely popular genre in the Weimar cinema. Kracauer envisioned *Tartarin sur les Alpes* as an international comedy in which the national heroism and the pompous battles of man against nature are replaced by accidental achievements and *dei ex machina*. For Kracauer, comedy was not only a subversive means to critique German mountain films for their phony and commercialized pathos of the sublime. He also recognized the comic as a domain that, as Esther Leslie puts it, could showcase cinema's "capacities to chop, merge and rearrange space and time" (2016, 123) along with its analytical and constructive power of reinventing nature.

In his 1931 essay "The Case of Dr. Fanck," Béla Balázs argues that Arnold Fanck's mountain movies of the 1920s reveal the "countenance" of landscape (2016, 69). If cinema imbues mountains with a human face or lets us see – as Balázs puts it – "the soul of things" (1952, 59), it does so by showing us exterior and material relations. Notably, cinema shares this material investment with humor. Physical comedy in particular affords us with a bottom–up, deeply embodied, materially sensitive, and heterarchical approach to mountain environments. While twentieth-century theories of humor have largely focused on linguistic premises of jokes, earlier theories of humor developed in the eighteenth century offer a productive framework for integrating non-verbal and non-intentional forms of humor. They promise to be particularly instructive for understanding the creative matrix of cinema and the ways slapstick comedy interlinks different environmental, personal, and semiotic realms.

In the *Act of Creation*, Arthur Koestler points out that although "we all know that there is only one step from the sublime to the ridiculous … the possible gains which could result from the reversal of that step" have been surprisingly ignored (1976, 32). Following Koestler's suggestion, the first half of the chapter explores the comic as a creative model to filmic understanding of "mountain being." It will do so by tracing the figure of the Chimera from its mythological origins as a mountain being to its invocations in biotechnological domains and theories of humor. Cutting across mythological, biological, and comic domains, chimeric figuration in film can help us to better grasp both the heterogenic processes of cinematic creativity and the heterarchical basis of non-binary being.

Although Kracauer's scenario never materialized, there is a group of mountain films that follow this route. In the second half of this chapter, I discuss Buster Keaton's *Our Hospitality* (1923), an early comic intervention that targets the film tradition of the mountain melodrama set in the US South, as a chimeric assemblage that places the protagonist in ever-changing technical and technological relations to mountains. I argue that the film de- and re-territorializes Appalachia through humorous de- and re-coding of genre and gender as well as national and personal histories. Humor, I claim, is crucial to grasping the multidimensionality of environments.

Ecocriticism is in dire need of humor, not simply because, as Friedrich Nietzsche knew best, "humans alone suffer so deeply that they had to invent laughter" (1999, 571, my translation) or because, as Virginia Woolf maintained, laughter reveals true tragedies (1986, 59). In *Bad Environmentalism*, Nicole Seymour (2018) argues that an increasingly apocalyptic and moralizing discourse of environmentalism may run the risk of failing us altogether. In her study, she sifts through witty, ironic, and downright irreverent forms of ecocriticism that refuse to feed on "guilt, shame, didacticism, prescriptiveness, sentimentality, reverence, sincerity, earnestness, sanctimony, self-righteousness and wonder" (4). These forms not only broaden the affective range and sensibilities of mainstream environmentalism but also deconstruct its "heteronormativity and whiteness" (4). The comic not only lends itself to subversive critiques of hierarchical and binary orders, but – as I show in my discussion of *Our Hospitality* – it can also help us conceive of non-binary and heterarchical modes of being.

From Mountain Being to Being Funny

In modern alpine encounters, mountains are frequently objects of territorialization and individuation. They are prominent terrains for imperial, scientific, and economic explorations as much as they serve as sites of (typically male) rituals of self-discovery and purification. A Chimera can be thought of as an embodiment that relates to both of these processes. It represents a mythical mountain being and is an allegory of a mountain as being. In Greek mythology, Chimera emerges as the monstrous progeny of Gaia and Pontus (earth and sea). She is typically depicted with a lion's head, the body of a she-goat, and a snake as the tail. At once tame and wild, she moves lightly and with great speed. As Ginevra Bompiani points out, like Sphinx, Chimera "has always been preceded in translations by the definite article, making it a common noun, a multipliable entity ... the prototype of every possible composite, every hybrid (including the contemporary hybrids of genetic engineering)" (1989, 376). Chimera has also come to signify monstrous illusions and excessive flights of imagination. She was killed by the deluded Bellerophon, whose hubristic attempt to fly to Mount Olympus left him blind and selfishly embittered.

What makes the Chimera particularly pertinent to ecocriticism is that she addresses both the heterogeneous compound of nature and culture as well as the compounding nature of imagination. Renaissance mythographers decoded the Chimera as a mountain in Lycia with a sun-glazed summit, and fauna and flora that included mountain lions near the top and pastures with goats but also venomous snakes near the bottom, which kept people away until Bellerophon made the mountain inhabitable. The allegory endows the mountain and its disparate elements with a sense of organic unity. The rhetorical principle that informs such allegorical interpretations decodes Chimera as a figure of speech, which is another meaning she assumed during the Renaissance. The rhetorician Emanuele Tesauro calls the Chimera "a hieroglyphic of insanity" (quoted in Bompiani 1989, 392) that reveals the ingenious power of metaphor and poetic invention that transforms one thing into something entirely different or even impossible.

In *When Species Meet*, Donna Haraway draws on this old figurative use of Chimera to support her materially grounded semiotic approach:

> Figures collect the people through their invitation to inhabit the corporeal story told in their lineaments. Figures are not representations or didactic illustrations, but rather material-semiotic nodes or knots in which diverse bodies and meaning coshape one another. For me, figures have always been where the biological and the literary or artistic come together with all the force of a lived reality. My body itself is just such a figure, literally.
>
> *(2010, 4)*

Developments in microbiology contemporaneous to Haraway's famous "A Cyborg Manifesto" (1985) help to illustrate the conceptual shift in this metaphor from denoting something exceptional, impossible, and specifically female to describing a ubiquitous or default model of heterogenesis. The momentous attribution of the X chromosome as "female" in the late 1950s laid the groundwork for biological characterizations of the female sex as chimeric or mosaic, as much as it fueled long-standing stereotypes that portray women as bipolar, unstable, impure, and uncontrollable (Grosz 1994, 203; Richardson 2013). This line of reasoning is, of course, questionable; it would be more plausible to refer to the male XY chromosome pair as a hybrid.

By contrast, in more recent microbiological developments, symbiotic processes and gene-modifying bacteria have gained importance. If the chimeric metaphor has followed a colonial or imperial gesture that like Bellerophon's mythical conquest appropriates the land as an incongruent body or territorializes the Other body, one may recognize a decolonial turn in modern biological conceptions of the body as landscape. Notably, Dorion Sagan compares the living body to both a "pointillist landscape" (1992, 363) and a chimera: "Like that many-headed beast, the microbeast of the animal cell combines into one entity bacteria that were originally freely living, self-sufficient and metabolically distinct" (364). He sees this new biology following suit psychoanalytical and phenomenological theories that have turned against monolithic models of subjectivity. Gilles Deleuze and Félix Guattari's *A Thousand Plateaus* (1980) can be regarded as a hallmark in this reorientation. Equally programmatic are Guattari's essay *The Three Ecologies* (1989) and, of course, Haraway's "Cyborg Manifesto" which attests the late twentieth century a cybernetic ontology: "we are all chimeras, theorized and fabricated hybrids of machine and organism; in short, we are cyborgs" (1991, 150). Notably, the microbiological re-description of the body as a Chimera is made within a referential frame of landscape, which provides a heterarchical model of ecological distribution. The re-evaluation of chimeric metaphors accompanies an epistemic shift in biology that is increasingly turning away from vertical, hierarchical models toward horizontal, heterarchical ones (Müller-Wille and Rheinberger 2012, 205).

Chimeras also play a key role in the history of the comic and its gradual recognition as a serious subject matter of aesthetic and ecocritical theories. The idea that laughter arises from the concoction of disparate elements into a unified plane of being can be found at the beginning of Horace' *Ars Poetica* (19 BCE), where he introduces a grotesque Chimera as an illustration of what happens when compositional principles of unity and coherence are violated:

> Imagine a painter who wanted to combine a horse's neck with a human head, and then clothe a miscellaneous collection of limbs with various kinds of feathers, so that what started out at the top as a beautiful woman ended in a hideously ugly fish. If you were invited, as friends, to the private view, could you help laughing?
>
> *(1988, 279)*

What makes this picture a laughing matter is not simply the combination of incongruous elements but their forced or contrived co-existence as a singular being. In 1779, the poet and philosopher James Beattie referred to this passage to express what is sometimes cited as the first reference to the incongruity theory of humor (see Morreall 2009, 12):

> Any one of the parts of the Horatian monster, a human head, a horse's neck, the tail of a fish, or the plumage or a fowl, is not ludicrous in itself; nor would those several parts be ludicrous, if attended to in succession, without any view to their union. For to see them disposed on different shelves of a museum, or even on the same shelf, no body would laugh, except perhaps the thought of uniting them were to occur to his fancy, or the passage of Horace to his memory. It seems to follow "that the incongruous parts of a laughable idea or object must either be combined so as to form an assemblage, or must be supposed to be so combined."
>
> *(Beattie 1779, 320)*

Revisiting the Horatian monster, Beattie stresses the importance of unity, which humor, at least to some extent, shares with poetry.

It is mainly through such contrastive analysis that humor enters European eighteenth-century discourses on art and gradually establishes itself as an aesthetic subject matter. For Immanuel Kant, jest and wit belong to the agreeable arts, a subgenre of aesthetic forms which he defines in contradistinction to the fine arts. Humor merely pleases through its free play of sensations and our engagement of the body. Unlike the fine arts, it does not propel insight or cognitive powers (Kant [1790] 1987, 172–173 and 203). Drawing on John Locke's distinction between judgment and wit, in 1744 Corbyn Morris published an inventory of existing humor theory that seeks to elevate humor as a form of an absurd reasoning: "WIT is the LUSTRE *resulting from the quick* ELUCIDA-TION *of one Subject, by a* just *and* unexpected ARRANGEMENT *of it with another Subject*" (1). While Locke notes that judgment discriminates matters and wit confounds them, Morris particularly emphasizes the enlightening function of wit.

In his exploration of humor as a fundamental pattern of creativity, Koestler revisited such neoclassical theories of humor. In *The Act of Creation*, he regards humor along with art and science as one of three elementary domains of creativity. If humor surprises us by making connections across seemingly incompatible frames of reference, scientific discoveries elaborate such connections through analogical reasoning. Art, by contrast, creates a surplus or excess of meaning, by forging not singular or analogical, but multiple connections. For Koestler, interlinking different matrices or frames of references through creative acts of bisociation reveals the multidimensionality of reality. He coined the term bisociation in contradistinction to habitual associations that operate within the same matrix. Bisociation marks "an escape ... from boredom, stagnation, intellectual predicaments, and emotional frustration" of established routines of thinking (1976, 45). By juxtaposing different matrices and their respective rules of articulations, bisociation creates meanings that are double-coded and sometimes even decode another: "The bisociative act connects previously unconnected matrices of experience; it makes us 'understand what it is to be awake, to be living on several planes at once' (to quote T.S. Eliot, somewhat out of context)" (45). As a means of escaping trivial routines, bisociation implies a strategic dimension; it responds to intellectual impasses by embracing multidimensional challenges of life.

For Koestler, bisociative activity not only spans an entire spectrum of conscious and unconscious activity, but it also includes the molding and re-molding of structures on all levels of biological evolution: "The transformations of fins into legs, legs into arms, arms into wings, gills into lungs, scales into feathers, etc., while preserving certain basic structural patterns were eminently 'witty' answers to the challenges of environment" (466). Koestler offers a theoretical basis for film theorist Noël Carroll's notion of adaptability as a form of bodily or concrete intelligence in his reading of Keaton's comedic style (2009, 7). If Bergson believed humor would result from the absence of "wideawake adaptability" or from "a certain *mechanical inelasticity*" (1914, 10), Carroll argues that the opposite may be equally true. Rather than being the result of maladaptation caused by inattentive or automatic routines, laughter may also be a response to successful adaptation gags that exhibit a remarkable degree of bodily intelligence and virtuosity (2009, 49). Thus, situating humor in a wider spectrum of adaptive processes allows us to better appreciate the heuristics of humor on a developmental or evolutionary plane, which Koestler sought to outline.

The developmental dimension of Koestler's concept of bisociation not only connects with eighteenth-century theories of humor in insightful ways, but it also comes close to the notion of *agencement* that Deleuze and Guattari introduced in *A Thousand Plateaus* (see Goehring 2019, 210–218), and that Manuel DeLanda and others have expounded upon in the name of assemblage theory. Koestler's matrices can be productively compared to Deleuze and Guattari's notion of planes of consistency and development that provide horizons of understanding. For Deleuze and Guattari these planes, which function like the intersecting matrices in Koestler's model, make up an abstract machine. While "concepts are concrete assemblages, like the configurations of a machine, ... the plane is the abstract machines of which these assemblages are the working parts" (1994, 35). Assemblages are different from the environment in which they are created. As Deleuze and Guattari point out, they "operate in zones where milieus become decoded: they begin by extracting a *territory* from the milieus. Every assemblage is basically territorial" (1987, 503).

To illustrate this eco-concept in the context of neoclassical humor theory, we may review Beattie's reconstruction of the Horatian monster quoted above. As Beattie points out, there is nothing humorous about the disparate body parts that are stored on one or several shelves of a museum, a milieu that may be described as a repository preserving select items of cultural significance. Imagining these items to form a hybrid monster means viewing them along a different (organizational) plane. Instead of seeing them as parts of a collection in a cross-sectional view afforded by the (consistent) layout of the shelf, the disparate animal parts are *contemplated* along an organic plane as a unified organism. This shift in perspective, which encodes the discrete body parts into a grotesque figure, presupposes decoding of the museal milieu that allows for a reading "across" and "in between" the archival grid of shelf spaces and allows for an ecocritical rendering of humor theory.

As Beattie remarks, the new organic alignment may be the product of fancy or triggered by the memory of the opening passage of *Ars Poetica*. In the latter case, the configuration of body parts undergoes a conceptual concretization. In Beattie's essay, or in Salvador Dali's 1972 lithograph *Le Chimere d'Horace*, the compounds are "grasped" by phrases like Horatian monster or Chimera. Such phrases and visualizations stabilize (or, in Deleuze and Guattari's terminology, territorialize) the assemblage of a fleeting, fanciful whim, a process. Such a conceptual concretization also lends itself to be reviewed along other planes that may de- and re-territorialize the monster's milieu. For instance, the Horatian monster may appear as a compound in a cross-section of hybrid beings that help to develop non-binary notions of embodiment and subjectivity.

Incongruous assemblages of humor tend to have a low degree of internal homogeneity. Theorists of humor from Beattie to Koestler speak of flashes of insight and contrast them to sustained efforts of reasoning. This is particularly true of accounts that describe humor within theories of release. Following Kant, who regards the humorous interlinking of otherwise incompatible frames as a shortcut that leads nowhere or even disappears into nothing (1987, 204), Freud describes this shortcut also as a highly charged short-circuit that brings relief to a sustained cognitive effort. Neither of them, however, considers the productive powers of a sustained humorous effort. If Kant distrusts the pre-judgmental correlations of humor as an intellectual impasse (203), Koestler embraces them as a creative starting point and basis for cognitive adaptability to a multidimensional universe. In what follows, I propose to view Buster Keaton's film *Our Hospitality* not simply as a series of funny moments that lead into nothing (Kant 1987, 204) but as the moving parts of an ecological machinery that can help to rethink our conceptions of nature, technology, and gender.

Our "Horsepitality," or Buster Keaton's Chimera

Approaching slapstick as assemblages that forge new connections across different frames or planes can help to account for a felt disparity between the technical ingenuity in Keaton's comedies and the sophisticated interpretations his work has received (see esp. Trahair 2002; Carroll 2009; Fay 2018). While Keaton was deeply invested in creating surprising connections on material and technical levels, he resented addressing their deeper philosophical and ideological implications (Meade 1995, 112, 113). *Our Hospitality* offers its own version of a Horatian monster. The heterogenesis of Keaton's Chimera is not a singular act of creation but a continuous process of transformation that entangles the protagonist in ever-changing technological relations with his environment. Attempts at adapting and assimilating are constantly thwarted by frames of reference that are often at odds with a particular milieu and decode it.

Our Hospitality recycles and combines shopworn plot devices of the Southern mountain melodrama, which by the time the film was released had already passed its peak of popularity: the country girl who escapes to the city, the city boy who inherits a feud along with a star-crossed romance (see e.g. *Ferdie's Family Feud,* 1912 or *Mountain Mary,* 1915), and the urban dandy immersing himself in mountain life (*The Cub,* 1915). Having lost her husband in a Kentucky feud, Mrs. McKay (Jean Dumas) takes her baby son, Willie McKay (played by Keaton's son), to New York, where he grows up with his aunt. Twenty years later, Willie (Keaton) returns to Kentucky to inherit his father's estate. On the train ride to Kentucky (operated by Keaton's father Joe), Willie falls in love with a charming girl, who turns out to be the feudist's daughter, Virginia Canfield (Keaton's first wife, Natalie Talmadge). In a curious metaleptic twist, the film considers the feuding narrative so outdated that the rivaling families are represented as civilized urbanites and aristocrats who have long outlived their uncouth days. It is rather Willie's "toxic urbanism" that sends the Canfields back to their mythical tribal past.

To complicate matters, civil progress has over-coded the social mores of revenge and re-territorialized the Canfield estate as a Christian home of neighborly love, which forbids Willie from being shot as long as he stays in their house. Once Willie understands this he decides "to become a permanent guest". Ironically, the moral perversity of the situation reinforces the cultural opposition between the safe domestic milieu and dangerous wilderness as much as it exposes its artificiality, which lends itself to playful decoding. By quickly running out one door and entering the house through another, Willie occupies Virginia's father and brothers in a cat-and-mouse game.

Keaton's liminal gender performance plays a key role in the film's decoding of domestic and public milieus. His accentuated white make-up not only highlights Willie's urbanite dandyism but also presents him as a comic double of Virginia (Linville 2007, 275). Throughout the film, Willie disarms the Canfields' malicious intentions by undermining their manliness. He repeatedly fixes the stoppages of Canfields' single-shot peashooter pistols. Willie eventually manages to leave the house cross-dressed as Virginia. Yet, he is soon recognized by her brother and a spectacular chase through the wilderness begins.

This final chase sequence, which makes up about one-fifth of the film, can be described as a series of chimeric assemblages. By entangling Willie in shifting configurations of mountains and technology, Keaton reveals to us deep conceptual affinities between engineering and cinematic poetics (particularly those of humor). Willie does not conquer his sweetheart and win her family's consent by pursuing a well-thought plan. Rather, his successful escape and concomitant explorations of the mechanics of mountains are the outcome of skillful *ad hoc* responses and almost involuntary reflexes to increasingly pressing and dangerous situations. At one point the Canfields seem to catch up with him as they see the back of a figure walking through the woods in the same dress. When the father is about to fire his gun at whom he believes to be Willie, his target takes a turn and reveals itself as a horse onto which the dress and umbrella had been appended (see Figures 8.1 and 8.2).

Keaton's ridiculous contraption not only recalls a Chimera for its illusory quality and its allegorical organicity, but it is also characteristic of Keaton's playful perspectival deceptions and encapsulates the story. Combining Virginia's dress with Willie's umbrella, the masqueraded horse prefigures the happy ending of the romance and the reconciliation of the feuding families. The horse is also emblematic of the many means and modes of transportation (such as trains, horseback, canoeing, running, climbing, swimming, and diving) and their makeshift qualities (e.g., derailed trains turn into an automobile and a boat). In similar ways, film sets and props are constantly transforming. The face of the rock from which Willie descends is filmed in vertical and horizontal

FIGURE 8.1   Keaton's Chimeric Horse (back view).

FIGURE 8.2   Keaton's Chimeric Horse (side view).

orientation. Similarly, a waterfall set construction is used for different locations (Bengston 2000, 131–133): Willie's fishing scene and Virginia's rescuing scene (described below). Perhaps the best example of perpetual reappropriation can be seen in the various uses that a rope serves throughout the chase sequence. Virginia's brother Lee uses it to get a hold of Willie, who got stuck descending a mountain's face. Willie gratefully accepts the rope and swings over to another part of the cliff only to find out that the rope was not meant to rescue him but rather to capture him. Once the ambiguity or ambivalence of the rope as a rescuing or capturing device is exposed or decoded, the rope becomes a connotative bond that unites two enemies. When Willie pulls on the rope, he causes Lee to fall off the cliff, who in turn makes Willie fall, and so forth. Enacting what in classical mechanics is referred to as the two-body problem, Willie and Lee continually trade the roles of a central body and spacecraft.

The generous timing given to Willie's acts of perception, comprehension, and reaction certainly adds to the humor of the scenes. It also draws attention to Keaton's bodily or concrete intelligence (Carroll 2009, 5–7), which in highlighting inertia and gravity emphasizes the body's alignment with environmental forces rather than its opposition. Although Willie is frequently the cue ball or object that suffers from a change in fortune, he always retains a pragmatic understanding of a situation and its shifting intentionalities. In the remainder of the chase sequence, the rope extends its network of affiliation. A train not only severs the bond between the enemies but also entangles Willie with the train. Later the rope gets stuck in the riverbed and throws him off the boat. And while his attempt to tie himself to a log turns out to be a trap, it also provides him with the means to rescue Virginia who has ventured into the river to rescue Willie. By swinging out on the rope, he saves her from being swept down an enormous waterfall. After this spectacular rescue, Willie and Virginia return home and get married just before Virginia's father and brothers return.

Keaton's circular chase pokes fun at the nostalgic trope of the lost home (Linville 2011, 26). The home has always been there; it is Hollywood's othering gaze that has made it disappear. By casting his wife, son, and father in the film, Keaton revisits his own family history and artistic career and rediscovers them in the story of the famous Hatfield-McCoy feud. The elopement of Buster's parents Joseph and Myra Keaton against her father's will bears an uncanny resemblance to Buster's marriage to Natalie, of which Natalie's mother disapproved. Appalachian clichés and legends become a vocabulary for coded personal expressions as well as subversive cultural techniques. The allusion to the Hatfield-McCoy feud, which Keaton redates to have it coincide with the technological novelty of trains, includes an autobiographical dimension. Changing the name McCoy to McKay can be seen as an inside joke that refers to the famous animator Winsor McCay, best known for his animated dinosaur Gertie. McCay's lasting influence on Keaton's conception of film can be traced back to 1914, when the Three Keatons (Buster, Myra, and Joseph) performed alongside McCay in vaudeville theaters (Crafton 2013). In his first feature film *Three Ages* (1923), Keaton paid tribute to McCay by entering the film as a caveman riding on a dinosaur.

In contrast to Bellerophon, territorialization in *Our Hospitality* does not mean conquering a monstrous allegory of nature. Rather, it evolves through situational experiences of the self as being part of a diverse techno-cultural gender complex. The cross-identification with our own heterogeneous monstrosity critiques early Hollywood's appropriation of

Appalachia as a national other. Frequently, the southern clichés presented in *Our Hospitality* merely provide a starting point for addressing larger technological, political, and cultural frames. Willie's attempt at trout fishing provides an illustrative case in point. Lacking the patience for fishing, he soon throws the rod into the water, only to find out later that a fish has taken the bait. He jumps into the river to retrieve the rod and discovers a very small fish at the end of the line. In the meantime, two mountaineers have blown up a dam upstream to irrigate the valley. Willie believes the nearing flood to be the onset of rain, but it rapidly turns into a waterfall that creates a timely hiding place for Willie from the Canfields. If the coherence of this gag had to be spelled out, one could say that an anti-governmental eco-terrorist attack sabotages a dandy's fishing attempt while saving him from his pseudo-aristocratic enemies. Although such an interpretation most likely exceeds Keaton's intentions in engineering this gag, it shows the cross-sectionality of his chimeric comedies and their power to reveal the dense ecological network of Appalachia.

Conclusion

Keaton's engagement with landscape brings out hidden and surprising interrelations that complement and revise phenomenological and vitalist approaches to mountain cinema of the 1920s. While Balázs discovered in mountain films a new way of revealing the soul of nature, he looked at the agency of mountains in anthropomorphic terms as a human interface with the countenance of mountains (Balázs 2016, 69). Similarly, Bergson's conception of the comic as a mechanical lapse of the human can only be applied to an already anthropomorphized nature. Keaton's comedies show us a different route that cuts across binaries in both Balázs' and Bergson's frameworks. Instead of endowing mountains with spiritual human-like agency top-down, Keaton's engineering wit innervates landscape bottom up. As I have illustrated with reference to *Our Hospitality,* by way of theories of the eco-comedic, Keaton complicates and develops the basic syntagma of the chase sequence into an elaborate chimeric organism. This strategy can also be found in many of his mountain chases, most notably, in the spectacular boulder scene of *Seven Chances* (1925). In these scenes, the landscape changes from an attractive setting to be traversed and a backdrop for Keaton's spectacular stunts into a carefully created obstacle course that directs surprising turns of actions and shifts in intentionality. Not only is Keaton's comic assemblage of mountains composed of a diverse array of elements and discourses, but it also evolves and transforms through surprising bisociations among them, thus opening up new ways of reading film as ecocritical.

Notes

1 The research for this chapter was supported by the Austrian Science Fund (P32994-G).
2 Following Gilles Deleuze' philosophy of cinema, various attempts have been made to reconceptualize Bergson's dualism. In regard to Bergson's theory of laughter, see Flaig (2021).

Works Cited

Balázs, Béla. [1931] 2016. "The Case of Dr. Fanck." In *The Promise of Cinema: German Film Theory, 1907–1933*, edited by Anton Kaes et al., 68–70. Oakland: University of California Press.
———. 1952. *Theory of the Film: Character and Growth of a New Art*. New York: Dobson.
Beattie, James. 1779. *Essays: On Poetry and Music, as They Affect the Mind; on Laughter, and Ludicrous Composition; on the Usefulness of Classical Learning*. London: E. and C. Dilly.
Bengston, John. 2000. *Silent Echoes: Discovering Early Hollywood through the Films of Buster Keaton*. Santa Monica: Santa Monica Press.
Bergson, Henri. 1914. *Laughter: An Essay on the Meaning of the Comic*. Translated by Cloudesley Brereton and Fred Rothwell. New York: Macmillan.
Bompiani, Ginevra. 1989. "The Chimera Herself." In *Fragments for a History of the Human Body, Part One*, edited by Michel Feher, Ramona Naddaff, and Nadia Tazi, 365–409. New York: Zone.
Carroll, Noël. 2009. *Comedy Incarnate: Buster Keaton, Physical Humor, and Bodily Coping*. Chichester: Wiley-Blackwell.
Crafton, Donald. 2013. "McCay and Keaton: Colligating, Conjecturing, and Conjuring." *Film History* 25.1–2: 31–44.
Deleuze, Gilles and Félix Guattari. [1980] 1987. *A Thousand Plateaus: Capitalism and Schizophrenia*. Translated by Brain Massumi. Minneapolis: University of Minnesota Press.
———. 1994. *What Is Philosophy?* Translated by Hugh Tomlinson and Graham Burchell. New York: Columbia University Press.
Fay, Jennifer. 2018. *Inhospitable World: Cinema in the Time of the Anthropocene*. Oxford: Oxford University Press.
Flaig, Paul. 2021. "Bergson's Boffo Laughter." *JCMS: Journal of Cinema and Media Studies* 60.2: 4–31.
Freud, Sigmund. (1905) 1999. *Der Witz und seine Beziehung zum Unbewußten*. Frankfurt am Main: Fischer.
Goehring, Billy. 2019. "Repurposing Deleuze and Design." PhD diss., University of Oregon.
Grosz, Elisabeth. 1994. *Volatile Bodies: Toward of Corporeal Feminism*. Bloomington: Indiana University Press.
Guattari, Félix. [1989] 2000. *The Three Ecologies*. Translated by Ian Pindar and Paul Sutton. New Brunswick: Athlone Press.
Haraway, Donna Jeanne. [1985] 1991. "A Cyborg Manifesto: Science, Technology, and Socialist-Feminism in the Late Twentieth Century." In *Simians, Cyborgs, and Women: The Reinvention of Nature*, 149–182. New York: Routledge.

————. 2010. *When Species Meet*. Minnesota: University of Minnesota Press.

Horace. [19 BCE] 1988. "The Art of Poetry." In *Ancient Literary Criticism: The Principal Texts in New Translations*, edited by Donald Andrew Russel and Michael Winterbottom, 279–291. Oxford: Oxford University Press.

Kant, Immanuel. [1790] 1987. *Critique of Judgment*. Translated by Werner S. Pluhar. Indianapolis: Hackett.

Koestler, Arthur. [1964] 1976. *The Act of Creation*. London: Hutchinson.

Leslie, Esther. 2016. *Liquid Crystals: The Science and Art of a Fluid Form*. London: Reaktion Book.

Linville, Susan E. 2007. "Black Face/White Face: Keaton and Comic Doubling." *New Review of Film and Television Studies* 5.3: 269–284.

————. 2011. "Buster Keaton's Comedies of Southern History: *Our Hospitality* and *The General*." In *Historical Comedy on Screen: Subverting History with Humour*, edited by Hannu Salmi, 23–35. Bristol: Intellect.

Locke, John. [1690] 1997. *An Essay Concerning Human Understanding*, edited by R. S. Woolhouse. London and New York: Penguin Books.

Meade, Marion. 1995. *Buster Keaton: Cut to the Chase*. New York: Da Capo Press.

Morreall, John. 2009. *Comic Relief: A Comprehensive Philosophy of Humor*. Chichester: Wiley-Blackwell.

Morris, Corbyn. 1744. *An Essay towards Fixing the True Standards of Wit, Humour, Raillery, Satire, and Ridicule*. London: Printed for J. Roberts, at the Oxford-Arms, in Warwick-Lane; and W. Bickerton, in the Temple-Exchange, near the Inner-Temple-Gate, Fleet-Street.

Müller-Wille, Staffan and Hans-Jörg Rheinberger. 2012. *A Cultural History of Heredity*. Chicago: The University of Chicago Press.

Nietzsche, Friedrich. 1999. *Nachlaß 1884–1885. Kritische Studienausgabe*, edited by Giorgio Colli and Mazzino Montinari. Berlin: de Gruyter.

Richardson, Sarah S. 2013. *Sex Itself: The Search for Male and Female in the Human Genome*. Chicago: University of Chicago Press.

Sagan, Dorion. 1992. "Metametazoa: Biology and Multiplicity." In *Incorporations*, edited by Jonathan Crary and Sandord Kwinter, 362–385. New York: Urzone Books.

Seymour, Nicole. 2018. *Bad Environmentalism: Irony and Irreverence in the Ecological Age*. Minneapolis and London: University of Minnesota Press.

Trahair, Lisa. 2002. "The Ghost in the Machine: The Comedy of Technology in the Cinema of Buster Keaton." *South Atlantic Quarterly* 101.3: 573–588.

Woolf, Virginia. [1905] 1986. "The Value of Laughter." *Essays of Virginia Woolf*, volume 1, edited by Andrew McNeillie, 58–60. London: The Hogarth Press.

9

THE MATRIX OF ECOMEDIA

Fan Worlds as Environments

Anthony Lioi

The most venerable ecological catastrophe in *Star Trek* occurs in the 1967 episode "The Trouble with Tribbles," in which the titular furballs, always hungry and born pregnant, create a Malthusian disaster by eating all the grain intended to avert a planetary famine. I experienced my own trouble with them in 1976, when my sister took me to a *Trek* convention in Madison Square Garden. I was 8 years old. Even then, a convention involved thousands of fans, more people than I had ever seen in one place. Inevitably, I got lost in the crowd and found myself in a hall filled with Tribbles scattered across the floor. Tawny Tribbles, black and white Tribbles, particolored as far as the eye could see. I resolved to steal one. As I reached down to snatch my favorite, I found myself surrounded by Klingons – convention staffers in cosplay (a portmanteau: costume + play) – who had noticed the lone child and led my sister back to me. They glared in mock disapproval, made more impressive by professional-level makeup. I managed to escape with Tribble in hand and fancied myself very clever. I had survived my first encounter with a fan world.

An imaginative otherworld such as *Star Trek's* Federation, the Old Republic of *Star Wars,* or the England of *Bridgerton* becomes a fan world when communities arise into these stories and co-inhabit them. In a robust fandom that persists over decades, the fan community becomes powerful enough to decide what is and is not a legitimate version of the world, sometimes usurping the original author, director, or showrunner entirely. Such fan worlds are media matrices in the way a forest ecosystem is made of plants, animals, fungi, and bacteria. Economies of attention and poiesis run between the nodes of a media matrix in the way metabolites course through networks of tree roots and mycelia. Canceled television series live again because fan communities feed them attention. Climax storyworlds can become endangered when the author makes the wrong

DOI: 10.4324/9781003246602-12

move politically in the "real" world ostensibly outside the matrix of media. For example, will J.K. Rowling's becoming a "TERF" (trans-exclusionary feminist) to former fans threaten the longevity of *Harry Potter* (Duggan 2021)? Fan worlds can emancipate themselves from the dictates of the author, living or dead. Such stuff as dreams are made of no longer depends on a canonical text written by a genius, even when we academics continue to pretend that it does. Fan worlds are a mosaic of different versions of the story, different aspects of the storyworld, in print, digital, video, film, and fan fiction forms, each form revising and impinging upon the others. Every fan knows this: Emma Watson *is* Hermione Granger in the "Potterverse," even and especially when we try to imagine Hermione otherwise. However, for theories of ecomedia, the fact of a shared world made inextricably from different media has more serious implications. I argue that the media matrix of fan worlds obliges environmental humanists to move beyond the study of isolated works to a model of a network of environments. Such a vast network of fan worlds has emerged since the early days of *Star Trek* conventions that we ecocritics require a change in strategies of interpretation, theories of environmentality, standards of canonicity, and models of materiality as they were received from print culture. Ecomedia studies must not erase the literary; we should connect it to these other technologies of world-building.

For much of its history, ecocriticism has conceived of "environment" as the *oikos*, the biophysical systems in which human cultures and the arts are enmeshed. For scholars of wilderness literature or nature writing, the nineteenth-century Anglo-American separation between nature and culture still looms as a value persisting into the present, even when one tries to deconstruct it. Ecomedia studies troubles this separation because cinematic, digital, and augmented environments are not, like wilderness, "out there," not simply representations of "actual" environments. Media environments surround us, exerting a pull on the perception of the "real world." They are also environments that we inhabit. Ecocriticism has a Walter Benjamin problem: aware of the profusion of "copies" in the midst of "originals," it assumes that value and meaning decrease the farther we get from the original, that is natural, environment. Moreover, the infinite reproducibility of digital environments – such as the way the world of *World of Warcraft* can be on many screens at once – introduces a communal aspect of the experience of ecomedia that makes it fundamentally different from the experience of reading a print book by oneself. All of these problems for ecocritics are amplified in the case of fan worlds generated by contemporary popular culture. While these worlds may include literary elements, they cannot be reduced to any one medium, existing in a matrix of print, filmic, televisual, digital, and material–cultural elements such as toys and souvenirs. Fans can enter such a world through multiple doorways and take many paths through its "matrix of media." The multifarious nature of fan worlds creates a set of phenomenological, interpretive, and ethical questions with which ecomedia studies must grapple.

In the next section of this chapter, I consider what it means to grapple with these questions of a world constituted by a matrix of media. First, I ground the question of the matrix as a form in the semiotics of Roland Barthes and Julia Kristeva. I then examine the idea of a narrative world form via the narratology of Erin James and the media theories of Alenda Chang and Adrian Ivakhiv. In the subsequent section, I use two artifacts of the Marvel Cinematic Universe (MCU) – *Black Panther* and *WandaVision* – to understand the matrix of ecomedia as empowering archive, impediment to interpretation, and irreducible multiplicity. These artifacts illuminate the challenges presented by the fan world for fans, critics, and the "aca-fans" like myself who seek to interpret such media matrices as clouds of fun-knowing.

A Matrix of Theories

Ecocriticism never really had its structuralist moment, but Roland Barthes is ready for his close-up. In *S/Z*, his 1970 essay (or "attempt") to understand Honoré de Balzac's *Sarrasine*, Barthes gives us a crucial tool for understanding the matrix of media that makes up a fan world: the idea of the *writerly text*. By this, Barthes means a text in which the reader becomes another writer: "Why is the writerly our value? Because the goal of literary work (of literature as work) is to make the reader no longer a consumer, but a producer of text" (Barthes 1974, 4). He does not say that the goal of *a* literary work, singular, is to make the reader a producer of text. Rather, it is a literary kind of work that makes the reader a writer. As opposed to the idea of the author (or auteur) as a genius or great man, Barthes's idea of literary *labor* is to make the reader a maker of text, anticipating Henry Jenkins's concept of the fan as *prosumer* (producer-consumer). While Jenkins situates the prosumer in a capitalist system of media production as the default setting of textual work (2008), Barthes figures the reader as a worker who makes something of equal value to the original or great work of art (1974). This principle is both semiotic and Marxist. Thus, the Barthesian model of the reader as producer upends both the reign of the Author as the arbiter of textual meaning and the hegemony of the "culture industry" as critiqued by the Frankfurt School. Fan communities stand inside-outside the traditional hierarchies of the American culture industry, transferring part of the means of production from the Hollywood machine to artisanal collaborators. This principle helps us define the makers of the matrix of media, the community of audience-creators and creator-audiences, as a dispersed network of textual producers no longer dependent on a singular moment of creation that defines the authentic version of work forever. In a Barthesian framework, the matrix of media expands at the speed of readership/viewership, and the story-world can be entered at any moment through any of its nodes, from cosplay and fan fiction to more traditional broadcast or print media. In Barthes' terms, the "pitiless divorce which the literary institution maintains between the producer of the text and its user, between its owner and its customer" is overcome (1974, 4). Readers gain access to the "magic of the signifier, to the pleasure of writing" (4). It is not that the matrix of media has no maker, but that it has a plenum of makers that is infinitely dense in potential.

This relationship of readers-as-writers to literature is balanced by the relationship of texts to other texts that they echo, imitate, depart from, and transform. In French semiotics, this interrelated constitution of texts is called *intertextuality* by Julia Kristeva: "a mosaic of quotations; any text is the absorption and transformation of another. The notion of *intertextuality* replaces that of intersubjectivity, and poetic language is read as at least *double*" (1980, 85). Two clarifications: by poetic language, Kristeva does not mean poetry as a mode, but all language that engages in *poiesis*, the process of making. So, alongside the Barthesian idea of readers as writers, there is also the idea of texts as the poets of other texts. This is not a destruction of authoring, but a distribution of it through the action of language itself. Second, intertextuality thrusts aside the idea that literature is the by-product of titanic minds competing with one another for a place in Parnassus in favor of a model of memetic self-generation, in which tropes, plots, character types, and the rest pass through authorial subjects on the way to becoming other texts. This model elegantly describes not only how the *Iliad* becomes the *Aeneid* which becomes *The Divine Comedy,* but also how *The Godfather* becomes *The Sopranos* which becomes *The Many Saints of Newark*. Kristeva explains:

> To interpret a text is not to give it a (more or less justified, more or less free) meaning, but on the contrary, to appreciate what *plural* constitutes it. Let us first posit the image of a triumphant plural, impoverished by any constraint of representation (of imitation). In this ideal text, the networks are many, and interact, without any one of them being able to surpass the rest; this text is a galaxy of signifiers, not a structure of signifieds; it has no beginning; it is reversible; we gain access to it by several entrances, none of which can be authoritatively declared to be the main one.
>
> *(1980, 5)*

This system of systems, for Kristeva, frees interpretation from monolithic meaning into a pluriverse of polysemy. The principle of the text as *triumphant plural* that we can enter through many doors is the right way to understand matrices of media, both in and of themselves and as already inhabited by a pleroma of fandoms.

This semiotic way of understanding art as a network of intertexts written by its readers has sometimes been understood by media scholars in a disembodied manner, as if the system were only data held in an imaginarium beyond matter. Were this the case, the idea of a matrix of media would be an inappropriate way to understand fan worlds within an ecomedia framework that is obligated to take into account the material components in any system of mediation. However, the tools that depend upon the concept of the matrix of media as an inhabited environment already exist to employ the semiotic-intertextual approach within a new materialist paradigm. The bridge between the storyworld and the material world can be built with reference first of all to the econarratology of Erin James. In *The Storyworld Accord*, James writes:

> Like the similar terms *story* and *fabula*, *storyworld* is a term narrative theorists use to discuss what happens in a narrative. But more so than other terms, the storyworld highlights the world-making power of narrative texts. Storyworld scholars argue that narrative comprehension relies upon readers interpreting textual cues to make mental models of a text's world and inhabiting those models emotionally. To understand a narrative, such scholars suggest, we must lose ourselves in the same environment and experiences as a narrative's characters.
>
> *(2015, 14)*

Unlike *story* (or syuzhet), which emphasizes the narrative as recounted, and unlike *fabula*, which denotes the events in a story in chronological order – both of which are terms related to time – the concept of the storyworld emphasizes space, in particular, the space that readers enter to immerse themselves in the story-as-environment. For James, the most important aspect of immersion is loss of control or, we might say, a degree of participation in the environment of the characters such that emotional understanding becomes possible.

The ability to inhabit a mediated world over a long period of time is crucial to the idea of a fan world. It is not just that individual readers or viewers immerse themselves for as long as the book, film, or game lasts. Instead, immersion in the storyworld persists even when the text at hand ends. It is this persistence that allows fans to share a storyworld IRL, "in real life," even as they move between particular instances of that world in the media matrix. This space-between-nodes might be the time between the episodes of a television series that airs weekly, or the moments between reading *The Lord of the Rings* and watching the Peter Jackson films. The storyworld persists in the community of fans as an experiential environment IRL (here I raise my hand in the Vulcan salute: *Live long and prosper*) and in this sense inhabitation of it resembles a mode of augmented reality *avant la lettre*. The fan world is not a shared hallucination but a form of culture.

Videogame theorist Alenda Chang goes at this dynamic from a different angle in her book *Playing Nature*. Chang wants to understand games, not as imaginary gardens with real toads in them, *pace* Marianne Moore, but as blends of real and simulated worlds. To understand games this way, Chang employs the term *mesocosm* ("medium-sized world"): "In ecology, mesocosms are experimental enclosures intermediate in size and complexity between small, highly controlled lab experiments and large, often unpredictable real-world environments" (2019, 17). To call a game a mesocosm is to distinguish it from the microcosm of the laboratory and macrocosm of the planet or universe. One is too controlled to be a useful analogy; the other is too autonomous. The game is a delimited environment of participation that allows for player choice without the possibility of getting truly lost (even if it preserves the possibility of getting truly stuck). Further, Chang underscores the way mesocosms structure relations between human and non-human agents in an actual world altered by fictional principles:

> Describing games as mesocosms is for me an ideal way to characterize the subtle negotiations that take place between human and nonhuman actors and technological assemblages during play, while also taking into account diverse situational and interpretive contexts. Rather than see games as real rules embedded in fictional worlds, as Juul does, we could make the case that games blend real worlds and fictional rules.
>
> *(2019, 21)*

Understood as mesocosms, the materiality of fan worlds encompasses not only the energy required by server farms to facilitate online storyworlding (via chat rooms, social media, fan websites, video-sharing platforms, etc.) but such IRL forms as conventions, Live Action Roleplaying ("LARPing") spaces, and cosplay contests. In each case, there is a building, a field outdoors, or a room in which a storyworld manifests in a well-defined public space refigured by the rules of that world. Inside such "magic circles," as defined by historian Johan Huizinga (1955), players become the Sailor Scouts of the televised anime *Sailor Moon* or members of the Fellowship of the Ring or Jedi Knights of *Star Wars*. Such spaces are meso*cosmic* – a local ordering force – in an important social sense: the fictional rules reframe social space so that certain relationships and communities that may be absent or impossible to form in hegemonic social spaces become possible in this augmented real life. This is different from the creation of shared virtual space. The Facebook group *Queer Nerds United*, for instance, creates an online community for a kind of queer person not valorized in homonormative cultures. However, when Gay Nerds of New York meets at the annual New York Comicon, their shared space becomes mesocosmic, asserting an alternate set of rules in person. When the mesocosm becomes powerful enough to spawn a network of such spaces, the effects can become political. Such is the case with the Harry Potter Alliance, an international group of fans who share charitable and political projects (Jenkins 2008). In the wake of the controversy over J.K. Rowling's support for "gender-critical" feminists, whom many fans understand as an anti-transgender hate group, the Alliance declared its support for trans fans, effectively severing their mesocosm from the author of the original storyworld (Hoffman 2020).

If we combine the semiotic, intertextual, narratological, and mesocosmic understandings of fan worlds, it becomes possible to see that matrices of media are, in Adrian Ivakhiv's terms, both interobjective and intersubjective (2013). They are interobjective in the sense that they are made of books, films, television shows, podcasts, et cetera, and all the material relations that go into their production, distribution, and maintenance. They are intersubjective in that they produce social environments in the way outlined above. The missing element that bridges the objective and subjective dimensions of a media-matrix is the *perceptual*. Because film is a medium of images, Ivakhiv says, it is tempting to think of it as non-material and purely subjective. However, "the perceptual or mental realm is not the realm of ideas or meanings *as distinct from* matter. It is the interactive dimension among living things, which are material bodies perceived, or "imaged," and responded to by other material bodies" (36, italics in the original). It would be a mistake, therefore, to assume that the materiality of fan worlds begins when a mesocosm is constructed from a storyworld. Instead, especially where film, television, and video nodes of a matrix are concerned, materiality begins with the event of perception. "The perceptual interactions among image-matter bodies are where the action occurs, and it is out of those relations that the specifically material, or interobjective, and social, or intersubjective, dimensions emerge" (36). In Ivakhiv's account, semiosis is perceptual, and therefore material, all the way down. Likewise, any account of the intertextual relationships in a matrix must also assume the node of any text as a series of perceptions that lead to other nodes that are also a series of perceptions. Understood this way, the formation of a fan world in general and a mesocosm specifically is a culmination of a vast web of events that are objective and subjective, material and social, at once. The media-matrix of any given fan world surrounds fans with objects, events, perceptions, and responses, some of which the individual fan contributes to the system. This dizzying array of interactions, constantly evolving, is a more accurate way of understanding fan worlds than the ideal of the solitary reader or viewer along with their own imagination. If it ever was a good model of codex readership, it is certainly not a model that can accurately describe the function and effects of shared storyworlds in the early twenty-first century. I now provide two case studies drawn from the MCU of the effects of the ecomedia matrix on audience experience.

Black Panther: The Matrix as Empowering Archive

To theorize the structure of a media matrix is not to say how matrices function in practice. To do the latter, we need to examine individual cases because a matrix is not just a structure but a process located in a history of reading, viewing, and playing. The first example I offer, MCU film *Black Panther* (2018), helps us understand the media matrix as empowering archive, a case in which audiences enter through a popular doorway that leads to intertexts that enrich engagement with the storyworld.

Neither ecocriticism nor the environmental humanities possess an auspicious record of engagement with the art and cultures of the African diaspora. *Black Panther*, as an icon of the resurgence of Afrofuturism, presents us with an opportunity to correct those omissions. Scholars such as Mark Dery and Ytasha Womack assert that Afrofuturism endeavors to resignify a diasporic past occluded by white supremacy and enslavement to recreate a future in which Black people become subjects of their own history through the use of high technology and its narrative tropes (Dery 1994; Womack 2013). *Black Panther* tells the story of T'Challa, the ruler of Wakanda, an African kingdom that never suffered colonial rule because it is the most technologically advanced civilization on earth. This advancement is due to the mineral vibranium, sourced from a meteorite that forms the physical foundation of Wakanda's capital city. Vibranium is a metal that absorbs and re-emits kinetic and electromagnetic energy, making it the perfect basis for advanced electronics and weaponry. In short, Wakanda is a nation that functions as an advanced civilization from the future, a contemporary scientific utopia, and a global superpower. However, this power has not been shared with the African continent or anyone else: Wakanda is a xenophobic culture that hides its riches from the world under an illusion of backwardness. This illusion is shattered when Eric Killlmonger, T'Challa's American cousin, reappears to challenge his rule to deploy Wakanda's wealth and power to help the African diaspora. Killmonger is right that Wakanda needs to take responsibility for its suffering relatives, but wrong to model that response around reverse colonialism designed to subjugate the planet to the Wakandan throne. Though he dies in an effort to seize that throne, Killmonger succeeds in opening up Wakanda to the world, and the film ends with T'Challa opening a science education center, led by his sister Shuri, in a historically Black neighborhood in Los Angeles.

Black Panther earned 1.8 billion dollars worldwide and 700 million dollars in the United States, surpassing the gross profit of *Avengers: Infinity War* (2018). Audiences responded enthusiastically to the story of a Black superhero, his family, and its history, though a number of African critics protested the diasporic syncretism in the representation of Wakanda's culture. If we think of the film as a door into the media matrix of the Black Panther storyworld, which originated in the medium of comic books, we observe that this storyworld was flooded by new inhabitants entering through that cinematic gate. In this case, the matrix as archive functioned to enrich audience experience in the following ways: through the comic book origins (from 1966) and extensions of the storyworld; through fan culture; and through connections to a larger world of Afrofuturism. (It also accelerated the consumption of merchandise, which might give ecomedia scholars pause.) As dense as the matrix of *Black Panther* is, it attains its true potential as empowering archive in the Black diaspora by being connected to the work of Afrofuturism at large. The resurgence of Afrofuturism stimulated by the success of the film would not have been possible without decades of work by graphics artists, musicians, writers, and scholars. In turn, the new wave of Afrofuturism has been noticed by the doyens of high culture: in 2022, the Metropolitan Museum of Art debuted an Afrofuturist Period Room, and Carnegie Hall sponsored a three-month-long festival of music and visual art anchored by "The Black Angel of History," a live and virtual exhibit characterized by Wakanda-inspired images and comic book explainer pages (Carnegie Hall 2022).

Though unfamiliar to the general audience of the film, Black Panther is one of the oldest heroes of the Marvel Silver Age, introduced into *Fantastic Four* in 1966, first as an antagonist and then as an ally. He is not at all obscure, but comic books are still such a demeaned medium that millions of people who saw the film had never heard of the character. In this sense, the matrix of media for the film constitutes an empowering matrix because fans could find decades of comic book backstory by artists such as Christopher Priest and John Romita Jr., as well as new comic book material by Black literary figures such as Nnedi Okorafor and Ta-Nehisi Coates. The most obvious level of the Black Panther matrix is intertextual in the literary sense, but fans have made the next level mesocosmic.

Black Panther sponsors more than one mesocosm, but the most prominent is Wakandacon, a Chicago fan convention that began in 2018, funded by Ali, David, and Matt Barthwell and their friends (Gibbs 2019). Its homepage asserts: "Wakandacon creates a supportive space for black-identified people to come together, educate each other, cultivate positivity, celebrate the beauty of Blackness and the future of the entire diaspora!" (Wakandacon). This event was inspired by the end of the film, when T'Challa decides to open Wakanda to the world through outreach to the Black diaspora. Technically, the convention is a non-persistent but recurring mesocosm that appears once a year, confined to a hotel. Within that annual space occur typical convention events such as cosplay, a merchant's room, and appearances by actors, writers, and other artists associated with the Pantherverse. Wakandacon goes a step further, featuring self-defense lessons taught by the stunt coordinators of the film in the style of Wakandan warriors; "Shuri's Room," a space in which children can learn to code; women in STEM; and explorations of more esoteric subjects such as Black polyamory and the history of Afrofuturism. However, like many mesocosms built by fandoms, Wakandacon's effects are not only material but also sociopolitical. Fans who participate in the convention do not confine their work together to the convention but build an annual schedule of collaborations around the appearance of Wakandacon. It is this level of activity that leads to the third level of the matrix, Afrofuturism itself.

Though Afrofuturist culture existed as such before and after the scholar Mark Dery named it in the 1980s, *Black Panther* created a worldwide surge of interest. Afrofuturism contains obvious roots in the Black Arts Movement of the 1960s, but asserts a much stronger reach into popular culture through musicians Sun Ra, Parliament-Funkadelic, and Janelle Monae; writers such as Octavia Butler and Samuel Delany; and television shows such as *Star Trek, Battlestar Galactica, Cowboy Bebop,* and *Doctor Who.* At this level, the matrix of media that extends as far back as W.E.B. DuBois and Pauline Hopkins in the early twentieth century to a history of African political excellence combines with a vision of diasporic technocultural achievement. The Black Panther matrix opens into an intertextual archive so vast that it embodies the Barthesian galaxy of signifiers. In this view, one has not understood *Black Panther* the film until one has encountered its media matrix. At the same time, it raises questions of material presence that include resource consumption by fan communities as well as the consciousness of the extractive relationships with which white media and governments have burdened Black communities in general and Blerds (a portmanteau of "Black" and "nerd") in particular.

WandaVision: The Matrix as Impediment to Understanding

Though they take place in the same storyworld, *Black Panther* and *WandaVision* produced quite different effects in the matrix of Marvel media fandom. If *Black Panther* entered the canon of Afrofuturist empowerment, *WandaVision* – despite its excellence as a television show – sponsored a meltdown in the matrix, as fans of its comic book and filmic sources second-guessed the writers and showrunners, spun out wild plot theories that could not have come true, and stymied their own enjoyment through expectations that could not be met by one show. *WandaVision* premiered in 2021 on the Disney+ Channel as a series about the life of Wanda Maximoff, the Avenger known as the Scarlet Witch in Marvel Comics, after the events of *Avengers: Endgame* (2019) that led to the death of her husband, Vision. The show reveals that Wanda sought refuge in a small New Jersey town that she transformed into a television utopia through her magic. The town is separated from the world by an energy barrier. Inside the walls, Wanda and Vision – mysteriously alive again – live an idyllic suburban life as a couple and eventually as parents to twin boys, who also appear by "tv magic." In this illusion, Wanda hides from her grief and trauma, forcing the other residents to participate in false lives that protect her from the truth. At the start of the show, neither Wanda nor the audience understands that she is responsible for the magical mesocosm that creates a storyworld in which none of the Avengers died and everyone is sitcom-happy. As the show progresses, the mesocosm transforms into a sitcom from the 1950s through the 1990s, mirroring Wanda's viewing as a child in Eastern Europe who dreamed of escaping to an America she knew only through television. Eventually, she is forced to recognize her delusion and the costs it inflicts on her neighbors, and the mesocosm comes to an end, having made its point about the price of evading grief through media consumption.

This plot is original to the series, but the details of the episodes contain strong intertextual allusions to the *Avengers* comics and additional television series the writers employed to signal viewers about the nature of Wanda's environment. The allusions to television sitcoms, from *I Love Lucy* to *Full House*, operate clearly enough to signal the comforts of television suburbia and the race-, gender-, and class-based tensions Wanda's storyworld tries to efface. The comic book intertexts are the source of the true problem of the media matrix as an impediment to understanding, produced when the hermeneutics of desire – what the audience *wished* would happen – overran the series in real time as the episodes ran from week to week. The writers drew on various *Avengers* comics, as well as maxi-series such Jamie Robinson's *The Scarlet Witch* and the X-Men drama *House of M*, to signal that the origins of Wanda's powers and the source of her pain are complex and misunderstood, especially by the protagonist herself. The profusion of references includes versions of Wanda as the mutant daughter of the villain Magneto, a sorcerer brainwashed by Hydra, a devoted wife, and an angry little girl trapped in a dying nation in the Eastern Bloc. There are also references to comic books in which Vision creates a family of artificial life-forms like himself, which is strangely echoed by the human children, Tommy and Billy, who are superheroes in the main Marvel comic book continuity ("Earth 616") in which Vision is not their father.

In an attempt to decode or harmonize the intrusion of the matrix into the false mesocosm of the show, fan speculation ran rampant through social media in real-time response to the show. On Reddit, Twitter, Facebook, websites, podcasts, and other media, professional critics and traditional fans formed theory after theory of what was "really" happening onscreen. Because the season was not available to binge on Disney+, but dropped episode by episode once a week, the online speculation reached a fever pitch just before each episode premiered, only to generate another round of debunking and speculation once new events were digested. Based on the comics, fans speculated that Billy and Tommy had been created to torture Wanda by Mephisto, a devil-like villain familiar to *Avengers* and *Doctor Strange* fans. Agatha Harkness, a character from *Fantastic Four*, who is the true antagonist of *WandaVision,* never blossomed into the role of mentor that she serves in the comics. Emma Caulfield, an alumna of *Buffy the Vampire Slayer*, appears as a neighbor that fans misunderstood as Clea, an extradimensional sorceress from the Marvel Universe, because she had played a vengeance demon on *Buffy*. Ironically, the penumbra of critical and fan speculation created its own delusion step by step, even as the plot unraveled Wanda's delusion inside the mesocosm she had created to avoid her own pain.

This is the sense in which the matrix of media can form an impediment to understanding and ecocritical interpretation. Instead of reflecting on the way

WandaVision materializes the avoidance of grief through the television parodies and the false mesocosm, fans and critics became overwhelmed by the fake clues planted by the writers to playfully mislead the audience as a way to relieve the somber nature of the storyworld. As Marc Faletti, host of the critical podcast *Marvelous TV Club*, observed, "Those of us who got theory-obsessed maybe lost track of the basic rules of every television show or book we've read or film we've watched" (Faletti 2021). *WandaVision* is a meditation upon the ways television and comic books can comfort us in the midst of grief with fictional friends who, when grasped too closely, can mislead us into the hell of avoidance, misperception, and communal suffering. The title reflects this complexity by referring to Vision, the dead husband Wanda refuses to mourn; her vision of suburban utopia that is so unlike the life she has actually lived; and the false mesocosm of the town itself, made material by the magic Wanda has forgotten she ever used. Premiering during the height of the COVID-19 lockdown, pre-vaccine, and in the aftermath of the Trump presidency, characterized by fake news, conspiracy theories, and demagogic manipulation of public perception, the stakes in the fabula of *WandaVision* could hardly be more serious. It is only at the very end of the season that viewers, through Wanda herself, come to understand the true order of events that led to Wanda's delusional world, a revelation that leads to the undoing of the storyworld itself. But as the mystery is revealed episode by episode, the allusiveness of Wanda's vision worked to obscure the point of the narrative. Caught up in speculation about Mephisto, the Fantastic Four, Doctor Strange, and the rest, the online fan community mystified itself in real time, avoiding Wanda's avoidance, which was the pivot of the plot. In other words, the phenomena of the show itself were partially displaced by the echoes of the Scarlet Witch/Avenger media matrix. Thus far, that displacement has prevented a grappling with the ecocritical questions the show suggests but does not engage, such as: In what sense does suburbia itself constitute a fantasy of a perfectly safe and controlled environment? Were Wanda's neighbors vulnerable to her mental domination because they were already in the midst of their own fantasy of small-town life? In what sense are suburban mesocosms already an ideological and material refuge from the Anthropocene, and how long can that illusion last? It may only be possible to answer such questions after we encounter the show the second time around, once viewers have freed themselves from the trap of the story's intertexts. The eldritch spellbook, called the Darkhold, that Wanda reads at the end of the last episode can be taken as a warning of the dangers of getting lost in the spell of limitless semiosis.

Conclusion

Though there is a matrix of consequences in working within a matrix of fan worlds, I want to conclude this chapter by highlighting the three most important takeaways for ecocinema studies and all students of popular culture and multimedia:

1. **The matrix should change the way we read and view.** Most scholarly ways of reading and viewing are stuck in a Modernist paradigm that privileges the great writer or auteur filmmaker and their discrete works. By focusing on one important text at a time, readers and viewers can be sure that they have a sharply defined focus and do not need to engage other readers or viewers to understand the work. The matrix of media model complicates this process by assuming that the individual work is not autonomous, but always-already a part of a system that includes other media objects, material components such as memorabilia or convention centers, and entire communities of others engaged with the matrix. Scholars and students must grapple with new ways of engaging the matrix that takes into account a systemic level of complexity that, in principle, may have no outer boundary.

2. **The matrix should change the way we interpret.** A matrix of signs connected intertextually to one another and to mediated environments, including mesocosms, must change our idea of the phenomenological encounter and the means of interpretation. It should still be possible to interpret individual works by themselves, but other questions must now arise: What other versions of this storyworld exist, and how is each instance of it connected to the matrix? Are there material instantiations of the storyworld? Has it produced mesocosms? To what extent does the matrix impinge on our ability to make meaning out of an encounter with a node in the system? To some extent, these questions already arise in the disciplines of comparative literature and comparative film studies. They rest on a foundation of traditional questions of allusiveness, quotation, variora, lineage, and the affects of influence. But unlike the Modernist literary and anthropological urges to reduce complex patterns to one paradigm, the matrix forces us to make meaning from a network to which we, by definition, never have total access or complete comprehension. In this way, the matrix of media model harkens back to the medieval European models of fourfold exegesis and cosmic correspondence, but without the hierarchies of value and substance implied by these earlier interpretative systems. The matrix destabilizes the *mono-* in "monograph."

3. **The matrix raises tricky theoretical questions of what is now meant by "environment."** What would it mean to take mediated, networked environments seriously without the shadow of Baudrillardian simulacra stalking us? Any matrix is itself a vast environment of signification, but that fact does not dissolve the environmental status of the nodes. There are textual environments – the book itself – and imaginary, televisual, mesocosmic-material environments in a matrix. We must become used

to the idea that all of these nodes environ the reader–viewer–participant, and that there are many paths through these environments. For instance, a child taken to Disneyworld may encounter Cinderella's Castle as a castle first, before reading Grimm or Calvino or even seeing the animated film *Cinderella* or its live-action descendant, *Maleficent*. We are used to taking print environments as the proper way to enter a storyworld, but this assumption becomes less and less tenable as a matrix increases the kinds of environments it includes. As fan communities expand, coalesce, and diverge from one another and the originary auteur, influence over the matrix of environments becomes more decentralized and more extreme. Fans of Spider-Man, Studio Ghibli, *Firefly*, and *Doctor Who* (among others) call forth new nodes in the storyworld through activism, patterns of consumption, Twitter campaigns, and sheer obsessiveness. This does not negate the traditional relationships between text and landscape or film and place that ecocritics have traditionally traced, but it does create a deeper, higher, more dense ecology of signs to contend with.

Works Cited

Barthes, Roland. [1970] 1974. *S/Z: An Essay*. Translated by Richard Miller. New York: Hill and Wang.

Carnegie Hall. 2022. "The Black Angel of History." https://artsandculture.google.com/story/mgWBi7ccMEXisA

Chang, Alenda Y. 2019. *Playing Nature: Ecology in Video Games*. Minneapolis: University of Minnesota Press.

Dery, Mark. 1994. "Black to the Future: Interviews with Samuel R. Delany, Greg Tate, and Tricia Rose." In *Flame Wars*, 179–222. Durham: Duke University Press.

Duggan, Jennifer. 2021. "Transformative Readings: Harry Potter Fan Fiction, Trans/Queer Reader Response, and JK Rowling." *Children's Literature in Education* 2021: 1–22.

Faletti, Marc, et al. 2021. "Theorycast: The Messy Obsession with Theories in *WandaVision*." *Marvelous TV Club*. Podcast. https://marveloustvclub.libsyn.com/theorycast-the-messy-obsession-with-theories-in-wandavision

Gibbs, Adrienne. 2019. "'Come Find Your Tribe': Wakandacon Takes Over Chicago and *Black Panther* Fans Rejoice." *Forbes*, July 24, 2019. https://www.forbes.com/sites/adriennegibbs/2019/07/24/come-find-your-tribe-wakandacon-takes-over-chicago-and-black-panther-fans-rejoice/?sh=1220d93f2db0

Hoffman, Jordan. 2020. "How the Harry Potter Fandom Is Reacting to J.K. Rowling's Anti-Trans Statements." *Vanity Fair*, June 14, 2020. https://www.vanityfair.com/style/2020/06/how-the-harry-potter-fandom-is-reacting-to-jk-rowlings-anti-trans-statements

Huizinga, Johan. 1955. *Homo Ludens: A Study of the Play-Element in Culture*. Boston: Beacon Press.

Ivakhiv, Adrian J. 2013. *Ecologies of the Moving Image: Cinema, Affect, Nature*. Ontario: Wilfrid Laurier University Press.

James, Erin. 2015. *The Storyworld Accord: Econarratology and Postcolonial Narratives.* Lincoln: University of Nebraska Press.

Jenkins, Henry. 2008. "The Moral Economy of Web 2.0 (Part 2)." *Confessions of an Aca-Fan,* March 19, 2008. http://henryjenkins.org/blog/2008/03/the_moral_economy_of_web_20_pa_1.html

Kristeva, Julia. 1980. *The Kristeva Reader,* edited by Toril Moi. New York: Columbia University Press.

Metropolitan Museum of Art. 2022. "Before Yesterday We Could Fly: An Afrofuturist Period Room." https://www.metmuseum.org/exhibitions/listings/2021/afrofuturist-period-room

Wakandacon Homepage. 2018. https://wakandaconforever.com/

Womack, Ytasha L. 2013. *Afrofuturism: The World of Black Sci-Fi and Fantasy Culture.* Chicago: Chicago Review Press.

PART III
Ecocinema Communities

10

INDIGENOUS COSMOLOGIES AND COMMUNITIES

The Digital Art of Jonathan Thunder and Missy Whiteman

Angelica Lawson

This chapter considers the ecological dimensions of the artistic collaborations of Ojibwe animator Jonathan Thunder and Arapaho and Kickapoo media artist Missy Whiteman. Locating Thunder and Whiteman's work at the intersections of ecocinema and Indigenous digital studies, I examine how artistic communities and collaborations create ecomedia that highlights Indigenous cosmologies in sharp contrast to settler colonial industrialism and capitalism. Though Whiteman and Thunder are both active in a large network of artist communities, for the sake of brevity I will focus on their work. Whiteman is a Northern Arapaho and Kickapoo photographer, filmmaker, and digital media artist raised primarily in Minneapolis and currently living and working in Minnesota. Thunder is a Red Lake Ojibwe painter, animator, and digital media artist who grew up in the Twin Cities and is now living in Duluth, Minnesota.

An Indigenous studies lens provides language for assessing how digital media contributes to decolonial efforts by illuminating Indigenous histories and environmental issues affecting Native American communities. Environmental justice scholar Kyle Powys Whyte's (Potawatomi) concept regarding "industrial settler campaigns" (2017) helps us unpack settler colonialism's environmental impact on Indigenous communities and artistic responses to these campaigns. By focusing on the ecological dimensions of Whiteman and Thunder's work, I consider how their art presents alternative worldviews rooted in Indigenous thought that are "valuable as a means to confront Western notions of linear progress, which not only tend to ignore the cyclic rhythms of earth's biogeomorphic systems but do so with dangerously myopic focus" (Monani and Adamson 2017, 15). These cinematic renderings challenge simplistic notions of Western progress and bring important concepts regarding Indigenous relationality back into focus.

DOI: 10.4324/9781003246602-14

Ecocinema scholar Salma Monani's analysis of Indigenous film provides a framework for thinking about how Indigenous ecocinema "unsettles" Western boundaries between human/non-human to address "vital, entangled, and multifaceted aspects of our environmental relations" through various cinematic techniques (2017, 2). Indeed, an analysis of directorial choices, editing, sound, and image, along with ecological messages that are attentive to Indigenous epistemologies provides a more nuanced reading of images and soundscapes in Indigenous media than reading such media through canonical Western lenses can. This combination can bring to light not only layers of meaning but also highlight the layers of collaboration and community practices that create the final product. In performing an ecocritical reading of Thunder and Whiteman's dynamic Indigenous media, I contribute to larger conversations about ecocinema communities and practices through a capacious reading of what might be considered Indigenous ecocinema. Specifically, in this chapter, I focus on the music video "Time Dreams" (dir. Whiteman 2016), Minneapolis digital billboards, and Thunder's art installation *Manifest'o* to show how together they emulate cinema's aesthetics and creative teamwork to animate and Indigenize urban landscapes while illuminating the ethics and values of Indigenous cosmologies. These projects demonstrate community activist practices that create works of art that not only critique settler colonialist anti-environmental practices but also remind Indigenous audiences that "ancestor memories" hold valuable knowledge for living as a responsible relative on this earth. I begin with a close ecocritical reading of the music video "Time Dreams" to consider not only poem content but also how cinematic aspects, such as layered images and soundscapes contribute to the overall ecocinematic affect.

"Time Dreams"

"Time Dreams" weaves together the spoken word poetry of Native American activist John Trudell, vocables of singer Quiltman, and the music of the band The Pines. "Time Dreams" juxtaposes images of industry and capitalism with multiple generations of Indigenous people. The layering of Indigenous song, language, poetry, and images, both ancient and contemporary, produce a "site of Indigenous instruction" (Allen 2002, 184). These layers of artistic contribution are significant in the context of an ecocinema and Indigenous studies reading. The list of collaborators includes Indigenous artists, activists, and allies who deeply admired Trudell and his work. Such layering also visually represents multiple generations via archival footage, images of Trudell, and ending with Missy Whiteman's son—intentionally dressed like Trudell-signing the words "friend, together, and peace" in Plains American Indian sign language. According to the introductory text that accompanies the video on YouTube, this ending "represent[s] the younger generations connection to Trudell's message" (Whiteman 2016).

Lakota activist John Trudell was a leader of the American Indian Movement founded in Minneapolis. He met members of the Indie transcendental folk band The Pines in Ojibwe author Louise Erdrich's bookstore Birchbark Books, and soon they devised a plan to collaborate. Trudell's poem became the last song on their album. According to David Huckfelt:

> "Time Dreams" had a powerful magic to it from the first rehearsal together, and we agreed to record it, with plans to make an entire record of John's words and our music… When he fell ill, "Time Dreams" was the only song we had time to get recorded, and it ended up being the closing track to our 2016 record *Above the Prairie*.
>
> *(Jacobs 2016, 2)*

After Trudell's passing in 2015, The Pines sought out Missy Whiteman to create a music video in his honor. As someone deeply inspired by Trudell's poetry, Whiteman was an excellent choice. In an interview with *Indian Country Today*, Whiteman said,

> his words meant a lot to me… when John's music came into my life, it helped me out during a very difficult time… John taught me the foundation of being a human is the connection to Spirit and all of creation.
>
> *(Jacobs 2016, 2)*

The resulting music video which includes footage from multiple sources – a live performance at the Cedar Cultural Center, Heather Rae's documentary *Trudell*, historical TV and film footage, original footage by Whiteman, as well as Jonathan Thunder's animation – was nominated for an Emmy and is a stunning experimental-like rendition of Trudell's poem and message.

The opening sequence of the music video visually and audibly indicates the earth and sky as vibrant living beings connected to humans. Trudell's lyrics, "Time dreams/our memories come from the earth and return to the earth/ in the reunion our pulse comes from the sky/and returns to the sky/reflections of ancient sunlight" are paired with images of a sunrise and a birds-eye view of the poet standing on a hill in a large open field. As the camera pans across the field, we hear Quiltman's vocables layered underneath the lines, "in the re-union our pulse comes from the sky/and returns to the sky." Vocables, which are "composed of non-literal vocal sounds rather than actual words" are an important component of Native American singing as relevant today as in ancient times (Harris 2016, 4). As one singer states, "the story taught to me… was that vocables were more powerful than any other language because they're the way that we communicate to our creator" (4). This layering of Indigenous sound over land and sky captures and conveys important Indigenous concepts. In *Mapping Indigenous Presence*, Assiniboine scholar Kate Shanley notes, "For

Indigenous peoples—people vitally connected to geographical locations—place means both an imagined home and a vibrantly interactive space inhabited by many sentient beings... Place means kinship in its broadest terms" (2015, 6). This relational aspect of Indigenous identity is clearly implied as the video begins.

However, as the images shift from land and sky to animated space, the viewer narrowly passes a satellite before encountering a barrage of layered archival images including warplanes. The juxtaposition of the natural world with the technologies of war reminds the audience that Indigenous people were dispossessed of their lands and homes via settler colonial violence. As Phil Deloria et al succinctly state, "Land lies forever at the heart of America's problem with Indians. The United States and the American dream – of freedom, democracy, a divine mandate to lead the world – are built on Indian land" (2018, 14). This concept is visualized in perhaps one of the most striking sequences in the video. The introductory visual and aural representations of Indigenous concepts of time and land are sharply contrasted with the linear concept of settler time visualized through images of technological advances such as the invention of cars, skyscrapers, satellites, and rockets. The framing of these "advances," begs the question as to whether they are equally beneficial to all. When paired with images associated with the violence of settler colonialism, such as the Indian wars and nuclear bomb testing, we begin to see the costs of such technology. This sequence of images creates a visual representation of what Kyle Powys Whyte calls "industrial settler campaigns":

> I use the term *campaigns* because these waves of settlement are sustained, strategic and militaristic... As a means of carving out settler home-lands from Indigenous homelands, waves of settlers harnessed industrial means, from military technologies to large-scale mineral and fossil fuel extraction operations to sweeping, landscape-transforming regimes of commodity agriculture.
>
> *(2017, 208)*

In one of the most dramatic sequences the lyrics, "Industrially darkened, re-formed humans" are paired with footage of a young Native American boy reenacting being shot in the chest alluding to playing cowboys and Indians, followed by archival footage of the Indian wars. The words "re-formed humans" operates on a number of levels. It implies the violent reshaping of Indigenous people through colonial violence in the form of westward expansion, and the assimilation policy period that followed. As the words "behaviors/morality/decided by punishment or reward" are spoken, footage of nuclear testing appears on screen, then followed by the refrain "punishment or reward" as images of more technology and American consumerism follow. According to Deloria et al, "American settlement histories are of necessity deeply ideological.

They frame Indian peoples around two distinct modes of disappearance: Indians can simply die or vanish; or they can assimilate into America, disappearing as distinct peoples into some vast melting pot" (2018, 14). The refrain "punishment or reward" underscores this idea by layering archival footage of the US cavalry charging straight at the viewer, while the words "decided by obediences/willingness to believe/using the lie/like a drug for the heart/silencing our feelings" indicates the violent force used to bring about assimilation.

Whyte elaborates on the concept of "industrial settler campaigns" to say, "These campaigns include both war-like violence and the tactics for suppressing populations that are used alongside belligerence, from assimilative institutions (e.g., boarding schools) to containment practices (e.g., reservations) to the creation of dependency (e.g., commodity foods)" (2017, 208). Dependencies are "like a drug for the heart" and the images on screen indicate this. However, as the content moves away from images of the violent technologies of colonialism, we are taken back in time with archival footage of our ancestors. Whiteman strategically uses archival footage of historical Native Americans as the lyrics shift from a critique of settler colonial industrialization, which creates "darkened re-formed humans" who live in "fear and doubt," to a reminder that self-pity, anger, and doubt disconnects us from "time dreams/the medicine of dreamtime." In this shift, we are reminded that answers for a better future lie in our "ancestor memories," represented through this archival footage followed by multiple layered images of contemporary Native Americans, ultimately ending with footage of the filmmaker's own son. The poet tells us, "straight talk/ with ancestor memories/free without judgment" provides answers to questions and that the "medicine of dreamtime" is

> encoded in the DNA
> of human form
> spiritual umbilical cords
> inside human consciousness

According to Whyte,

> it would have been an act of imagining dystopia for our ancestors to consider the erasures we lived through today... Yet we do not give up by dwelling in a nostalgic past even though we live in our ancestors' dystopia... Our conservation and restoration efforts are motivated by how we put dystopia in perspective as just a brief, yet highly disruptive historical moment for us – at least so far.
>
> *(2017, 208)*

The combination of historical and contemporary images along with Trudell's lyrics help us to realize this is not nostalgia for the past, but a recognition that the past holds important knowledge – "ancestor memories" – that will lead us into the future.

As the poem nears the end, the director's young son Louis appears superimposed over an animated background blurring earthly realms and outer space. Thunder's animated Milky Way comes to life with floating stars as the poet speaks "dream time is a part of our pulse" before transitioning to a live-action sequence of Louis walking through a field, mirroring the poet earlier in the film. Soon, an animated horizon filled with ocean and clouds appears and then melts away from the center of the frame to reveal Thunder's animated Milky Way once again (Figure 10.1). This time, an animated moon cycles through rising and setting as the lyrics "our pulse comes from the sky/and returns to the sky" leads us to the final images in the film. As Quiltman's vocables become louder and stronger, we see Louis putting on a leather jacket, knit cap, and sunglasses – intentionally dressing like the poet Trudell – before signing the words, "friend, together, and peace" in Plains American Indian sign language (Figure 10.2). Whiteman, who nearly always includes some form of Indigenous language in her work, used the most universal of Native American languages to say goodbye to Trudell. The signing parallels the earlier archival images, creating visual continuity from our ancestors to the present represented by Indigenous youth. The inclusion of children in Indigenous new media importantly challenges centuries of stereotypes of vanishing Indians. As film and media scholar Joanna Hearne states, "envisioning Native families… is always a political act, and representations of youth in particular stake claims about the future of Indigenous nations as legitimate, and legitimating heirs to the land" (2012, 9),

FIGURE 10.1 Milky Way animation in "Time Dreams"; courtesy of director Missy Whiteman.

FIGURE 10.2 Louis Whiteman signing in "Time Dreams"; courtesy of director Missy Whiteman.

thus ending the music video on a hopeful note. Indeed, the traditional style vocables, which become louder as Louis signs, indicate this style of singing is as important today as in ancient times. Importantly, Quiltman's vocables challenge and replace Hollywood "Indian music" which is a fabricated construct, with real Native American songs. The combination of the youth signing and Quiltman's vocables indicate that though Trudell has passed, a new generation will take up his message and his activism with the lessons they have learned connecting with "ancestor memories" to lead us into the future. The "Time Dreams" music video would not be the only collaboration between Whiteman and Thunder. In this next section, I consider how Indigenous media artists and communities engage with the digital in large-scale public art works.

"We Are Still Here"

Not long after "Time Dreams" premiered, Whiteman and Thunder worked together again on a two-year project sponsored by the Hennepin Theater Trust and All My Relations Gallery in Minneapolis, Minnesota. This time Thunder would serve as a mentor to Whiteman and two other Indigenous artists on a multi-dimensional project called "We are Still Here." According to the press release, this project is designed to "promote native storytelling for the built environment along Hennepin Avenue and "bring large-scale, high-profile public artworks to the Hennepin Theatre District" (Hennepin Theatre Trust 2022). The Native American artists selected for this cohort are mentored by Jonathan Thunder and create digital billboards, animations, projections, and building-size banners and murals in an effort to Indigenize and decolonize the urban landscape, in particular Hennepin Avenue.

"Whirlwind Woman – Neyóóxetíísei-n"

Whiteman's digital billboard for the "We are Still Here" project indicates Arapaho creation stories through Whirlwind Woman symbology. She designed an abstract animated version of a quillwork medallion representing Whirlwind Woman juxtaposed over a night sky that alludes to an Arapaho creation story symbolically, rather than literally. As the medallion moves on the digital billboard it enacts the spinning out motion of this creator who designed the earth as we know it through her cycles of spinning and resting (Anderson 2013, 112). The image is based on medallions created in quillwork societies for teepee decorations and ceremonial purposes, but Whiteman's digital version is abstract, original, and does not appropriate historical designs, thus protecting sacred knowledge. However, the allusion is significant. Whirlwind Woman's cinematic "radiating outward motion" is associated with female creation, creativity, and power. As Anderson notes, "there is a deep connection, then, between women's artwork in paint and quillwork, and the original formation of the earth's surface" (112). Whiteman's digital medallion signals a formidable counterpoint to settler colonial erasure of Indigenous presence on the land.

The significance of Indigenizing Hennepin Avenue was important to Whiteman (Personal communication, December 17, 2020). The name Hennepin signals colonial mapping over Indigenous lands. In an article titled, "Legacy of Father Hennepin Looms Large on the Mississippi" Catherine Goetz describes the Recollect friar as

> gaining fame in the seventeenth century with the publication of his dramatic stories of the exploration of the Mississippi River. Father Hennepin spent only a few months in Minnesota, but his influence is undeniable. While his widely read travel accounts were more fiction than fact, they allowed Hennepin to leave a lasting mark on the state.
>
> *(2013)*

Indeed, Hennepin Avenue, Hennepin County, and other places in the Midwest are named for this friar, who spent only a short time in the area, yet his published writings "detailed his travels, his experiences living with the Dakota, and his discovery of St. Anthony Falls" (2013). This "discovery" ultimately contributed to settler colonial practices which led to the exploitation of the water and land in the 1800s with Euro-American settlement of the area. During this time, Dakota people were forcibly removed and exiled to Canada (Westerman and White 2012). As Whyte notes, "industrial settler campaigns *both* dramatically changed ecosystems, such as through deforestation, overharvesting and pollution, *and* obstructed indigenous peoples' capacities to adapt to the changes through such removal and containment on reservations" (2017, 209). The removal of the Dakota from the landscape and the settler colonial claiming and re-naming of their sacred sites, such as the falls on the Mississippi River, are examples of *disappearing* Native people and places.

Particularly troubling for Missy Whiteman, who grew up in the Twin Cities, is the knowledge that this avenue was largely superimposed over a natural Dakota footpath that led from the sacred falls to what is now called Lake Calhoun (Personal communication, December 17, 2020). This lake was the place of a Dakota village, called "Cloud Man's" village, and Native elders and storytellers note the importance of the Mississippi River and this footpath for their world making (Boden n.d.). Over time, the appropriation of this footpath for the creation of Hennepin Avenue led to significant ecological devastation, including its role as a neighborhood for lumberjacks and eventually lumber barons who exploited the land for economic growth. The falls made economic development possible. According to Sarah Boden, "The cascading water provided settlers energy to build milling and lumber empires. In fact, Minneapolis was a world leader in the lumber industry during the first half of the twentieth century" (n.d.). What once was a natural footpath from waterfall to lake now represents a notoriously famous avenue symbolic of ecological devastation on many levels.

Whiteman challenges the dominant story of Hennepin's "discovery," his naming of the falls, and the erasure of the sacred Dakota footpath by returning to the original Indigenous maps and knowledge that storied the land. "Reclaiming Native cartographies is key to decolonizing the spatial disruptions caused by settler colonialism and to promoting broader forms of spatial justice" (Goeman 2012, 90). Fully aware of how settler colonial identities have been layered over Indigenous stories of the land, Whiteman seeks to reverse this. She re-maps the space, bringing us back full circle to original Dakota and Arapaho knowledge and an "animated celestial night sky of Dakota and Arapaho stories" that reference Mississippi sacred sites and Arapaho creation stories (Personal communication, December 17, 2020). Whiteman's decision to include Arapaho stories speaks about the knowledge the Arapaho people have of once living in the Great Lakes areas with Dakotas and reasserts their presence on the land from which they were also erased (Personal communication, December 17, 2020).

Through imagery of star maps and constellations, Whiteman re-maps and re-visualizes the landscape from Dakota and Arapaho perspectives. The ancient trailways that led from the sacred falls on the Mississippi River to Cloud Man's village on the lake are re-asserted and made known. Re-storying the land with reference to Whirlwind Woman, an Indigenous female creator, contrasts the recent colonial mapping of Hennepin's "discoveries" and reclaims the sacred sites along the avenue. Whiteman's digital quillwork medallion reflects

Channette Romero's concept of an Indigenous feminine animation aesthetic, which references "Indigenous women's historic roles of utilizing stories and domestic arts to help humans negotiate their relations with each other and the land" (2017, 58). Arapaho women's quillwork societies played a critical role in creating art for both daily and ceremonial life. Whiteman's medallion extends Arapaho quillwork to the digital realm through creative animation. Indigenous knowledge shines bright from the billboard creating and telling new stories linking our past to the present and future.

The Return

In a more playful take on these responsibilities, Jonathan Thunder's digital billboard *The Return* features parachuting buffalo in aviator goggles falling from the sky. Thunder originally created this design as a wood panel triptych delightfully titled "The Return of the Freaky Deaky *Mashode Bizhiki*." The colorful images of parachuting buffalo allude to activist movements taking place among various Native American nations that are acquiring buffalo "seed herds" to strengthen economic and cultural sovereignty. Thunder digitized these images for the billboard project, and in his artist statement, he says, "This series is dedicated to the bison who provided food, clothing, and shelter for generations prior to their calculated extermination by the U.S.A. as a way to starve tribes into dependence and submission" (Hennepin Theatre Trust 2022). In referencing their calculated extermination, Thunder notes the ecological devastation created by this practice as well.

The near elimination of the bison and their replacement with domesticated cattle negatively impacted the earth's physical environment and ozone layers. In addition, the "removal" of bison from the land paralleled the removal of Native people. Historians note the appearance of bison along the Mississippi River prior to the removal of the Dakota and the near extinction of the bison afterward (Westerman and White 2012, 43) In our efforts to reestablish our presence and our connections to the land, many tribal people see the return of bison to communities as an effort to live up to our responsibilities and reciprocal relationships with the earth:

> To many Plains Indian nations, bison are traditionally sacred animals. Many reservations are building on the tradition and have established tribal bison ranches. Hopes are that these cooperatives will provide jobs and other economic opportunities, but also that the renewed connection to the animals will bring cultural restoration with it.
>
> *(Braun 2004)*

Thunder's billboard complements Whiteman's work in that both address the violent removal and destruction of Indigenous peoples, animals, and ecosystems. Yet, both offer hope in connection to "ancestor memories" which include Indigenous knowledge and languages as the key to restoring those ecosystems and cultural connections.

Manifest'o

Focusing on Indigenous knowledge and languages is a notable aspect of Thunder's work, and in 2018 he premiered *Manifest'o*, a mesmerizing multimedia installation originally on view at the Tweed Museum in Duluth, MN. Thunder created three animated vignettes along with 3D sculptures for a glass display case on the museum's second floor. The animated films wrapped completely around the case creating 120 feet of transcendent Indigenous landscapes and immersive soundscapes. Part of the beauty of these short films is how their luminous simplicity alludes to ecological issues. In describing Indigenous song, Maria Chona said, "the song is very short because we understand so much" (Underhill 1979) and though she was speaking specifically of O'odham songs, the sentiment applies here as well. These animations are brief and play on a loop, but for those literate in the symbols from Anishinaabeg storytelling traditions, these brief images are laden with meaning and ecological references, and for those not familiar with those symbols they may be encouraged to find out more.

In "Gold Finch Counts the Leaves", a tiny bird hops from branch to branch counting in Anishinaabemowin (the Ojibwe language) as an owl appears and disappears. Thunder added the owl as a threatening figure whom the finch carefully avoids indicating the vulnerability of the language and its endangered status (Combs 2018). The word for the gold finch in Anishinaabemowin is "the one who counts the leaves" and finches are considered the spirit keepers of the language (Jones 2012). As discussed earlier in this essay, Indigenous languages contain within them critical environmental knowledge. Language revitalization or resurgence is an important part of current Indigenous movements (Kelly 2020). As the gold finch animation plays on repeat the audience learns Anishinaabemowin. In addition, scholars of Native American oral texts note the use of repetition as not only a mnemonic device but also one that may induce a trance-like state (Allen 1993; Simpson 2017). The repetition of these vignettes, along with their soothing soundscapes and calming colors "transfixed" museum audiences and transformed the space (Combs 2018).

The vignette featuring Star Woman is perhaps the most mesmerizing of the three. Both soundscape and landscape hypnotize the viewer as they watch a small rocket descend ever so slowly from the sky to land on the shore of a lake. As this happens bells chime every few seconds while a woman exits the spaceship and enters the water. There she disappears before reemerging as a waterlily floating on the water's surface. The color palette of the film in addition to the chiming bells has a calming effect even as they command the viewers' attention and focus. In "The Star People are Always Watching", Leanne Simpson relays how a new star in the night sky wanted to come live with the Annishnabeeg. After describing how the star chose to live on the water she says,

> After that, the Nishnaabeg gave her a new name: Nibiish Waawaasgone, Water Flower. Nibiish Waawaasgone reminds the Nishnaabeg of the beautiful Sky World and her people, and she reminds us to always live in a careful, gentle, and loving way. In her thankfulness Nibiish Waawaasgone often gives her roots so that powerful medicines can be made.
>
> *(Simpson 2013, location 891)*

This story highlights connections between humans and more-than-humans and implies our ecological responsibility.

Thunder's third vignette features Mishu Bizhiw,[1] an underwater being who is part serpent and part lynx. Thunder notes, "One of his roles is to protect the copper in the lake from mining" (Bermas 2018). Thunder was inspired to create a vignette of this figure after visiting a school where none of the children knew the story, despite living so near Lake Superior (Combs 2018). In her chapter, "The Hydromythology of the Anishinaabeg: Will Mishipizhu Survive Climate Change, or Is He Creating It?" ecologist and Anishinaabeg scholar Melissa Nelson asks,

> how shall we relate to water to protect and nurture it for future generations? It is our human responsibility, indeed perhaps one even vital to our cultural continuance, to keep those Ojibwe hydromyths and other narratives of moral ecologies alive.
>
> *(2013, 229)*

The Mishu Bizhiw stories teach us not to exploit and plunder our environments. They also teach that interaction with our environments must be done in a respectful way. Historically Anishinaabeg and other Indigenous people offered tobacco and prayers before setting out on the waters of Mishu Bizhiw and in doing so acknowledged both the gifts and dangers of such an environment.

Mishu Bizhiw stories appear in many places from ancient petroglyphs to the novels of Louise Erdrich. Most recently, Thunder installed *Manifest'o* at the Minneapolis International airport where travelers encounter him as they glide on moving walkways through the B concourse. This seems fitting. According to Nelson, this underwater lynx is "a protector of natural resources and a mediator between the water, land, and sky beings" (2013, 213). It makes sense that those visiting the city should encounter this protector and be reminded, if only briefly, of our responsibilities to this earth. As Nelson notes, "Today we are in dire need of good medicine stories, new myths of resilience for these unprecedented times" (2013, 21). Thunder's *Manifest'o* may prompt travelers to learn more about these stories, after all, how can one "swim" with a water lynx and not want to learn more? In their seeking and questioning, they will discover more about these "narratives of moral ecologies."

Both Whiteman and Thunder continue to collaborate with many artists, activists, and Indigenous communities throughout Minnesota on projects ranging from multimedia live performances to children's books. Their work frequently highlights Indigenous cosmologies, communities and languages which emphasize our responsibilities to this earth and our more-than-human relations so we can move in a positive direction for the future. These digital media projects created by Thunder and Whiteman, through their retelling and rewriting/righting Indigenous stories, inherently address our interconnectedness and interdependence with our environments and more-than-human-beings. Whiteman and Thunder's ecocinema aesthetics go beyond being beautiful works of art to remind us of the necessity of being in good relation with our world. By considering the ecological dimensions of their artistic collaborations with each other and other Indigenous artists in Minnesota we can learn the stories of Indigenous resilience and resistance through stories that travel via creative technologies and ideas.

Note

1 Spellings of Mishu Bizhiw vary among Indigenous authors and artists.

Works Cited

Allen, Chadwick. 2002. *Blood Narrative: Indigenous Identity in American Indian and Māori Literary and Activist Texts*. Durham and London: Duke University Press.

Allen, Paula Gunn. 1993. *Studies in American Indian Literature: Critical Essays and Course Designs*. New York: MLA.

Anderson, Jeffrey D. 2013. *Arapaho Women's Quillwork: Motion, Life, and Creativity*. Norman: University of Oklahoma Press.

Bermas, Jakob. 2018. "Tweed Museum Celebrates New Native American Exhibits." *The Bark*. November 14. https://www.thebarkumd.com/arts-entertainment/2018/11/13/tweed-museum-celebrates-new-native-american-exhibits

Boden, Sarah (producer). n.d. "An Architectural and Cultural History of Hennepin Avenue." Accessed October 24, 2021. https://ampers.org/mn-art-culture-history/an-architectural-and-cultural-history-of-hennepin-avenue/

Braun, Sebastian Felix. 2004. "Contemporary Tribal Bison Ranching on the Great Plains: Economic, Ecological and Cultural Restoration?" *Société suisse des Américanistes/Schweizerische Amerikanisten-Gesellschaft* 68: 23–26.

Combs, Marianne. 2018. "Duluth Artist Uses Modern Tech to Connect with Native Traditions." *MPR*. November 15. https://www.mprnews.org/story/2018/11/15/duluth-artist-uses-modern-tech-to-connect-with-native-traditions

Deloria, Philip J., K. Tsianina Lomawaima, Bryan McKinley Jones Brayboy, Mark Neil Trahant, Loren Frank Ghigliones, Douglas L. Medin, and Ned Blackhawk. 2018.

"Unfolding Futures: Indigenous Ways of Knowing for the Twenty-First Century." *Daedalus.* 147.2: 6–16.

Goeman, Mishuana. 2012. "The Tools of the Cartographic Poet: Unmapping Settler Colonialism in Joy Harjo's Poetry." *Settler Colonial Studies* 2.2: 89–112.

Goetz, Kathryn. 2013. "Legacy of Fr. Hennepin Looms Large on the Mississippi." *Minnpost.* April 27. https://www.minnpost.com/mnopedia/2013/08/legacy-fr-hennepin-looms-large-mississippi/

Harris, Craig. 2016. *Heartbeat, Warble, and the Electric Powwow: American Indian Music.* University of Oklahoma Press.

Hearne, Joanna. 2012. *Native Recognition: Indigenous Cinema and the Western.* Albany: SUNY Press.

Hennepin Theatre Trust. 2022. "We Are Still Here." Press Release. https://hennepintheatretrust.org/we-are-still-here/

Jacobs, Alex. "John Trudell Music Video 'Time Dreams' Now Released on Winter Solstice 2016." *Indian Country Today.* December 2, 2016. https://indiancountrytoday.com/archive/john-trudell-music-video-time-dreams-released-winter-solstice

Jones, Dan. 2012. "Gold Finch—Spirit Keeper." *Ojibwedigitalarchive.* https://www.youtube.com/watch?v=XOIkiKol38&list=PLBH6YBR53QZN1TTCZ2CzbpkD-pboY6z6VT&index=16

Kelly, Phineas. 2020. "Ceh'eɜteekuu!—Listen—This Is Arapaho Land." *American Indian Quarterly* 44.4: 415.

Monani, Salma. 2017. "The Cosmological Liveliness of Terri Calder's *The Lodge*: Animating Our Relations and Unsettling Our Cinematic Spaces." *Studies in American Indian Literatures* 29.4: 1–28.

Monani, Salma and Joni Adamson, eds. 2017. *Ecocriticism and Indigenous Studies: Conversations from Earth to Cosmos.* New York: Routledge.

Nelson, Melissa. 2013. "The Hydromythology of the Anishinaabeg: Will Mishipizhu Survive Climate Change, or Is He Creating It?" In *Centering Anishinaabeg Studies: Understanding the World Through Stories,* edited by Jill Doerfler, Niigaanwewidan James Sinclair, Heidi Kiiwetinepinesiik, 213–234. Lansing: Michigan State University Press.

Romero, Channette. 2017. "Toward an Indigenous Feminine Animation Aesthetic." *Studies in American Indian Literatures,* 29.1: 56–87.

Simpson, Leanne. 2013. *The Gift Is in the Making: Anishinaabeg Stories.* Kindle edition. Winnipeg: Highwater Press.

———. 2017. *As We Have Always Done: Indigenous Freedom Through Radical Resistance.* Minneapolis and London: University of Minnesota Press.

Shanley, Katheryn W. 2015. "'Mapping' Indigenous Precence: The Declaration on the Rights of Indigenous Peoples at Rhetorical Turns and Tipping Points." In *Mapping Indigenous Presence: North Scandinavian and North American Perspectives,* edited by Kathryn W. Shanley and Bjørg Evjen, 5–25. Tucson: University of Arizona Press.

Underhill, Ruth Murray. [1936] 1979. *Autobiography of a Papago Woman.* Tucson: University of Arizona Press.

Westerman, Gwen and Bruce White. 2012. *Mni Sota Makoce: The Land of the Dakota.* Minnesota Historical Society Press.

Whiteman, Missy (dir). 2016. "Time Dreams." Music Video. The Pines Featuring John Trudell and Quiltman. Poet Tree Publishing/DRV Music and Pines Publishing Farm. https://www.youtube.com/watch?v=fRTMe_EPgSM.

Whyte, Kyle Powys. 2017. "Our Ancestors' Dystopia Now: Indigenous Conservation and the Anthropocene." In *The Routledge Companion to the Environmental Humanities (1st ed.)*, edited by Ursula Heise, Jon Christensen, and Michelle Niemann, 206–215. New York: Routledge.

11

OF TOXIC DUST AND SAD PLACES

Ecochronicity and Debility in Julio Hernández Cordón's *Polvo (Dust,* 2012)

Aarón Lacayo

Polvo (*Dust,* Julio Hernández Cordón, 2012) is a fiction film that recounts the impossibility of shooting a documentary about the legacy of the Guatemalan Civil War (1960–1996). Ignacio (Eduardo Spiegeler), a Ladino filmmaker, follows Juan (Agustín Ortíz Pérez), a young Mayan musician searching for the remains of his father, who disappeared during the war while Juan was still a child.[1] What gets in the way of the documentary is dust itself, which debilitates both protagonists, accursing Ignacio with allergies and Juan with crippling migraines and insomnia. In the case of Juan, this disabling state leads him both to commit murder and make several suicidal attempts. He struggles with an urge both to take his own life and to seek revenge on Basilio (Carlos Gómez Subuyuj), a neighbor at least partly responsible for his father's disappearance. Basilio reported his father and two other men – with the same names – to the military.

In this chapter, I argue that *Polvo* revisits the legacy of Guatemala's civil war and its impact on the country's Indigenous Mayan community by interweaving disability and environmental concerns. I consider the political and ecological dimensions of dust using Elizabeth Freeman's notion of chronicity (a state of endurance that occupies some shape of time) and Mel Y. Chen's work on how toxicity circulates among bodies and debilitates them. I also examine how *Polvo* instantiates a "dirty" aesthetics of dust by way of Heather I. Sullivan's dirt theory. From this vantage, we can interpret Juan's increasingly violent attacks, both against others and against himself, as an unbearable chronic condition or, more precisely, as a toxic and ecological debility – an *ecochronicity* – brought about by sad memories.

By ecochronicity, I refer to the process through which bodies become increasingly debilitated in toxic environments. In *Polvo*, this ecochronicity

DOI: 10.4324/9781003246602-15

is carried out in the aftermath of the civil war and its legacies of violence: dust disables weak bodies, fertilizer acts as a toxin, and the Mayan Highlands become a nonhuman casualty of war. I situate ecochronicity at the intersection between the fields of disability studies and ecocriticism. In their introduction to *Disability Studies and Environmental Humanities: Toward an Eco-Crip Theory*, Sarah Jaquette Ray and Jay Sibara acknowledge the material effects of political violence on those who endure repressive regimes: "the slow violence of military legacies, to use the postcolonial ecocritic Rob Nixon's term, manifest most often as physical and mental disabilities, both domestically and abroad" (2017, 2). In *Polvo*, dust registers Guatemala's debilitatingly slow chronic violence.[2]

The dust that circulates in *Polvo* and powders the filmic image is composed not only of particles from the earth but also of the unaccounted victims of the war. Rather than any unspecified dust, this particular dust is lifted from a land marked by the forced disappearance, torture, and murder of civilians and leftist fighters, as well as the National Army's strategic genocidal campaign against various Maya groups. The war holds a singular place in twentieth-century Cold War conflicts in the Americas given that the United Nations–sponsored Truth Commission specifically classified the war as genocide "because the population, lived spaces, and culture of Maya people were disproportionately targeted by government forces" (Gould and Estrada 2014, 102). The Maya suffered most of the violence and accounted for more than 90% of the casualties. The human rights reports of both the United Nations and the Guatemalan Catholic Church attest to a strategic genocide against the Maya in the early 1980s (Carey and Little 2010, 5). During that decade, "over 150,000 people were killed or disappeared, over 440 villages were destroyed, over one million people were internally displaced, and up to 500,000 people were forced into exile in Mexico and other countries" (figures quoted in Rodríguez 2009, 107). The Guatemalan Peace Accords, signed on December 29, 1996, officially ended the war.

Director Julio Hernández Cordón – who identifies as Mesoamerican – has approached the repercussions of Guatemala's civil war through disability in other films. In his first feature, *Gasolina* (*Gasoline*, 2008) a teenage protagonist suffers from asthma. Neurodivergent characters appear in both the comedy *Las marimbas del infierno* (*Marimbas from Hell*, 2010) and the mixed-media fictionalized documentary *Hasta el sol tiene manchas* (*Even the Sun Has Spots*, 2012). In fact, in a scene in this film, Hernández Cordón announces that with a proper budget, he would film a story in which all the characters would share one thing in common: asthma. We can trace the trope of a chronic malaise – or dis-ease – to a master text of Guatemalan cinema, Luis Argueta's *El silencio de Neto* (*The Silence of Neto*, 1994). Argueta's landmark film depicts the coming-of-age story of a Ladino boy with asthma and his struggle and triumph over his disabling condition in the context of the 1950s. In 1954, the US CIA orchestrated a coup against President Jacobo Arbenz, which ended a decade of progressive democracy and social reform in Guatemala, destabilizing the country and setting off a long war. *Polvo* diverts from *El silencio de Neto* by centering on a Mayan protagonist and by situating the story in the Mayan Highlands.

This chapter analyzes three crucial narrative elements, or eco-scenarios, in *Polvo* that illustrate the dynamics of ecochronicity: a visual leitmotif of a man in the forest that runs through the filmic narrative, a conversation in an automobile in which Juan and Ignacio discuss their allergies and migraines, and the climactic episode in which Juan consumes fertilizer. I conclude by discussing how dust in *Polvo* portrays a country of sad places but also the possibility of reclaiming a lost home.

The Man in the Forest: Debility, the Chronic, and Dirt Theory

In *Polvo*, the concept of disability or in-capacity, mental or physical, carries an ecological dimension. A recurring visual and aural motif of a young man in a forest – what we could call an ecochronic image or ecochronic memory – begins and haunts the film's narrative. In various instances, the man appears up in a tree, lying on the ground with bound wrists, or walking into the woods. The soundscape accompanying these forested images is stripped down to a flat-line pitch, reminiscent of a heart monitor after death, which evokes a surreal sensation between life and death. Whether these images form part of Juan's childhood memories of his father, flashbacks to the fate of a tortured parent, or hallucinations remain unclear. But they are most likely a recurring series of dreams because the film begins with a shot of a man climbing the branches of a tree but cuts directly to Juan sleeping while reclined against the exterior walls of his house. The flatline sound is briefly superimposed with the wailing of a crying child that takes over the soundscape as Juan wakes up.

Juan's initial dream of the woods speaks to an uncertain association between protection and confinement. The forest signals life – a green shelter that protects from harm – as well as an ominous landscape. When *Polvo* begins, Juan lives in his father's hometown with his mother, wife, and infant son. After hearing the baby cry, Juan enters his house and slits his wrists with a knife while his family sleeps. Although he becomes unconscious, the cut does not prove fatal. His wife, Manuela (Claudia Oron Cuc) tells him, "You did it again," indicating that Juan has attempted suicide before. Seeking help, she carries his seemingly moribund body on a wheelbarrow. The wheelbarrow, usually utilized for plowing or gardening, foreshadows the scene in which Juan eats fertilizer.

Like many Indigenous Guatemalans who were directly affected by the war, Juan has no access to mental health resources. Although Juan seems intensely depressed and anxious, it remains unsaid whether he might suffer from conditions such as autism, mania, bipolarity, or post-traumatic stress disorder. No one seems to acknowledge or understand his condition. Later in the film, Ignacio's girlfriend, Alejandra (Alejandra Estrada), who is helping Ignacio with the documentary, tells Juan's mother, Delfina (María Telón Soc), that she thinks

Juan is "strange" because he does many things she cannot understand. His mother tells her that his father, who also suffered from headaches like Juan, behaved similarly.

The term *debility* better describes Juan's conditions than the term *disability*. Following Jasbir K. Puar, I understand debility not only as a "needed disruption" but also as a "collaborator" of the ability/disability categorical binary (2017, xv). In *The Right to Maim: Debility, Capacity, Disability*, Puar makes clear "that while some bodies may not be recognized as or identify as disabled, they may well be debilitated, in part by being foreclosed access to legibility and resources as disabled" (xv). Accordingly, Juan has been debilitated by his circumstances. Without proper medical care, Juan's condition remains undiagnosed. While the film suggests that Juan may have inherited his migraines from his father, his chronic condition is also linked to the violence of physical displacement since the war uprooted his family from his mother's hometown (his birthplace).

In "Theorizing the Chronic," Elizabeth Freeman (2011) understands *the chronic* as a form of continuity not rooted in a predetermined notion of time but aligned with a sense of endurance, as "a state of keeping on" that disrupts differences between living and dying (222). Although the term chronic originally meant "of time" (since at least the year 1600), by the eighteenth-century use of the word shifted to describe persistent medical conditions (Freeman 2019, 125). What interests me about Freeman's concept of chronicity is its transgressive ability to disrupt the boundaries that favor the abled body over a disabled one marked by the "reproduction of the status quo, capacity and debility, action and passivity" and its potential for an ecstatic experience of pain with pleasure – a form of *jouissance* – that can "narrow some capacities while enlarging others" (2011, 222).

What form of chronicity does Juan enact in *Polvo*? And, in Freeman's terms, what kind of capacities does this chronicity amplify or reduce? Juan carries out toxic chronicity by way of ecological signs as he struggles to make sense of his past and his future, thus performing a form of ecochronicity. In *Polvo*, such "eco" signs include the haunting forest that triggers Juan's migraines, a school bus filled with dung that becomes a graveyard, and Juan's consumption of fertilizer that provokes a toxic reaction. The forest, manure, and fertilizer form a series of images linked to dust that affect Juan, constituting what Heather I. Sullivan would call an aesthetics of dirty matter. In "Dirt Theory and Material Ecocriticism," Sullivan calls for a "dirty aesthetics" that includes dust, dirt, and other matter such as soil, earth, and sand (2012, 515). As a form of ecological thinking, dirt theory is more concerned with an embodied process – of dust moving with and on bodies – than with a fixed sense of place (515–516). Sullivan's emphasis on living with dirt in all its generative potential and lethal toxicity resonates in *Polvo* because it seems that Juan can only engage with the world through dust. Juan's ecochronicity reveals a damaged relation to dust that has been circulating in the air since the war. It is not just any dust but *this* particular dust that has displaced so many that also disables Juan as he tries to move forward with his life.

Sullivan's dirt theory cautions against nostalgia for a "pure, clear nature" somewhere "far-away" (515). In the case of *Polvo*, the mobile and pervasive dust can never reconstitute a physical place torn by war (Juan's destroyed hometown) no matter how much Juan longs for it. Instead, the dust of history is dispersed everywhere throughout Guatemala in the film, manifesting in toxic ways via Juan's debilitated body. What would it mean to consider *Polvo ecocritically* through the lens of "dirty" aesthetics? The answer may lie in the (im) possibility of making a film about a substance that is both everywhere and yet not really anywhere.

Terrain, Dust, and Debility

Like the leitmotif of the man in the trees, the scene featuring an automobile road trip through the countryside renders Juan's mental and physical unease in ecological terms. Juan travels with the filmmakers in Ignacio's car, a pistachio-colored Mercedes-Benz, to a remote forest to shoot a scene for the documentary. The car serves as the location for various scenes in *Polvo* that show the protagonists having conversations while driving somewhere, waiting for something, or taking a break from filming. Juan uses a specific word in Spanish (*terreno*) to speak about the difficult stretch of land they drive on. *Terreno* and its English equivalent "terrain" refer to all things terrestrial, including a piece of land, territory, ground, and in this case, dust. Moreover, *terreno* also carries the sense of *terrane*, a fault-bounded area with a distinctive stratigraphy and geological history. To Juan, this terrain speaks to his own family's scarred history. While they drive, Juan recounts: "Speaking of the terrain, you can hear laments on the tops of the trees; that's why my head hurts when I come here." Juan cannot explain the cause of his headaches in physiological terms; instead, he associates them with the voices he always hears when he visits this forest. Alejandra suggests that the voices might belong to Juan's father. Juan replies that, although this is a possibility, he would rather think that his father went elsewhere or that he left with another woman. Despite Juan's ambivalence, this haunting scene suggests that the trees register the ghostly presence (and express the pain) of those who disappeared or died during the war. The weight of this pain also permeates Juan's dreams through the recurring visual motif of a man in the trees. Whichever condition Juan may have inherited from his father manifests itself through an ecochronicity of recurring headaches and lingering laments in the forest.

Polvo also traces the relationship between two young fathers, since both Juan and Ignacio are each expecting their second child. The automobile scene marks a turning point in this developing friendship between Ignacio as director and

Juan as the subject of the documentary. The conversation in the car unfolds as an intimate and uncoerced piece of testimony unfilmed by Ignacio. Juan willingly shares how his father's disappearance continues to affect him. This scene also offers an insight into Ignacio's own condition with allergies, since he almost died once from an asthma attack. While they talk about their children, Alejandra worries that her unborn child may inherit his father's allergies. She tells Juan: "I hope he won't turn out allergic to dust like him. He gets like a fish out of water." Alejandra's choice of the words "a fish out of water" describe an allergic reaction in terms of a living organism being "out of place" from its surroundings. In *Dust*, a series of meditative essays on the complex ways that human life is enmeshed with this substance, Michael Marder defines an allergy as "the biological alarm that sounds when the boundary between the inside and the outside is breached" (2016, 52). Ignacio's allergies might be caused by any possible outside substance affecting a hypersensitive body. What causes an allergic reaction, Marder explains, is not so much the dust per se but a "living element" *within* dust "that functions as a trigger be it fungus, pollen, or dust mites" (52). Just as Juan's mother suggests that Juan inherited his strange behavior from his father, Alejandra fears that Ignacio's compromised immunity might be passed down to her own children. In this regard, the possibility of a future allergy to dust also triggers her parental fear of a vulnerable, transmittable heredity within her family.

Despite their similarities, dirt and dust differ in a crucial way. Dirt is heavier and more grounded whereas dust is lighter and more mobile. As Marder explains, "When it does not hang in the air, dust mixed with moisture turns into dirt" (2016, 4–5). Hernández Cordón reinforces the hazy appearance of particulate matter floating in the air in the automobile scene by the use of lighting, framing, and focus. As Alejandra speaks, her face stares to the right side of the frame in profile while the camera captures the sun's blinding light behind her. The rays seem to pass through her while their reflection on the windshield gives the appearance of translucent yellow spheres of light suspended in mid-air. This murky effect is repeated later in the scene when Juan narrates how his father was taken by the military. The car windows reflect the passing trees while Juan speaks. The car's rear window, caked with a layer of dust, appears behind Juan's shadowy figure in the glare of strong light. That there is so much dust on these roads may indicate the process of soil degradation. Interestingly, the word *dust* still meant "garbage" in nineteenth-century English (Marder 2016, 58). The mise-en-scène draws a nuanced parallel between illness and the difficulty of driving through unsteady roads. The terrain leads Juan to think of his headaches while Ignacio struggles at the wheel to get the car past the rough stretch. Juan's migraines and Ignacio's allergies both have unclear or unknown causes and vary depending on the weather, time of day, or related to a specific location. More importantly, these conditions are both ecochronic.

Filming the Documentary: Trauma, Politics, and Meta-Narratives

Juan's chronic headaches are inextricably entangled in the making of the documentary. His trips to the forest and the instances in which he shares too much of his life in front of Ignacio's camera set off his headaches as they bring forth painful unreconciled memories. Through the film-within-a-film, *Polvo* offers a metacommentary on its own form, revealing the potentialities and limits of ecochronicity as a performance of the possible. As Valeria Grinberg Pla (2018) argues, *Polvo* stages Juan's reluctance to share his life on film against Ignacio's efforts to make this important story public (208). This recurring friction between the act of filming and giving testimony – what may be possible to shoot but impossible to testify – plays out as a chronic tension between filmmaker and witness to make a story visible. Grinberg Pla suggests that *Polvo* is for Hernández Cordón, "a self-critical and meta-reflective act through which…[he]…makes his own dilemma over his right to recount the trauma of the direct victims' public" (208), raising the question of the proper ethical and aesthetic ways of filming victims of trauma. I would add that the question pertains not only to the act of bearing witness to a political crime but also to an ecological one.

The chronic lends structure to the film as a persistent interruption of time. As *Polvo* progresses, Ignacio's film becomes delayed, blocked, and ultimately unfinished due to budget constraints and Juan's eventual refusal to participate. Halfway through *Polvo*, it seems clear that the documentary will not be produced. Ignacio's failed attempt at successfully finishing the movie and completing a narrative mirrors Juan's failed efforts at making peace with his own life and of finding a way to move forward as a father, a husband, and a son. As a director, Ignacio is always looking for the perfect shot and the best conditions to shoot Juan's story. In various scenes, Ignacio carries a surgical mask (but not over his face) while filming outdoors, to keep the dust out. In one particular scene, Ignacio films Juan standing in the middle of a cemetery while he asks him how many times he has attempted suicide. Juan hesitates, refuses to answer, and runs abruptly into the cemetery. Ignacio tells Alejandra that he does not understand what is going on with Juan since "Everything's perfect, the light; it's the cemetery…" What better setting than a cemetery for a scene in which a man recounts his suicide attempts? What Ignacio fails to see, despite finding the most appropriate location, is that Juan cannot reconcile his ambivalent feelings about telling his life story in *any* setting. Put differently, no mise-en-scène, regardless of its aesthetics, could properly frame Juan's story.

The location of the outdoor scenes mentally unnerves Juan and debilitates him physically. Juan's mother tells Ignacio that speaking in front of the camera leaves him exhausted, with headaches that do not let him sleep at night. Juan finds himself trapped in a precarious socioeconomic cycle of debility: he is forced to buy pills to ease the pain of his migraines, yet he cannot afford the pills without a job. Furthermore, the production company that has commissioned Ignacio's documentary has not paid Juan and his mother for agreeing to appear in the film. Delfina doubts Ignacio's honesty, convinced they must be getting paid for their work. Ignacio tries to assure Delfina by saying that they are actually getting paid very little and that making the film is just a job like any other for them. What is a source of modest income for Ignacio and his young family is something altogether different for Juan. Juan participates in the documentary as both a Mayan ethnographic subject and a survivor of war, putting the painful material of his family's past in front of a camera for others to view. Although Ignacio never discusses the film's target audience, he films Juan speaking only in Spanish – notably, not in his Mayan language – which suggests a Spanish-speaking national (and/or international) audience but not necessarily the country's non-Spanish-speaking Mayan minority groups.

Juan's wavering involvement in the documentary illustrates a chronicity of in/action between a "would" and a "would not," following Freeman's suggestion of a "defective chronicity" (2019, 148). Freeman understands this defective chronicity as "a commitment to ongoing intensity, to the emphasis that keeps one alive if not precisely going anywhere amid constraining conditions" (148). Freeman's lexicon of "ongoing intensity" aptly describes Juan's ecochronicity that keeps him alive but not really living. Juan's homicidal and suicidal tendencies reach an intensity between living, dying, and "not precisely going anywhere" in the most visceral and ecological terms when Juan kills Basilio's son and then proceeds to eat fertilizer.

The Bad Harvest, Eating the Toxic

After announcing that he is quitting the documentary, Juan buys fertilizer from a local store that sells various agricultural and gardening products. On the left side of the store's facade, the list of chemicals available for purchase includes fungicides (such as Antracol) and plant fertilizers (Bayfolan). To the right of the door, large faded red letters indicate the store's name: *LA BUENA COSECHA*, which translates to "The Good Harvest." When a passerby sees Juan carrying the sack of fertilizer and asks if he has bought some land, Juan responds that he will soon find out. After buying the fertilizer, Juan walks toward Basilio's son, who is washing the school bus that his father owns. Juan attacks him, dragging the boy inside the bus as he struggles. The camera discreetly depicts this episode from outside the vehicle, only showing Juan through the windows while he kicks the boy relentlessly and bashes him with what seems to be a large heavy metal appliance. We see only the boy's legs, immobile, on the floor surrounded by newspapers. Juan runs to the town announcing that a thief has made his way into the bus. The townspeople, gripped by a mob mentality, destroy the bus and set it ablaze. The bus, which has been Basilio's source of income, becomes his son's tomb.

A vehicle as the site of a crime is not unusual in the cinema of Hernández Cordón. Automobiles also play an important role in the relationship between mobility, agency, and violence in other films. In both *Gasolina* and *Atrás hay relámpagos* (*Lightning Falls Behind*, 2017), cars are implicated in criminal acts. In *Polvo*, Hernández Cordón presents the mise-en-scène of the murder in the bus as a culmination of a disturbing array of repellent scatological images. In a previous scene, before killing the boy, Juan wrecks the bus's interior by throwing chunks of dirt and animal excrement all over its walls, seats, and floor. In that scene, the beige leather seats covered in chunks of manure resemble the carcass of a dead animal around which flies gathered. When Basilio's son initially finds the defiled bus, he vomits in disgust.

While the bus burns, Juan runs to the field where he left the sack of fertilizer and stuffs chunks of it into his mouth. His compulsive eating makes him vomit. The recurring image of the man on the treetop reappears as if witnessing Juan's poisoning. Ironically, Juan consumes a bag of fertilizer in the form of dirt (most likely mixed with synthetic chemicals), instead of a more organic fertilizing substance like animal dung. I interpret Juan's compulsive eating as a distorted process of self-fertilization as if he were a plant or a plot of land – not wanting to "buy" land, as his neighbor had asked, but wanting to *become* the land that surrounds him. However, this non-organic self-fertilization immediately becomes toxic in(di)gestion, as he expulses it from his body. This convulsive act of in(di)gestion, the last in a series of self-harming acts, culminates Juan's ecochronic journey: instead of a repository of a good harvest, Juan's body has run amok, something of a *bad* harvest.

We can understand Juan's body as a somatic nexus in which contradictory violent urges are negotiated. Juan relates and reacts to his surroundings in *Polvo* in an ecochronic manner: trips to the forest trigger Juan's headaches, he uses animal dung to damage Basilio's bus and eats fertilizer immediately after killing Basilio's son. Juan's behavior in these eco-scenarios, in one way or another, consists of fits and starts that as Freeman puts it in terms of the chronic, are both "paradoxically ongoing *and* unusual" (2011, 222), leading to attempted suicides, self-sabotage and eventually kidnapping and murder. Considering Freeman's definition of the chronic as an "ecstatic experience of pain with pleasure," one could consider Juan's paradoxical actions as a form of cathartic *jouissance*, combining intense pain and pleasure (222). Juan's violent impulses intensify through the course of the film, concluding with the murder of Basilio's son, setting the neighbor's livelihood (his bus) on fire, and one last failed suicide attempt, which leads to Juan's stomach getting pumped. At the same time, Juan's sense of reason and responsibility diminish, oblivious to the consequences of his actions or the ways they affect his family's future. In these episodes, dust accumulates but it never really settles, all the while clouding Juan's judgment.

We can further situate Juan's toxic in(di)gestion of fertilizer in relation to Mel Y. Chen's understanding of the chronic. In "Unpacking intoxication, racializing disability," Chen (2015) considers the concept of toxicity and intox-ication under the lens of a racialized geopolitical circulation of opium in both England (as a medical suppressant in Langdon Down's clinic for idiocy in England) and China (via the British Empire's importation of the substance) under Queen Victoria's rule. Chen is interested in chronicity as "simultane-ously an occasion for thinking about the temporalities of disability and debility imposed from without" (28). As a global and local toxin, opium chronically suppressed at least two different populations, the English and Chinese, at the same time (28). Following Chen, through his act of self-fertilization Juan enters a state of toxicity, "thinking with its [the toxin's] inter-human temporalities, its urgent demands, its soothings, its very pace" (29).

In *Polvo*, dust circulates as a toxin throughout Guatemala's recent history by way of dead bodies, destroyed villages, and unbreathable air. Dust is, one could say, ingrained in the soil, the skin, and the lungs. In the particular case of Juan, dust enacts a simultaneous chronic suppression and overexposure within his debilitated body. Juan acts and reacts to his own choices and circumstances ecochronically, through fits and starts, rehearsing a state of keeping on with the dust somewhere between living and dying, not getting sicker but not getting cured or better either. Juan's overexposure to dust reaches its most acute point the moment he eats fertilizer. Chen's call for acknowledging *and* consuming the toxin also resonates with Sullivan's dirt theory, which calls to fully embrace dirt by taking in "the full range of life-sustaining and toxic agencies in the soil without flinching" (2015, 516). In this light, Juan's consumption of fertilizer gestures toward an act of abandoning oneself to a toxin, of giving in to the ecochronic.

Exhausted Dust, Exhausting Precarity

In the context of postwar Guatemala, ecochronicity can also be understood alongside the legacies of colonialism in terms of exhaustion and precarity. In "Exorbitant Dust," Christina A. León traces a "dusty poetics" in the liter-ary corpus of queer Puerto Rican author Manuel Ramos Otero (1948–1990) in relation to Puerto Rico's chronic precarity as a colonial state "always on the brink of exhaustion" (2021, 358). For León, the porous nature of dust marks the substance as both matter and metaphor – what she calls a "matter-metaphor" (358–359) – and provides a way for exploring how Puerto Rico forms part of an ecology of dust between the Atlantic and the Caribbean. Despite the differences between Puerto Rico and Guatemala, León's "thinking with dust" – with "perverse polvo" (372) – allows us to consider the dust in *Polvo* as the rem-nant of an exhausted condition of the Indigenous Mayan peoples vis-à-vis the white Ladino elite in postwar Guatemala. The 1996 Peace Accords officially concluded the civil war but did not restructure the ruling group's power over the country, where Indigenous groups are treated as second-class citizens after years of chronic disenfranchisement. Guatemala's chronic dust lingers between and beyond two crucial historical events of the twentieth century: the 1954 military coup that destroyed the country's hopes for progressive reform and the 1996 Peace Accords that failed to achieve a lasting peace. The circulating dust in *Polvo* also suggests that, as J. Kēhaulani Kauanui has argued about the endurance of Indigeneity in the face of settler-colonialism, Indigenous peoples continue to "exist, resist, and persist" (2016).

Polvo explores to what extent and in which ways cinema can tell the stories of those who survive genocidal violence. The film also proposes debility as a lens through which it might be possible to tell these stories. Guatemala's civil war, like its Central American counterparts in El Salvador (1980–1992) and Nicaragua (1979–1990), was characterized by a general disregard for life. Out of the many thousands killed and forcibly disappeared or displaced throughout the Guatemalan countryside, the victims were not only humans. The National Army implemented an all-out strategy of eliminating humans, animals, and the physical environment that stood in their way. The army decimated their victims' livelihood by slaughtering countless animals and razing entire fields and crops. Members of the displaced population destroyed vegetation them-selves as they sought to escape the national government's orchestrated land-scorching tactics against targeted Indigenous groups (Rodríguez 2009, 107). Juan's mother alludes to the memories of this destruction in one poignant scene. Near the end of *Polvo*, when Alejandra asks her if she and Juan would move to Xetmanzana, their former village, if they were to find it, she responds: "We'll see; for me all places are sad."

Indeed, the film's final sequence reveals that Juan's childhood village has completely disappeared. In this regard, the terrain of Guatemala's country-side cannot be reduced to mere geography or landscape in *Polvo*. The Mayan Highlands not only serve as symbolic sites of remembrance for past atrocities but are themselves casualties of war. This dust also suggests that suffering in its many forms is not confined to the human but extends to the nonhuman and the more-than-human.

Conclusion: Every Place Is Sad, Reclaiming a Sad Place

To conclude, I would like to point out the sad joy that *Polvo's* final ludic scene offers: an intimate camaraderie marked by play and by time. Juan's disturb-ing violent episodes of self-harm, kidnapping, and murder are interspersed throughout the film with scenes of people enjoying themselves while they play. In an early scene, Ignacio goes bowling with his daughter; in another, Juan teaches his mother how to make a shot during a game of basketball. In the film's final scene, Juan and Ignacio share a spontaneous moment of synchronized competition. Juan has brought his father's old bicycle, which he has dug up and repaired. As they stand in a sunny field, Juan learns that his village once stood in this place and decides that he will not tell his mother. He also confesses to the murder of Basilio's son. With this admission, Juan seems to finally be able to confide in someone. He watches Ignacio drive around in circles on the bicycle with his mask dangling from his neck. They discuss fertilizers and stomach pumps. Juan asks if Ignacio would help him build a house here. Ignacio agrees although he warns Juan that he just might be caught by the police soon. Juan responds by saying that even if such a moment of happiness (in a place where his family and his unborn child might make a home) were to last only for a short while, it would still be worth it.

They decide to compete, racing on the bike on a short piece of road. Ignacio goes first, Juan second. The act of competing in a timed and controlled match suggests that Juan and Ignacio want to grasp a piece of time to measure and record and enjoy it on their own. This moment of play suspends time, since Juan's future is still unknown, making the past and the future seem almost irrelevant. But if such a moment suspends time, it is no longer a suspension between life and death, between illness and cure, but rather between hope and something better to come. This film's coda signals the way the two different paths of the lives of Juan and Ignacio have managed to realign themselves into a synchronized understanding of their differences. The film ends with the final image of an open field with Juan driving away as Ignacio looks on.

In light of the COVID-19 pandemic, during which the act of breathing has become lethal for millions, a film like *Polvo* reminds us of the violent memories that remain entrenched and unreconciled in the body, in the air, and in the land. In *Polvo*, Guatemala remains a sad place haunted by a violent history and a difficult present. However, Juan's plight remains hopeful. His playful interlude with Ignacio suggests a desire to re-embrace life. He now wants to create good memories in the same place in which he experienced so much loss. Juan wants to build a house and make a home, to clear his head and plant the roots of a new life. In doing so, Juan negotiates directly with what dust – this dirty matter – can offer him in a generative, life-affirming way. This grounding of a new life evokes Sullivan's dirt theory, reminding us that "human bodies and minds are fully ensconced in material environments, which shape us just as vividly as we shape them" (2012, 528). This desire for a good harvest to come – of future memories for his family and himself – points to an urge for living against the violence and the pain that have not let him breathe in peace. Juan wants to recover his life precisely by reclaiming the land where his village once stood. In doing so, he embraces a sad, damaged place on his own ecochronic terms.

Notes

1 In Guatemala, *Ladino*, not to be confused with the medieval Judaeo-Spanish language, refers to a person of mixed Spanish and Indigenous heritage, similar to the term *Mestizo*. *Ladino* can also refer to non-Indigenous Guatemalans or white Guatemalans who speak Spanish.

2 For the sake of clarity, I will refer to the film by its title in Spanish (*Polvo*) and use its English equivalent—dust—to refer to the substance.

Works Cited

Argueta, Luis, dir. 1994. *El silencio de Neto* [*The Silence of Neto*]. Guatemala: Buenos Días. DVD.

Carey Jr., David and Walter E. Little. 2010. "Reclaiming the Nation through Public Murals: Maya Resistance and the Reinterpretation of History." *Radical History Review* 106: 5–26. http://doi.org/10.1215/01636545-2009-018.

Chen, Mel Y. 2015. "Unpacking Intoxication, Racializing Disability." *Medical Humanities* 41.1: 25–29. http://doi.org/10.1136/medhum-2014-010648.

Freeman, Elizabeth. 2011. "Theorizing the Chronic." In *Chewing the Scenery*, edited by Andrea Thal, 221–260. Zurich: Edition Fink.

Freeman, Elizabeth. 2019. *Beside You in Time: Sense Methods and Queer Sociabilities in the American Nineteenth Century*. Durham, NC: Duke University Press. http://library.oapen.org/handle/20.500.12657/24048.

Gould, Kevin and Alicia Ivonne Estrada. 2014. "Framing Disappearance: H.I.J.@.S., Public Art and the Making of Historical Memory of the Guatemalan Civil War." *ACME: An International E-Journal for Critical Geographies* 13.1: 100–134. https://www.acme-journal.org/index.php/acme/article/view/999.

Grinberg Pla, Valeria. 2018. "Against anomie: Julio Hernández Cordón's post-war trilogy – Gasoline/Gasoline (2008), *Las marimbas del infierno/The Marimbas of Hell* (2010) and *Polvo/Dust* (2012)." *Studies in Spanish & Latin American Cinemas* 15.2: 203–216. https://doi.org/10.1386/slac.15.2.203_1.

Hernández Cordón, Julio, dir. 2017. *Atrás hay relámpagos* [*Lightning Falls Behind*]. Guatemala: Melindrosa Films. DVD.

———. 2008. *Gasolina* [*Gasoline*]. Guatemala: Melindrosa Films. DVD.

———. 2012. *Hasta el sol tiene manchas* [*Even the Sun Has Spots*]. Guatemala: Melindrosa Films. DVD.

———. 2010. *Las marimbas del infierno* [*Marimbas from Hell*]. Guatemala: Melindrosa Films. DVD.

———. 2012. *Polvo* [*Dust*]. Guatemala: Melindrosa Films. DVD.

Kauanui, J. Kēhaulani. 2016. "'A Structure, Not an Event': Settler Colonialism and Enduring Indigeneity." *Lateral* 5.1. https://csalateral.org/issue/5-1/forum-alt-humanities-settler-colonialism-enduring-indigeneity-kauanui/.

León, Christina A. 2021. "Exorbitant Dust: Manuel Ramos Otero's Queer and Colonial Matters." *GLQ: A Journal of Lesbian and Gay Studies* 27.3: 357–377. muse.jhu.edu/article/797161.

Marder, Michael. 2016. *Dust*. London: Bloomsbury Academic.

Puar, Jasbir K. 2017. *The Right to Maim: Debility, Capacity, Disability*. Durham: Duke University Press. https://doi.org/10.1215/9780822372530.

Ray, Sarah Jaquette and Jay Sibara. 2017. "Introduction." In *Disability Studies and the Environmental Humanities: Toward an Eco-Crip Theory*, edited by Sarah Jaquette Ray and Jay Sibara, 1–25. Lincoln: University of Nebraska Press.

Rodríguez, Ana Patricia. 2009. *Dividing the Isthmus: Central American Transnational Histories, Literatures, and Cultures*. Austin: University of Texas Press.

Sullivan, Heather I. 2012. "Dirt Theory and Material Ecocriticism." *Interdisciplinary Studies in Literature and Environment* 19.3: 515–531. http://www.jstor.org/stable/44087133.

12

INDIGENOUS POST-APOCALYPTIC FILMMAKING AT STANDING ROCK

Emily Roehl

"I want to tell you a story." So begins the 2016 video *We Are in Crisis*, a three-minute montage of drone footage of the landscape surrounding *Mni Sose*, the Missouri River, in southern North Dakota. This is a story of oil – imagined as a voracious beast – and water – imagined as a life-giving fluid. The story is accompanied by a visual catalog of lines across the land: railroads, power lines, furrows in a field, the fresh earthen cut of a pipeline right of way, the long diagonal shadows of earthmovers. It is a story that weaves past, present, and future resource histories into a narrative, sonic, and visual tapestry. Created by the artist collective Winter Count as a gift to Water Protectors resisting the Dakota Access Pipeline (DAPL) during the fall of 2016, the filmmakers use apocalyptic narrative, evocative soundscape, and aerial artistry to envision an Indigenous future.

From the summer of 2016 through the winter of 2017, the Standing Rock Sioux Tribe and their allies set up camps in opposition to the DAPL, a 3.7 billion dollar infrastructure project that can transport 470,000 barrels of oil a day from North Dakota to storage facilities in Illinois and on to refineries. Water Protectors from the Standing Rock reservation, joined by Indigenous and non-Indigenous people from across the continent and globe, camped along the proposed pipeline route between the summer of 2016 and the winter of 2017. In December of 2016, the Obama Administration ordered a halt to construction awaiting an environmental impact study; within days of taking office, President Trump signed an Executive Order fast-tracking the pipeline, and the camps were cleared beginning on February 22, 2017.

While state operatives implemented measures to ground drones and other forms of Indigenous media-making at Standing Rock, Winter Count grounded their collaborative artistic practice in Indigenous storytelling and used drone

DOI: 10.4324/9781003246602-16

footage to claim both land-based and representational sovereignty. By super-imposing a narrative voiceover and soundscape of water and drums over drone footage of landscapes indelibly marked by energy extraction past and ongoing, the artists of Winter Count trace the contours of an Indigenous future. They do so by reframing the body of the land, bodies of water, and the bodies of Water Protectors as agents of relational, historically-informed Indigenous resistance in the face of their erasure as victims of extraction and objects of police vio-lence. Through its evocative layering of soundscape, landscape, and narrative, *We Are in Crisis* braids past and present into a future where Indigenous com-munities continue to thrive in the midst of the failing infrastructures of settler colonialism.

We Are in Crisis not only reimagines the role of the drone in relation to bod-ies on the ground, a relationship that has long been characterized by military-industrial violence, but also imagines a distinctly Indigenous future that assesses the wreckage of the past while building communities that can continue to sur-vive the apocalypse of settler colonialism. This essay reads *We Are in Crisis* into long traditions of Indigenous filmmaking and resistance to what Grace Dillon (2012) and Kyle Powys Whyte (2018) describe as an apocalypse that has already occurred. The video's apocalyptic narrative, woven through its aerial imagery and soundscape, tells a story of the land and the many bodies that inhabit it: water, humans, animals, machines, infrastructure, and the body of the drone and the eye of the camera.

Documentary Drones and Indigenous Filmmaking at Standing Rock

Among those who gathered at Standing Rock were a number of artists and filmmakers who took part in direct action against pipeline construction, day-to-day life in the camps, and creative projects. During the fall of 2016, online arts magazine *Hyperallergic* reported on the activities of artists gathered at Oceti Sakowin, the largest camp along the pipeline route, where an art tent was set up as a place to make work in support of the #NoDAPL movement. There were many ways artists and filmmakers contributed to the #NoDAPL struggle; some of these included producing documentary shorts and feature-length films, broadcasting live video feeds on social media platforms, screen-printing signs, painting banners, donating supplies, selling work to raise funds, and making mirror shields – reflective boards that were used by Water Protectors as physical barriers that reflected the aggression of police back at the perpetrators of that violence.[1]

We Are in Crisis was filmed in September of 2016 and posted on Vimeo in October of the same year by Dylan McLaughlin (Navajo) and is attributed to McLaughlin as well as Cannupa Hanska Luger (enrolled member of the Three Affiliated Tribes of Fort Berthold; of Mandan, Hidatsa, Arikara, Lakota, and

European descent), Ginger Dunnill, Merritt Johnson, and Nicholas Galanin (Lingít/Unangax̂). This group of artists has worked together off and on as the collective Winter Count. The video was posted to Vimeo with the following caption: "In the effort we have made to gather image and sound for collective works to come, we wanted to first release this gratitude film in offering to the Water Protectors, the land and the water. #NODAPL #waterislife #mni-wiconi." *We Are in Crisis* has been shared online and exhibited widely. One of its first appearances was at Radiator Arts in New York for the show "My Country Tis of Thy People, You're Dying" (2017). The work of the collective has also appeared at Artists Space in New York City, the Center for Visual Arts in Denver, Washington Project for the Arts in Washington DC, The Museum of Capitalism in Oakland, and the Autry Museum in Los Angeles. In addition, the artists of Winter Count have produced a wide range of work related to their collective projects; for example, Canupa Hanska Luger's *Mirror Shield Project*, which includes drone footage of direct action at Standing Rock filmed by collective member Dylan McLaughlin, was shown most recently in an exhibition called "Land Art: Expanding the Atlas" at the Nevada Museum of Art (2021–2022).

The artists of Winter Count were not the only filmmakers using drones to document life at Standing Rock. Some of the most iconic images to emerge from the #NoDAPL struggle were captured by Indigenous filmmaker Myron Dewey (Newe-Numah/Paiute-Shoshone), who regularly broadcast live streams on Facebook during the encampments. Like the artists of Winter Count, Dewey returned to Standing Rock multiple times to produce documentary shorts and live streams, and some of this footage was used in the 2017 documentary *Awake: A Dream from Standing Rock*, which he co-directed with Josh Fox and James Spione. Dewey used cell phones and drones to document life in the camps; he also captured direct action, police violence against Water Protectors, and the routine surveillance that media-makers like himself faced from police and private security agents hired by the energy company.[2] Many of Dewey's videos were posted on the Digital Smoke Signals Facebook page, a platform for a media company Dewey founded with the mission of "Indigenizing Technology Through Indigenous Eyes."[3] One of Dewey's live drone feeds from November 20, 2016, revealed that the Morton County Sheriff's Department used water cannons and other crowd suppression devices against non-violent Water Protectors on a frigid late autumn night.

The way Dewey and Winter Count used drones to document at Standing Rock is part of a much longer practice of Indigenous filmmaking. This work can be understood as part of a tradition of Indigenous activist documentary, a form that filmmaker Danis Goulet (2021) argues "lends itself easily to social justice issues." In this work, according to Goulet, contemporary Indigenous filmmakers owe much to the "grandmothers of Indigenous cinema," Alanis Obomsawin and Merata Mita, whose work has been categorized as "fourth cinema," Barry Barclay's term to describe "Indigenous cinema created by Indigenous filmmakers for Indigenous audiences" (Turner 2013). This definition echoes Dewey's mission to produce films "through Indigenous eyes." Expressing a similar sentiment, the artists of Winter Count created *We Are in Crisis* as an "offering to the water protectors, the land and the water." Though the video has traveled to exhibitions and computer screens far from the banks of *Mni Sose,* it is part of a lineage of Indigenous filmmaking that exists in relation to social movements. As Goulet relates, she was inspired to create the short film *Wakening* (2013) in part by Idle No More, a women-led movement founded in 2012 in opposition to Canadian Bill C-45 and other efforts to erode Indigenous sovereignty in Canada (Monani 2016). She describes being "glued to live feeds" during direct actions, which included round dances at shopping malls. Goulet's most recent film, *Night Raiders* (2021), was inspired in part by the encampments at Standing Rock. Social movements like these provide a wealth of inspiration for filmmakers.

Drones have also been used in countless environmental documentaries since the technology became available to filmmakers (Kim 2022). A few examples that also address the issue of resource extraction include the films of Canadian aerial photographer Edward Burtynsky, which include *Manufactured Landscapes* (2006), *Watermark* (2013), and *Anthropocene: The Human Epoch* (2018). Each of these films, directed by Jennifer Baichwal, uses Burtynsky's drone footage of industrial operations to illustrate the massive scale of human impact on the landscape. Burtynsky has built his career on making beautiful pictures of battered places. In large-format, richly colored images of quarries, mines, refineries, factories, and other industrial landscapes, Burtynsky reveals the residues of resource extraction, manufacturing, consumption, and waste.

Burtynsky has established himself as one of the most iconic photographers of twenty-first-century industrial landscapes, with his photographs appearing in numerous exhibitions, catalogs, and photo books as well as the three feature-length documentary films mentioned above. A number of scholars, including Merle Patchett and Andriko Lozowy (2012) and Jill Gatlin (2015), have critiqued the "toxic sublime" in the work of Burtynsky, specifically the way scale and abstraction operate in his still and moving images to occlude context and accountability for industrial destruction (see also Crang 2010; Diehl 2006; Nickerson 2007; Peeples 2011). Dewey and Winter Count's work departs from the work of photographers like Burtynsky and filmmakers like Baichwal, who use drones to produce artful images of sublime landscapes absent of humans. The work of Dewey and Winter Count is better understood within the context of the long tradition of Indigenous struggle against settler infrastructure. Not only do they situate human bodies in relation to the bodies of oily machines and other-than-human bodies, Dewey and the artists of Winter Count were among those putting their bodies on the line, taking part in direct actions at Standing Rock. In the case of Winter Count, not only was *We Are in Crisis* produced as a gift to Water Protectors but also it was created from a distinctly Indigenous perspective that illustrates the relationship between the many bodies that met in the conflict at Standing Rock.

Bodies in Relation: A Close Reading of *We Are in Crisis*

We Are in Crisis opens with white text on a black background: a dictionary definition of "crisis." The text provides two definitions – first, crisis is "the point in the course of a serious disease at which a decisive change occurs, leading either to recovery or to death." Second, crisis is defined as "the change itself." The choice to use the medical definition of crisis proposes that the crisis the video addresses is a crisis of the body. The soundscape of the video is critical to communicating this idea. In the first few seconds of the video, as the definition of crisis fills the black screen, there is a low beat and the sound of water. The beat could be an elevated heartbeat or a drum, though it has the mechanical regularity of a piece of industrial machinery. The beat is joined by the buzz of an engine, which at times is indistinguishable from the sound of the water. After a moment, a man's voice joins the din with the words "I want to tell you a story." The quality of the voiceover is metallic; the voice carries a slight echo that mixes with the engine's whirr. Winter Count grounded their collaborative artistic practice in Indigenous storytelling, using

> screen media not to mask but to recuperate their own collective stories and histories—some of them traumatic—that have been erased in the national narratives of the dominant culture and are in danger of being forgotten within local worlds as well.
>
> *(Ginsburg 2002, 40)*

The story they tell in *We Are in Crisis* is a story of human rapacity and its effects on both human and other–than–human bodies. With this video, Winter Count "revitalize[s] storytelling modes that engage the human with the more–than–human, and draw into view earthly and cosmic 'persons' as allies in struggles against localized and planetary destruction" (Adamson and Monani 2017, 15).

As art historian Jessica Horton points out, the very name of the artist collective is a reference to "Plains pictographic calendars in which representations of a single important event for each year are arranged in a spiral" (2017, 107). The opening invocation "I want to tell you a story" establishes a relationship between the unseen narrator, or count keeper, and the imagined viewer, who might be a contemporary or far-future witness to the cycles of violence the narrative will recount. Traditionally, winter counts illustrate seasonal relations between humans and other–than–human relatives: for example the relationship between humans and buffalo. They are a form of Indigenous storytelling that both represents and maintains these relations over time. In *We Are in Crisis*, the count keeper depicts not only human and more-than-human bodies through voice, heartbeat, and drum but also the bodies of earth-moving machines and infrastructure through aerial footage captured by an "eye in the sky," the camera in the body of the drone.

In an article for *Art in America* on the work of Winter Count, Jessica Horton references Vizenor's concert of "survivance" and argues that "the drones of NoDAPL represent a complex scenario in which technologies with violent origins are bent to the work of 'survivance' by the populations they were designed to control" (2017, 104). Horton's analysis is not focused on what she calls the "pragmatic" uses of drones in conflict zones, which is to say it is not an on-the-ground analysis but a consideration of how drone images were appropriated by artists and circulated in art contexts. She sees Winter Count's *We Are in Crisis* as a paradigmatic example of a trend in Indigenous digital storytelling concerned with the environment since 2000. Horton writes that these works "are distinguished by two features: the artists' efforts to reframe the boom-and-bust cycle of 'disaster capitalism' as part of a continuous colonial history, and their use of digital technologies to communicate the regenerative potential of mythic forms" (105). For Horton, the artists of Winter Count "challenge to the primacy of military-industrial vision that delivers the same landforms as property and target" (107).

Like Horton, this essay is interested in how drones can be turned away from their military-industrial histories and uses. In Danis Goulet's 2021 science fiction/post-apocalyptic film *Night Raiders*, drones have achieved something like sentience, and though they are a fearful tool of an autocratic government, they have lively, relational potential. In an interview with the imagineNATIVE Film + Media Festival's Artistic Director Niki Little from 2021, Goulet talks about being at Standing Rock, being part of a community "from all over the place." Like Winter Count, Goulet counted herself among the many artists and filmmakers who gathered together on the banks of *Mni Sose* to ask the question, "what does it mean not just to survive but to thrive?" Reckoning with the ongoing history of settler colonialism, Goulet asserts, "We shouldn't have had to be this resilient...we deserve to have community...we deserve to have love... we deserve so much more than resilience and survival." The same sentiment emerges from *We Are in Crisis* when it is read through the web of relations that made it possible: the bodies on the ground "standing with Standing Rock."

As the voiceover continues, the black screen gives way to a drone's-eye-view of twin well pads with pump jacks. The drone approaches the pads swiftly, sweeping over a field of tall brown grasses as it draws close to the machinery. When the drone reaches the drill pad, the viewer can see the two pump jacks teeter-tottering, flanked by long lines of storage tanks. As the drone crests the hill, the river appears below, reaching out to the horizon. To assess the use of drones by artists like Winter Count, it is important to follow the lead of scholars like Katherine Chandler (2020), Caren Kaplan (2018), and Lisa Parks (2018), who have powerfully argued for situating aerial image-making devices within the context of the array of relationships each use activates. This includes but is not limited to the relationship between artists, activists, police officers, private security firms, energy companies, and the multiple distribution networks through which #NoDAPL media was shared: social media platforms, internal emails circulated among state agencies, and video sharing websites like You-Tube and Vimeo. Some scholars, including J. D. Schnepf, warn that we should approach drone footage with caution due to the way aerial vision teaches us, in Alan Sekula's words, to "see like a state" (Schnepf 2019, 749). Indeed, the energy company and state used helicopters and drones to intimidate and surveil Water Protectors throughout the encampment. Even so, Kaplan argues against a simplistic equation of drones with violence and calls for a "better understanding of the relational dynamics of the assemblage of airspaces, aerial vehicles, and their creators and operators" (2020, 50). In her recent work on #NoDAPL and drones, Kaplan writes,

> Claiming airspace, carefully surveying the land itself – referencing landmarks of special interest, noting places of significance to tribes, establishing a landscape aesthetic based on Indigenous sacred and political values, and sharing these images and narratives via social media—such practices not only disturbed the usual liberal discourse of "public order" but introduced new political actors, human and non-human, and an Indigenous "mediacosmology".
>
> *(2020, 54)*

This "mediacosmology" of human and other-than-human actors, of multiple watery bodies, is a form of what Dean Rader calls "engaged resistance" (2011, 1).[4] By using both Indigenous storytelling and Western image-making technologies, Winter Count asserts not only political sovereignty but also visual or representational sovereignty, identified by Joanna Hearne as "the conceptual center of gravity for Indigenous media studies" insofar as it "expands the framework of Indigenous nations' political sovereignty – their self-determination as nations within a larger nation-state – to intellectual and artistic analysis" (2020, 154).

In the opening shots of *We Are in Crisis*, the drone's camera seems to drift above the landscape like a bird flying in slow motion or like the world seen from the point of view of a paraglider. The movements of the drone are smooth and light. Whereas drones in the service of the energy company "encroach on sovereign air space in order to control natural resources on the ground," Winter Count's work with the drone is part of a media assemblage that includes cameras in the air as well as watery bodies on the ground (Schnepf 2019, 747). As Lisa Parks writes, "Much more than a sensor, the drone is a technology of *vertical mediation*: the traces, transmissions, and targets of its operations are registered in the air, through the spectrum, and on the ground" (2017, 136). Ultimately, for Kaplan, "Demonization of UAV systems is as pernicious as simplistic celebration" (2020, 55). It is true that drones are "historically militarized technologies and modes of seeing" that remain "imbricated in the workings of capital and empire" (Schnepf 2019, 747). However, in the hands of Indigenous artists and their settler allies in Winter Count, the drone "produce[s] new forms of relational experience as part of a networked citizen activism that challenges the militarization of civil society" (Tuck 2018, 173). This network at Standing Rock included activists on the ground, among whom these artists and filmmakers counted themselves. The network also extends to the digital distribution routes of social media platforms and the exhibition spaces that have shown the video. In each of these material and digital spaces, the drone imagery invites the viewer to witness state violence at "a safer distance than the activist on the ground" and in so doing grapples with the ongoing histories of extraction the narrative recounts (Zuev and Bratchford 2020, 453).

As the drone moves toward the drill pad, the narrator begins, tinny but determined: "A being was born out of the anxiety of separation. It is a fearful creature that we have nourished.... It grew powerful in the shadow of our wars, and it learned to crawl, aided by combustion engines." The voiceover conjures an image of an oily beast fueled by war as the scene shifts to a vertical shot of a railroad and road hemmed in by fields – one rough, one mowed. As the drone's camera travels up the railroad tracks, more lines become visible: the diagonal stripes of power lines. These lines across the land – the railroad, the road, power lines, the furrows in the mowed field – are the geometry of development, the traces of settler colonial occupation and systemic exploitation of the body of the earth. In an interview with *Hyperallergic*, Cannupa Hanska Luger discusses the name "Water Protector," which was taken up by many of those gathered at Standing Rock. He explains that it refers not only to the river and the danger the pipeline poses to this body of water but also to the water we carry in our bodies, which Luger describes as "vessels" (Vartanian 2016). This shift away from the violent bodies of machinery and toward the watery vessels of animals, humans, and the river is suggestive of Winter Count's vision of a Native post-apocalyptic future.

This video cinematically answers Sandy Grande's call for "resistance and refusal of the fast, quick, sleek, and spectacular," which secure settler futurity, "in favor of the steady, tried, consistent, and intergenerational," the materially and metaphorically "grounded" (2018, 14). Drawing on Glen Coulthard's concept of "grounded normativity," Grande argues that

> 'the movement' is not (only) about the present but rather demands both history and a ground(ing) that is both literal and metaphoric. The guiding vision is not human centered or derived but rather comes from land and all that sustains it.
>
> *(2018, 14)*

As Indigenous philosopher Kyle Powys Whyte (2017) has argued, it is not enough to point out that Indigenous cosmologies are relational. Relationality is a *type* of relationship, not a quality of relationships. The quality of relationality that Winter Count communicates in *We Are in Crisis* is a resilient relationality that is expressed as survivance, Gerald Vizenor's concept of "an active sense of presence … not a mere reaction … [but] renunciations of dominance, tragedy and victimry" (1999, vii). Faced with the crisis of fossil-fueled climate change, resilient relationality gestures toward the fact that, for the Indigenous peoples of North America, the apocalypse has already occurred, and yet *We Are in Crisis* reframes oily apocalypse narratives as narratives about water, life, and survival in the face of this already-past end.

Images of upstream and midstream energy extraction and shipment are combined in this video, as are images of energy produced by oil and water. As the drone's camera hovers over a hydroelectric dam, the voiceover catalogs the so-called "gifts" of the oily creature, which include "promises of leisure" and the notion that "the earth was here for our taking." Green water and white foam swirl near the dam, and power lines cut across the reservoir, linking this scene of energy extraction to the means of electrical transport. The inclusion of a hydroelectric dam in a video ostensibly about oil creates a critical historical link between these two forms of energy. The history of hydropower in the Great Plains and American West is a history of settler accumulation and Indigenous dispossession. It is a resource history of water used for the benefit of settler town electrification to the detriment of traditional ways of life for tribes. The Oahe Dam, built between 1948 and 1962, displaced Lakota and Dakota communities and destroyed fertile hunting grounds and timberlands (Estes 2019). Resistance to the DAPL is a contemporary iteration of a very long Indigenous struggle against settler colonialism in the form of energy infrastructure. Water power, too, is part of the "creature" described in the voiceover, a creature with many arms.

The next shot in the video, a vertical aerial view of a pipeline right of way being cut through a field, emphasizes the relationship between contemporary extractive projects like the pipeline and earlier incursions like the Oahe Dam. The voiceover says of the creature, "It lied and said we were created in its image and that we must consume as it consumes in order to survive." The word "consume" is starkly illustrated in this shot; as the drone travels along the cut, it reveals heavy machines, earthmovers, and cranes waiting to continue their work. Where the right of way frays, the vehicles sit, ready to consume more. The machines, mouths for a voracious monster called settler colonialism, cast long diagonal shadows on the ground, more lines across the land. This midstream scene in the midst of construction is the oily equivalent of the power lines that span the hydroelectric dam. It is here, with the drone's camera lingering over the pipeline right of way, that the voiceover first recites the words "we are in crisis." A reference to both the title and the opening text, this assertion is a turning point in the video. From here we travel away from energy infrastructure to an aerial view of a field of cows. The narrator speaks: "It is hard to remember the sound of our mother's heartbeat through embryonic fluid, but that is the first sound we ever heard, amplified by water." In the next moment, the viewer sees a closer shot of two cows, a mother and child, who move slowly across a scrubby field. From this point on, the bodies in the drone camera's lens are the bodies of animals, water, and Water Protectors, suggested by a long shot of the encampment at Standing Rock. At this fulcrum in the video, the drone camera's target is no longer the beasts of infrastructure but the beasts of water. By lingering on these animals and conjuring the sound of "our mother's heartbeat through embryonic fluid," *We Are in Crisis* connects these other-than-human mammalian bodies to human bodies and their shared experience of the crisis of extraction. The flesh and mineral bodies depicted in *We Are in Crisis* are enmeshed with the body of the earth and bodies of water for both good and ill.

In the final moments of *We Are in Crisis*, the drone travels from one end of the camp to the other, offering an oblique view that includes the encampment along the river and the horizon. As it reaches the road and bridge over *Mni Sose*, it begins to slowly rise, the horizon disappearing as the camera tilts downward. The voiceover ends here, the drone's camera poised over the river just beyond the camp, with the repeated phrase, "we are in crisis," followed by a black screen like the period at the end of a sentence. After a moment, white text appears on the screen: "No Dakota Access Pipeline." The final shot is a straightforward call to action, an answer to the question posed by the definition of crisis.

"The Change Itself": Diagnosing the Crisis to Heal the Body

In their introduction to the first volume of *Ecocinema Theory and Practice*, Stephen Rust and Salma Monani articulate the promise of ecocinema studies, a purpose that is echoed in the work of Winter Count and in this analysis of *We Are in Crisis*: "For eco-film critics, cinema and ecocinema studies enable us to recognize ways of seeing the world other than through the narrow perspective of the anthropocentric gaze that situates individual human desires at the center of the moral universe" (2013, 11). We ought to understand this video not only as a piece of filmmaking about ecological concerns but also as part of an on-the-ground struggle, as the work of a community of artists engaged in the #NoDAPL movement.

The engaged resistance of *We Are in Crisis* actively intervenes in settler narratives of land use, interrupting economic justifications for extraction and long histories of industry and military conquest. The artists of Winter Count counter official narratives of public lands seized through eminent domain for the "public good" and retell these stories on Indigenous terms. Winter Count uses a device associated with some of the most violent acts of war – targeted killings at a distance – and yet engages it as part of a complex web of relations in the air and on the ground that advocate against settler infrastructure and for Indigenous futures. By creating *We Are in Crisis* as an offering to Water Protectors, the artists of Winter Count align themselves with the #NoDAPL struggle while pulling the camera up and back to take in the much wider landscape and history of resistance to settler infrastructure.

Extraction continues in Alberta and North Dakota; both the Keystone XL and DAPLs were approved by former president Donald Trump, though the Keystone XL pipeline faced legal battles in Nebraska throughout the Trump presidency and President Joe Biden revoked the pipeline's permit in early 2021. Even so, a number of state legislators have proposed bills to discourage pipeline protests by punishing activists with felony charges and protecting drivers from being prosecuted for hitting activists with their vehicles. This legislation has been introduced not only in response to pipeline activism but also to the public demonstrations of the Black Lives Matter movement and other racial justice actions (Carpenter 2018). These circumstances suggest both the need for the kind of media activism that has emerged over the past few years as well as the very real challenges it faces.

One of the questions often asked of this kind of filmmaking is this: what does success look like? Even though DAPL is operational, recent anti-extraction media like the video produced by Winter Count has not failed. Socially mediated #NoKXL and #NoDAPL organizing and imagery, in particular, has contributed to a much broader divestment movement that calls on banks to end their relationships with energy companies like TransCanada and Energy Partners and calls on consumers to end their relationships with banks that fail to do so.[5] Building on the activism of groups like Idle No More in Canada, the #NoKXL and #NoDAPL movements have boosted the anti-extraction signal, drawing attention to the shared concern of Indigenous peoples across Turtle Island (Barker 2015).[6] The work of Water Protectors in North Dakota has even led some investors to put pressure on the board of oil companies; *Inside Climate News* reported in 2018 that Marathon Oil investors have asked the company to provide human rights risk reports for new infrastructure projects (Hasemyer 2018). While this move may be motivated primarily by economic interest, it nonetheless suggests that investors recognize the way anti-extraction media influences public opinion and policy.

In addition to inspiring divestment movements, artists and filmmakers engaged in the #NoDAPL struggle used aesthetic and political strategies to envision a distinctly Indigenous future, a world that recognizes Indigenous sovereignty while drawing attention to the long histories of resource struggle on Indigenous lands. Indigenous #NoDAPL media like *We Are in Crisis* reframes oily apocalypse narratives as narratives about water, life, and survival in the face of an apocalypse that has already occurred and continues to be endured. Through storytelling, soundscape, and aerial imagery, the artists and filmmakers of Winter Count diagnose the crisis of oil while modeling critically engaged aesthetic practice that is part of a much longer history of Indigenous resistance to settler colonialism. Although infrastructure projects like the DAPL attempt to secure settler futurity, the artists of Winter Count share Indigenous storytelling in service of a historically-informed Indigenous future.

Notes

1 Cannupa Hanska Luger, one of the artists of Winter Count, was inspired to create mirror shields by activists in Ukraine, who had used them against riot police. Writing for *Hyperallergic*, Erin Joyce (2016) describes these shields as "poetic armor" and notes that Luger also provides the voiceover for *We Are in Crisis*. Kate Morris begins her excellent book, *Shifting Grounds: Landscape in Contemporary Native American Art* (2019), with a rich description of the *Mirror Shield Project: Water Serpent Action* at Standing Rock.
2 Dewey had his drone seized by Morton County Sheriff's Department officers without a warrant, and he was charged with misdemeanor stalking due to his coverage of the #NoDAPL movement; the charges were eventually dropped by Morton County prosecutors.
3 The website of Digital Smoke Signals is no longer updated, as Dewey died in a car accident in 2021 (Schilling, 2021). The Digital Smoke Signals Facebook page, however, is still reposting content from around the internet. A moving tribute to Dewey and interview with Dewey's partner, Deborah Parker, was published on September 27, 2021, by *Indian Country Today*.
4 In their introduction to *Ecocriticism and Indigenous Studies: Conversations from Earth to Cosmos*, Joni Adamson and Salma Monani (2017) draw on Rader's work and describe "engaged resistance" as a "fundamentally Indigenous form of aesthetic discourse that engages both Native and Western means as resistance against 'colonial assimilation and erasure' and toward 'survivance'" (15).
5 Many of the social media accounts that documented the #NoKXL and #NoDAPL struggles, including Bold Nebraska and Indigenous Environmental Network's social media platforms, have also raised awareness about the #KeepItInTheGround movement.
6 Turtle Island is a term used by a number of Indigenous groups to refer to the North American continent; it has roots in the history and culture of the Iroquois peoples as well as the Anishinaabe.

Works Cited

Adamson, Joni and Salma Monani. 2017. "Introduction: Cosmovisions, Ecocriticism, and Indigenous Studies." In *Ecocriticism and Indigenous Studies: Conversations from Earth to Cosmos*, edited by Salma Monani and Joni Adamson, 1–20. New York and London: Routledge.
Barker, Adam. 2015. "'A Direct Act of Resurgence, a Direct Act of Sovereignty': Reflections on Idle No More, Indigenous Activism, and Canadian Settler Colonialism." *Globalizations* 12.1: 43–65.
Carpenter, Zoe. 2018. "Since Standing Rock, 56 Bills Have Been Introduced in 30 States to Restrict Protests." *The Nation*. February 16, 2018. https://www.thenation.com/article/photos-since-standing-rock-56-bills-have-been-introduced-in-30-states-to-restrict-protests/.

Chandler, Katherine. 2020. *Unmanning: How Humans, Machines and Media Perform Drone Warfare*. New Brunswick: Rutgers University Press.

Crang, Mike. 2010. "The Death of Great Ships: Photography, Politics, and Waste in the Global Imaginary." *Environment and Planning A* 42: 1084–1102.

Diehl, Carol. 2006. "The Toxic Sublime." *Art in America* 94: 118–123.

Dillon, Grace L., ed. 2012. *Walking the Clouds: An Anthology of Indigenous Science Fiction*. Tucson: University of Arizona Press.

Estes, Nick. 2019. *Our History Is the Future: Standing Rock versus the Dakota Access Pipeline and the Long Tradition of Indigenous Resistance*. London: Verso.

Gatlin, Jill. 2015. "Toxic Sublimity and the Crisis of Human Perception: Rethinking Aesthetic, Documentary, and Political Appeals in Contemporary Wasteland Photography." *Interdisciplinary Studies in Literature and Environment* 22.4: 1–25.

Ginsburg, Faye. 2002. "Screen Memories: Resignifying the Traditional in Indigenous Media." In *Media Worlds: Anthropology on New Terrain*, edited by Faye Ginsburg, Lila Abu-Lughod, and Brian Larkin, 39–57. Berkeley: University of California Press.

Goulet, Danis. 2021. "Futurisms: Danis Goulet." Interview by Niki Little. *ImagineNA-TIVE Film + Media Festival*, Facebook. Live stream, April 29, 2021. https://www.facebook.com/imagineNATIVE/videos/330921891698714.

Grande, Sandy. 2018. "Refusing the Settler Society of the Spectacle." In *Handbook of Indigenous Education*, edited by E.A. McKinley and L.T. Smith, 1–7. Singapore: Springer Nature Singapore.

Gregory, Derek. 2013. "Lines of Descent." In From Above: War, Violence, and Verticality, edited by Peter Adey, Mark Whitehead, and Alison Williams, 41–70. Oxford: Oxford University Press.

Hasemyer, David. 2018. "Oil Investors Call for Human Rights Risk Report after Standing Rock." *Inside Climate News*. February 6, 2018. https://insideclimatenews.org/news/06022018/marathon-oil-shareholder-resolution-human-rights-dakota-access-environment-social-risk-disclosure/.

Hearne, Joanna. 2020. "Indigenous Performance Networks: Media, Community, Activism." In-Focus Dossier. *Journal of Cinema and Media Studies* 60.2: 152–156.

Horton, Jessica L. 2017. "Drones and Snakes." *Art in America* (October) 105(9): 104–109.

Joyce, Erin. 2016. "Artists Join the Fight to Protect Standing Rock." *Hyperallergic*, November 22, 2016. https://hyperallergic.com/338755/artists-join-the-fight-to-protect-standing-rock/

Kaplan, Caren. 2018. *Aerial Aftermaths: Wartime from Above*. Durham and London: Duke University Press.

———. 2020. "Atmospheric Politics: Protest Drones and the Ambiguity of Airspace." *Digital War* 1: 50–57.

Kim, Jihoon. 2022. *Documentary's Expanded Fields: New Media and the Twenty-First Century Documentary*. Oxford: Oxford University Press.

McLaughlin, Dylan, Cannupa Hanska Luger, Ginger Dunnill, Merritt Johnson, and Nicholas Galanin. 2016. *We Are in Crisis*. Vimeo. October 17, 2016. https://vimeo.com/187762675.

Monani, Salma. 2016. "Feeling and Healing Eco-Social Catastrophe: The 'Horrific' Slipstream of Danis Goulet's *Wakening*." *Paradoxa* 28: 192–213.

Morris, Kate. 2019. *Shifting Grounds: Landscape in Contemporary Native American Art*. Seattle: University of Washington Press.

Nickerson, Sylvia. 2007. "Sublime Tar Sands? Edward Burtysky's Photography and Canada's Extractive Industries." *The Dominion* 48. http://www.dominionpaper.ca/articles/1438.

Parks, Lisa. 2018. *Rethinking Media Coverage: Vertical Mediation and the War on Terror.* New York and London: Routledge.

———. 2017. "Vertical Mediation and the U.S. Drone War in the Horn of Africa." In *Life in the Age of Drone Warfare*, edited by Lisa Parks and Caren Kaplan, 134–158. Durham and London, Duke University Press.

Patchett, Merle and Andriko Lozowy. 2012. "Reframing the Canadian Oil Sands." *Sighting Oil.* Special Issue of *Imaginations: Journal of Cross-Cultural Image Studies/Revue d'Études Interculturelles de l'Image* 3.2. http://imaginations.glendon.yorku.ca/?p=3869.

Peeples, Jennifer. 2011. "Toxic Sublime: Imaging Contaminated Landscapes." *Environmental Communication* 5.4 (December): 373–392.

Rader, Dean. 2011. *Engaged Resistance: American Indian Art, Literature, and Film From Alcatraz to NMAI.* Austin: University of Texas Press.

Rust, Stephen and Salma Monani. 2013. "Cuts to Dissolves: Defining and Situating Ecocinema Studies." In *Ecocinema Theory and Practice*, edited by Stephen Rust, Salma Monani, and Sean Cubitt, 1–13. New York and London: Routledge.

Schilling, Vincent. 2021. "Digital Smoke Signals Founder Myron Dewey Dies in Tragic Accident." *Indian Country Today.* September 27, 2021. https://indiancountrytoday.com/news/digital-smoke-signals-founder-journalist-filmmaker-myron-dewey-dies-in-tragic-accident.

Schnepf, J. D. 2019. "Unsettling Aerial Surveillance: Surveillance Studies after Standing Rock." *Surveillance & Society* 17.5: 747–751.

Tuck, Sarah. 2018. "Drone Vision and Protest." *photographies* 11.2–3: 169–175.

Turner, Stephen. 2013. "Reflections on Barry Barclay and Fourth Cinema." In *The Fourth Eye: Māori Media in Aotearoa New Zealand*, edited by Brendan Hokowhitu and Vijay Devadas, 162–178. Minneapolis: University of Minnesota Press.

Vartanian, Hrag. 2016. "The Roles of Art and Artists at the Pipeline Protests in North Dakota." *Hyperallergic Podcast*, December 2, 2016. https://hyperallergic.com/342677/the-roles-of-art-and-artists-at-the-pipeline-protests-in-north-dakota/.

Vizenor, Gerald. 1999. *Manifest Manners: Narratives of Postindian Survivance.* Lincoln and London: University of Nebraska Press.

Whyte, Kyle Powys. 2018. "Indigenous Science (Fiction) for the Anthropocene: Ancestral Dystopias and Fantasies of Climate Change." *Nature and Space* 1.1–2: 224–242.

———. 2017. "Resurgence from Within the Rust: Indigenous Science (Fiction) for the Anthropocene." Keynote Address. Association for the Study of Literature and the Environment Bi-Annual Meeting. Detroit.

Zuev, Dennis and Gary Bratchford. 2020. "The Citizen Drone: Protest, Sousveillance, and Droneviewing." *Visual Studies* 35.5: 442–456.

13

BLURRY STREAMS

The Pandemic Film Festival

Mila Zuo

It is April 2020. I am in our darkened living room, streaming part two of Wang Bing's 495-minute documentary *Dead Souls* (2018), which premiered at the Cannes Film Festival, on Ovid.tv. My laptop is connected via HDMI to a 55" Samsung flatscreen, set up with in-home surround sound speakers. Flanking my television are two *monstera deliciosa* plants with their messy roots and a few sunburnt leaves, waywardly reaching for the window. My eyes begin to roam and my thoughts follow suit: *I need to water the plants.* I try to focus, but the edges of the screen begin to bleed with the silent demands of plants, forming a roaming palimpsest of distraction. *Between Two Monsteras*, I think, and I'm reminded of comedian Zach Galifianakis' celebrity-roasting *Between Two Ferns* series. Meanwhile, the film image pixelates and blurs every few minutes, jolting me out of the film's difficult testimonies about Chinese communist hard-labor camps.

Thoughts meander during cinematic engagements in any exhibition space, but there are intrusive thoughts involving household management that can make for especially distracted home viewing. As such, by exploring the virtual pandemic film festival from the perspective of a filmmaker and festival programmer, this chapter revisits and adapts John Ellis' provocation that television's regime of vision is rooted in the glance, rather than the gaze (Ellis 1982). During the pandemic, I premiered and screened a narrative festival film (*Kin*, 2021) and participated in a commissioned omnibus (*Cinema-19*, 2019), which was released online. I also served as a narrative features programmer and co-captain for the Slamdance Film Festival and juried a film and television selection process for a federal subsidizing organization. Reflecting upon these experiences, I address the loss of the auratic or ritualistic experience of festival-going, with a replacement by the streamification, or what we might call the "Artflixing" of festival films. Using this concept and the analytic of the blur,

DOI: 10.4324/9781003246602-17

I contend that risk-averse ambiences become privileged within the domain of online-only film festivals, which are aesthetically and socially constrained, as well as ecologically problematic.

"Artflixing" in the Pandemic: The Netflixification of Art House Cinema

Artflixing produces an antithetical engagement to what Scott MacDonald describes as the ecocinematic experience "that models patience and mindfulness," in contrast to "the fundamentally hysterical approach of commercial media" (2013, 19). Analogous to the ways in which media devices within the middle-class home compete for attention (TV, computer, phone, tablet), slow art films, like *Dead Souls,* also compete with "hysterical" media objects.[1]

In another account of fragmented media consumption, John T. Caldwell describes the popular media management term "grazing" when describing the "rate at which viewers turn to and scan other channel choices while watching a show" (2003, 135). This also applies to the ways in which viewers graze and glance at media amidst other appliances and household items that remind one of their mundane, even if cozy, captivity. While grazing exploits the neoliberal illusion of choice, "binging" shows or series, for example, is a term that evokes late capitalism's engorging excesses. Binging hinges on unfolding revelations, whereas slow art cinemas often engage in the deflection of comprehension over time. Binge-y shows accommodate epistemophilia, even prestige or quality television shows which possess innovation and "narrative complexity," as Jason Mittell demonstrates (2015). "Artflixing" presents a paradox—slow and/or art cinema's attention needs clash with the particular design of Netflix (and other mainstream streaming platforms)'s triumphant-yet-ignored situatedness inside the home. In other words, streaming platforms oblige partial attention and encourage ambient mis/uses of media. Competing with epistemophilic desires and hysterical media, Artflixing (the household streaming of art cinemas) can therefore feel more like a household chore than a pleasure. As the above example demonstrates, Artflixing a slow eight-hour documentary centered on lengthy testimonials by camp survivors can feel compromised, and perhaps even inappropriate due to its casual domestic spectatorship. Although certainly there are exceptions to this, I contend that Artflixing is part of a larger movement toward a casualization of art cinema within a post-spectacular episteme that prefers ambience over aura, as I later explore.

There are also historical echoes in the concerns I will stage regarding the Artflixing of the pandemic film festivals with those concerning television in the twentieth century home, particularly in relation to its consumption by housewives. As Jane Feuer notes,

> The set is in the home, as part of the furniture of one's daily life; it is always available; one may intercept the flow at any point. Indeed, the

'central fact' of television may be that it is designed to be watched intermittently, casually, and without full concentration.

(1983, 15)

I am especially interested in notions of distraction, attention, and domestic labor, as those became heightened points of conversation during the pandemic. To what extent does televisual merriment at the expense/advantage of housework also apply to the viewer-in-lockdown? How do the ways in which 1950s housewives used television mirror pandemic streaming habits, and how do such habits influence content? As Lynn Spigel contends, mid-twentieth century television specifically appealed and catered to the multitasking housewife (1992). Notwithstanding the gendered division of labor in the home, which has persisted since the 1950s, it is also worth thinking about how the pandemic's blurring of work and home life has impacted most people.

The pandemic brought about the further domestication of media and people, who sheltered at home (for those fortunate enough to have a dwelling) from the rapidly-spreading disease. Many people, aside from front-line workers, began working from home, and articles touting a "blurred work-life balance" argued for the benefits of permanent WFH (work from home) arrangements, most notably by tech companies like Twitter and Microsoft (Gaskell 2020).[2] Along other fuzzy lines, the coronavirus and its aerosol spread constitute a blurring of boundaries and an expanse of body-hood and "personal space." Ecologically, where does one person begin and end, if their molecular reach is indeterminable? The beginning of the pandemic presented a blur of mis/information; for example, face masks were not initially recommended but were subsequently required as one of the safest protective measures.

Even within these blurs, boundaries become visible. Boundaries between nations suddenly sharpened into view as governments instituted travel bans, quarantines, and lockdowns, bringing to the fore the previous blurriness of globalization and international travel. The imaginary nation-state rose again to demarcate and re-entrench its borders, worsening the livelihood for nation-less migrants and refugees who were kept at crowded border holding places, making them vulnerable not only to statist violence and precarity but also to viral spread. Relatedly, ethnonationalist fervor rose in the West, which saw a significant uptick in anti-Asian violence and discrimination as a result of misdirected anger and perception of the "Chinese virus." Such racist backlash coincided with the growing visibility of systemic murders, oppressions, and dispossessions of Black Americans, and Native and Indigenous populations.

During the pandemic, film festivals shifted promptly to online streaming. This had the effect of domesticating in-person events and encounters, bringing global festival films into the home, though often with limited geo-blocked access and viewing times. Moreover, the blur, buffering, and glitching that often arises from digital streaming contributes to a "blurry effect" that we can relate to the impressionistic aesthetics of the pandemic itself, which blurs not only art and mainstream cinemas via streamification but also our sense of ecological impacts. Despite that travel to festivals diminished during the pandemic, thereby helping to reduce the carbon footprint produced by the aviation industry (which accounts for 2.4% of CO_2 emissions by humans), we must also consider streaming's ecological costs, as Laura U. Marks and others recently attest (Marks et al. 2020).

Although the virtualization of film festivals during the 2020–2021 cycles has ostensibly increased the international spectatorship of new, global cinemas, the loss of in-person gatherings results in further atomization for independent artists, while challenging works intended for theatrical viewing may recede into the margins when faced with streamification. Thus, blurring and boundary making also extend to a certain eco-aesthetic encounter with which we can discuss the virtual film festival.

Democratizing Fests?

Film festivals in 2020 were quick to respond and convert online. While CPH:DOX (Copenhagen International Documentary Film Festival) and Visions du Réel were the first to do so, others quickly followed suit. Discussing three film festivals, journalist Hannah Strong writes,

> all three festivals reported unprecedented levels of attendance.... Sundance reached an audience 2.7 times larger than its average 11-day physical festival in Utah, with over 250,000 views of its features and shorts. NYFF reported nearly 40,000 rentals across the US in addition to the 8,300 guests at COVID-safe screenings across New York—an increase of 9.15% over 2019. TIFF confirmed over 118,000 ticket sales.
>
> *(2021)*

The benefits of the online film festival included expanded viewership via the remote watch, increased accessibility via closed captioning options, and various kinds of interfestival collaboration, like the We Are One festival co-curated by 21 festivals and which screened over 100 international films on YouTube. The disadvantages included the lack of a communal viewing experience, and few, if any, networking opportunities where many filmmakers might meet their future collaborators and industry partners.

As social networking became challenged with the virtual film festival, ecological considerations reveal that streaming comes with another price. The global costs of streaming pornography and Netflix each equate to the generation of Belgium's annual CO_2 output (Le Page 2019). Marks cautions that streaming media contribute more than any other sector to the increase of computational energy consumption, which "currently emits 2.7–3.3 percent of global greenhouse gases and is cautiously projected to comprise 7 percent of global greenhouse emissions in 2030 and 15 percent in 2040" (Marks et al. 2020).[3]

Besides its ecological impacts, there are aesthetic-phenomenological constraints of home viewing that overpower the criteria of selections, to the detriment of including challenging, difficult, and provocative works. In 2021, the arthouse distributor Neon announced that Apichatpong Weerasethakul's *Memoria* (2021) would ever only be exhibited in movie theaters and would never be streamed or released on Blu-ray. *New York Times* film critic A.O. Scott describes the film as an "object and an experience [that] resists the rhythms of home viewing, to begin with," and as a result of its "delicate spell," may require a theatrical setting (2021). Watching "weird movies" in the company of strangers, Scott suggests, might restore something of the film's auratic life, or that which might never be comprehended but only fleetingly sensed. In response to the Twitter backlash of *Memoria*'s theatrical-only exhibition, which was rooted in accusations of the film's elitism and exclusionary practice, Scott describes such reactions as "a form of pseudo-populist techno-triumphalism that takes what seems to be the easiest mode of consumption as, by definition, the most progressive." Indeed, many like Strong embrace the virtualized film festival for "democratizing events that have long typified the more exclusive side of the film world," for example, panels and director Q&As (2021). What Strong's statement overlooks is the undemocratic selection process by many top-tier film festivals, which are already steeped in the politics of the marquee, financing, and the cult of the auteur. Moreover, with thousands of submissions a year at top festivals, it is unlikely that programmers watch screeners in their entirety (and if they do, they will often do so in a state of distraction or while multitasking).

Festival selection would become even more challenging if film festivals went permanently online (which is highly doubtful as their locations are so central to their geopolitical and vacation identities). Although online screeners have long been used to evaluate films for selection, deliberations are typically held in person. In 2020 and 2021, final deliberations for Slamdance's Narrative Features slate were held on Zoom, with programmers joining in from around the world. During those deliberations, as well as during the virtual deliberations for the jury selection of film and television awards in which I participated, the Zoomification of deliberations seemed to dampen vibrant frictions of in-person meetings. Individuals seemed to more often than not double down on their initial tastes and judgments, as the virtual meetings seemed to have lost some of the affective, and indeed auratic, components of fleshy persuasion.

Aesthetic objects in the home lose their *own* persuasive qualities insofar as they must compete with everyday objects, which makes for distracted viewing. Pointing to the oppressiveness of dumb aesthetic objects, Timothy Morton describes playing a climactic scene in Peter Jackson's *The Lord of the Rings: The Two Towers* (2002) at the same time as a Playskool Busy Ball Popper toy, observing that the toy's inane tunes "instantly undermine the coherence of Peter Jackson's narrative world" (Morton 2013, 105). That the inane will triumph over the complex is especially resonant within one's home when many wish to unwind and "turn off." The fragility of a cinematic world is subservient to its aesthetic effects, both within and without the film's text, as it blurs into its environment.

COVID-19 *Coyote*

Two experiences as a pandemic filmmaker further elucidate the blurry benefits and constraints of Artflixing. In June 2020, filmmakers Usama Alshaibi and Adam Sekuler commissioned a 190-second short from William Brown and myself for the anthology *Cinema-19,* a collection of 14 such films by 16 directors, which "do not attempt to summarize the pandemic, but instead focus on the personal, the political, the sensual, the distant, the abstract, and the absurd." We conceived *Coyote*, a personal film comprising two shots, which was produced while I was three months pregnant. The first take lasts roughly 180 seconds in duration and reveals an interaction whereby my character Vivi returns home from a walk with the dog, interrupting a conversation. He (played by Brown) is having over Skype with a friend (voiced by Aleks Krawec) in the United Kingdom. We proceed to vent petty jealousies over Paul and Karen, people from our respective pasts, before reconciliation over a foot massage He gives to Vivi after He ostensibly gives Vivi a reassuring, affectionate statement but displaces his regard to Trouble the dog. He then flatulates; she is grossed out. The film then cuts to an iPhone footage of a coyote scavenging for scraps, which Brown captured one night near our apartment complex.

 Coyote imaged our mundane lives, which included tensions and pent-up cabin fever "under lockdown," but which also gestures to larger contexts of the pandemic's racial reckonings as well as to post-pandemic worlds through the intimation of impending birth. As a televisual gesture of self-disclosure and as an exercise in embarrassment, we blur fact and fiction. We explore romantic tensions as a result of being in an interracial white-Asian couple, for example, being on the receiving end of a racist joke by one of Brown's white women friends, while situating this mundane insult against the backdrop of numerous accounts of anti-Asian violence in Vancouver during the pandemic (read out loud by actor Radhika Aggarwal on an iPad and over the final shot of the coyote). We acknowledge the coterminous Black Lives Matter (BLM) protests taking place around the world through a partially mirrored reflection of a television screen playing a video of BLM protests—a fragmented image that competes with the iPad on the couch. Bringing together various significations of the "inhuman" encounter, which spans the microaggressive and systemic racism against people of color as well as the ecological-animal impacts of the pandemic, the title refers to the encroachment of wild coyotes in our area as the

FIGURE 13.1   Shot on a mini–DV camera with a 4:3 aspect ratio, *Coyote* images our mundane pandemic lives under lockdown.

result of pandemic restaurant closures. Brown, drawing upon Native American mythologies of the coyote through Donna J. Haraway and Thomas King, explains that the coyote "emerg[es] when our attempts at planetary mastery have been thwarted and/or exposed as flawed" (Brown 2021). As a coyote, COVID-19 surfaced the racism and social inequities that only become more pronounced under such social duress while the *Cinema-19* anthology, in allowing the films to bleed into one another, with no demarcation of one film's beginning or end, enabled intertextual interpretations, a "stream of consciousness" that mirrors its streaming digitality.

Rather than waiting for film festival selection, which is far from certain and would take many months even for an online fest, Alshaibi and Sekuler seized upon partnering with the Anthology Film Archives in New York City, the Northwest Film Forum in Seattle, and the Zeitgeist Theatre and Lounge in New Orleans, to help promote and premiere the film online via Vimeo. This allowed the film to achieve a prescience and visibility prior to other inevitable pandemic films, and the film garnered attention for being "diverse and imaginative" (Macaulay 2020). After *Cinema-19* went "live" and was available for free via Vimeo, filmmakers participated in a moderated Zoom interview, which was recorded and made available on the film's Facebook page (Cinema-19 2020).

While *Cinema-19* took advantage of pandemic filmmaking, both in the sense of the immediacy of its production, and aesthetically, in embracing the stream/ing of consciousness, my short narrative film *Kin*, which was shot in the summer of 2019 prior to the pandemic, was ill-suited to the virtual film festival, even as it did make a few rounds at various virtual and hybrid festivals in 2021–2022.[4] *Kin*, set in rural Oregon, revolves around a love triangle of white

FIGURE 13.2   Still from *Kin* (2021).

20-somethings (starring Frank Mosley and Sophie Traub) that ends in mass violence. The film interrogates the libido of white supremacist desire and the teleologies of mass violence. By running counter to the subtle sentimentalism and humanistic mode of indie storytelling favored by many festivals following the Sundance model, *Kin* would have been a difficult selection any year, but especially so during the pandemic film circuit, as tastes seemed to shift under widespread duress. As North America was simultaneously hit with the viral pandemic and with renewed consciousness around racism and colonialism, it seemed as though festivals shied away from downbeat, difficult films. At least this was true for the final Slamdance slate of narrative debut features. Nevertheless, we might regard streaming platforms as a new "lipstick index" for pandemic times in light of the immense surge in streaming media, as worldwide subscriptions to streaming platforms reached 1.1 billion in 2020 (Watson 2021).

From Aura to Ambience

Bill Nichols describes the austerity and formalism of Iranian cinema that he encountered at international film festivals, remarking that the endings of many of the films move the spectators *"near* the characters rather than *with* them" (Nichols 1994, 26). How might we think about this unmasterful nearness through the spatial proximities of re-locating the film festival to home streaming devices? Are we still only *near* such characters when they are also within the intimate, messy spaces of our living room, for example? How does nearness truck with television's "metaphysics of presence," a term used by William Boddy to discuss early live television's ontology, and by Robert Stam to discuss television's phono- and logocentrisms (Boddy 1993, 82; Stam 1983, 34)? Indeed, the Internet's metaphysics of liveness is also predicated upon a certain contemporality (everyone is always *on*-line), and as Stam demonstrates with TV, similarly "prosthetically extends human perception" and grants feelings of narcissistic pleasure (24). Streaming platforms manifest this constant presence, as their texts wait to be activated (to stream or flow with the push of a button). Have we yoked streaming characters to *be with* us, rather than surrendering ourselves to be near them (and other strangers) in the auratic space of the cinema, as illustrated by a film like Tsai Ming-Liang's elegiac *Goodbye, Dragon Inn* (2003) about the delicately intimate experiences of moviegoing with strangers?

Those in the film industry also speculate on the appropriateness of streaming for various content. HollyShorts Film Festival hosted a panel at the Japan House Hollywood on September 25, 2021, entitled, "Pros and Cons: Streaming vs. Theatrical Releases" where producers Julianna Politsky and Lyn Sisson-Talbert, along with Head of Development at Treehouse Pictures Juliet Berman, discussed the industrial fallout from the Scarlett Johansson vs. Disney lawsuit, and in particular, the merits of streaming. Drawing together domestic labor, traditionally gendered feminine, with at-home spectatorship, Berman echoed some of the observations made by Feuer, Spigel, and other feminist television scholars, suggesting that rom-coms were a genre that thrived best in the streaming sphere, as a favored genre to watch "while folding laundry on the couch on a Sunday afternoon." Meanwhile, she contended that one might opt for a theatrical experience of other genres, like horror, to participate in a visceral community. When I asked about the place of art cinema, and specifically about slow cinema, in the streaming world, Politsky responded that with the absence of significant demand and private equity to support art cinemas, the space for the art streamer is limited. None of the panelists mentioned the Criterion Channel or MUBI, the London-based streaming distributor of global festival films.

Indeed, many rom-coms with their formulaic, heteronormative stories, quasi-witty banter, and displays of conspicuous consumption offer a kind of gentle, inoffensive atmosphere or ambience that acts as moving wallpaper for the home. Spectators can tune in and out as they get on with laundry or cooking or any other house doings. Reality television, particularly real estate shows or cooking shows like *The Great British Bake Off* (Love Productions, 2010–) also offer charming backdrops replete with expensively decorated homes and beautiful gardens that virtually expand one's physical space and emplace the viewer in their manicured settings, blurring us into luxury environments and vice versa.[5] Echoing Ellis' notion of the televisual glance, *New Yorker* writer Kyle Chayka credits Netflix for pioneering what he calls "ambient television," which capitalizes on boredom insofar as it "denotes something that you don't have to pay attention to enjoy it but which is still seductive enough to be compelling if you choose to do so momentarily" (2020).[6] Chayka observes that ambient television shows serve as functional screensavers which aim

> to erase thought entirely, smoothing any disruptive texture or dissonance… [Their] high-resolution shots are chopped and composed into lulling montages—slow motion, fast motion, drone footage—that numb

the senses with color and movement. [Ambient television] provides glossy, comforting oblivion, or, as Matisse once wrote, of his own paintings, "something like a good armchair".

(2020)

As Byung-chul Han reminds us, the aesthetic of smoothness is "an *optimized* surface *without* negativity," which therefore accelerates "the circulation of information, communication and capital" (2018, 10, 16). As Netflix added 26 million customers in the first half of 2020, it would seem strategic to provide such comfy escapism for those who felt "locked down." Such ambient engagement, however, runs counter to the ways in which MacDonald defines ecocinema, as one that might model "the attitude that this place *is* worthy of our sustained attention," through extended shots and forms of non-narrative immersion into natural scenes, as in the works by filmmakers like Andrej Zdravič, Peter Hutton, James Benning, J.P. Sniadecki, and Sharon Lockhart (MacDonald 2012, 21). If long takes, slower rhythms and a de-anthropocentric mise-en-scène attune us toward natural conservation, then distracted glances toward an ambient backdrop fold us back onto ourselves and our domiciliary concerns.

In this way, Artflixing might bend to ambientified pressures, privileging the good enough film or show that enables partial attention and willful distraction. Further to the idea of the "good enough," Spigel discusses the ways in which television producers of the 1950s drew upon "tropes of averageness" to lure and maintain female viewers without alienating them, while Rashna Wadia Richards describes the end of the golden age of TV as a result of a takeover by "least objectionable programming" (Richards 2021, 25; Spigel 1992, 84). Although there is plenty of prestigious, complex, and interesting television, as well as art streamers on Netflix and other platforms (like the aforementioned MUBI), the vast majority of what is offered on Netflix (and is therefore algorithmically pushed to the top), is what Internet slang deems as enjoyably "basic" (unoriginally mainstream) chiming with what Venkatesh Rao terms "premium mediocrity," which describes "a pattern of consumption that publicly signals upward mobile aspirations, with consciously insincere pretensions to refined taste, while navigating the realities of inexorable downward mobility with sincere anxiety" (2017). In Rao's neo-Bourdieuian take on the declining tastes of the shrinking middle class, someone who consumes premium mediocrity is well aware of her tastelessness but "pretends it is tasteful anyway." I would add that this is situated within the context of what Lauren Berlant incisively labeled capitalism's "cruel optimism," wherein subjects retain attachments to the very objects, ideas, and modes of life which inhibit their flourishing (2011). Streaming films can become such an object of cruel optimism, revealing viewers' strong cathexion to fantastic images of wealth and consumption to which they aspire but could hardly possess. Such aspirations transmute into moving wallpaper or screensavers (the screen's own efforts at not being ignored) for the home, as viewers flaunt their "consciously insincere pretensions to refined taste."

I adapt Rao's argument to suggest that premium mediocrity involves the Artflixing of cinematic tastes whereby middlebrow tastes hold distinct aesthetic limitations and thresholds. We/the Netflix generation will stream Alfonso Cuarón's *Roma*, which Jan Hanzlík and Ewa Mazierska argue marked the shift in "a growth in prestige of films by streaming platforms" (2021, 7), but few will stream an eight-hour Lav Diaz film or ten-hour Wang Bing documentary – and as noted above, no one will ever be able to view Apichatpong's *Memoria* at home. At the very least, were one to decide to stream such "high art" festival films at home, there is the strong possibility of consumption in bite-size installments and/or in a grazing state of distraction, thereby undoing much of their accretive unfolding force. On the other hand, one might binge eight hours of *Breaking Bad* (AMC, 2008–2013), revealing that it is not necessarily the duration that is the issue, but rather the seriousness, slowness, or perhaps the lack of discernible breaks within art cinema that make it an ill-fitting domestic object. In the age of cool media devices, aura is replaced by the ambience.

Indeed, many (myself included) will occasionally select a basic show to provide the luminescent banal chatter during which we conduct digital affairs on our smartphones. As Chayka explains, "the ambient era…succumbs to, rather than competes with, your phone" (2020). Netflix accompanies us while we do something else; one Netflix study found that 12% of streaming actually takes place in a public restroom (Rustad 2018, 505). Netflix itself is a companion device. The holographic persona generates parasocial relationships, for example with the pretty and pleasant-enough titular waif in Netflix's *Emily in Paris* (2020–), one of Chayka's examples of ambient television. While Chayka points out the overwhelming whiteness of ambient television, writing that "any diversity or discordance would disrupt the smooth, lulling surface," he misses the opportunity to critically engage with *why* whiteness is the aspiring standard for the ambient, "premediocre" digital homespace (2020). Indeed, there are two factors of ambient television that tend to overpower ideological critiques: whiteness and beautiful spaces, both of which are aspirational within white-heteropatriarchal neoliberal logics and are in fact embedded into the very "substrates of computational capital," to borrow from Jonathan Beller (2018). Beller suggests that the "prosthetics of whiteness" have long been engineered into digital culture through ongoing representational violence toward nonwhites ("machine-mediated beyond its comprehension"), which ultimately generates a kind of computational and unsustainable psychosis (155).

The sheer inanity of *Emily in Paris*, pivoting around a culturally ignorant, social media savvy 20-something white American, does nothing to dispel its appeal. Is the basic thus a way to relish in one's domesticity, or a way for us to *Enjoy!* (to borrow from Jacques Lacan and Slavoj Žižek) in a superegoic way our own disciplined and monotonous lives? Along other lines of ambience, Beller describes the new computational cinematic mode of production:

> now rendered fully ambient and ballistic by computationally cut and mixed data visualization….produced by the continued and near continuous arrival of information and affect bombs all competing—in increasingly self-conscious ways that are feedback loops of the market—for the capture and expropriation of human attention and neurological function.
>
> *(2018, 153)*

In lieu of the metaphysical nearness of which Nichols writes, so germane to the slowly unraveling mysteries of many arthouse films, the streaming home compels upon our virtual companions a "withness" that exemplifies our captivity to digital feedback loops and their administration over our nervous and limbic systems.

That is why besides the lulling calm of low-stakes ambient TV, hot media (McLuhan 2001) that holds one's attention hostage also works best at home (dramas, action, thrillers, horror, Fox News). *Squid Game* (2021), the narrative series that pits South Korean debtors against one another to the death, is at present the most watched Netflix show. *Squid Game* has exceeded the confines of ambient television, utilizing some elements of prestige cable with its melodramatic narrative arcs, sympathetic characters, and gripping cliffhangers. The series is a formal example of premium mediocre and of Melissa Phruksachart's related concept of "boba liberalism," even as its message seems to be an anticapitalist critique of classism and South Korean debt culture (2020). Phruksachart describes boba liberals as Asian diasporic subjects who desire power under the status quo, seeking "the financial wealth and media and political representation that constitute the usual citizens' spoils under neoliberal capitalism," citing *Crazy Rich Asians* (Chu 2018) as an exemplary text (60). Even though *Squid Game* overtly critiques South Korean debt capitalism and lack of social welfare, the show is nevertheless participatory in such a world through its complicity with financial capitalism (touting an expensive budget of $21 million), which Netflix estimates will generate almost $900 million for the streaming company. The irony of *Squid Game*'s success, as with Bong Joon-ho's Oscar-winning *Parasite* (2019), is that despite its overt ideological critiques, both texts exemplify the problem of popular culture and its relation to critique—that is, the problem of whether such films can transcend the very premises they allege to criticize because of their industrial and aesthetic participation within such economies. Within Jean-Louis Comolli and Jean Narboni's organization of ideological films, media like *Squid Game* fall into the category of having explicitly political content, "but which do not effectively criticize the ideological system in which they are embedded because they unquestioningly adopt its language and its imagery" (1971, 32). And indeed, this argument can also be made about many "high art," or Second Cinema films (to borrow their language) at premiere film festivals. These texts must look (or simply are) expensive to reach a certain saturation point with mass audiences, which means the films have exorbitant production costs to ensure profits for their makers, studios, and production and exhibition companies.

Although it might seem that I have taken a critical stance against Netflix and *Squid Game*, as a filmmaker I am very much also grappling with similar tensions and pressures. When recently I was asked whether I was reproducing the objectification of Asian women in my short film *Carnal Orient* (2016), I responded that I did not think cinema was wholly capable of critique because of the very nature of the apparatus to aestheticize (You 2021). This is even truer of *Kin*, which overtly represents white supremacist racism and violence through the seductions of beautiful vintage Cooke lensing. Nostalgic longing was engineered into the "look" of the film so that the film becomes an experiment in testing the boundaries of cinematic lure and sympathy. The narrative is set in contrast with the film's formal properties, deliberately, in the hopes of provoking critical thought about how and why white supremacy could flourish in the libidinal psyche and via cinematic spectacle. The seeming paradoxes between form, content, and ethics make it a difficult film for the home film festival. Rather than "unquestioningly adopt[ing]" the dominant language, however, I wished to test out the "master's tools," in the words of Audre Lorde (2018). With *Carnal Orient* and *Kin*, and perhaps also with *Squid Game*, such texts rest upon the conceit of smuggling in illicit, politically subversive content, even as this may not always "work" in any coherent or clear fashion.

Unlike *Squid Game*'s binge-y appeal, formally experimental films by unknown filmmakers risk being misread by festival programmers. However, I wish to suggest that these films are necessary for breaking new cinematic ground by modeling transitional plays. Mika Tajima's solo exhibition *After the Martini Shot* (2012) at the Seattle Art Museum featured structural panels made from reclaimed Herman Miller Action Office furniture, which the artist re-canvased and sculpted into interactive displays to comment on the collapse of Washington Mutual, once the center of the museum's financial portfolio. Vivian L. Huang reads Tajima's appropriation of Miller's designs as a form of transitional play after D.W. Winnicott; it is the idea that a child uses an object, which is imbued with fantastical powers, through which to explore a potential space that is neither internal nor external reality but rather an in-between space. It can be used to begin a process of autonomy from the mother (therefore the transitional object is both the mother and not the mother at the same time). In so doing, the child plays with "being alive" and "creative living." Huang thus describes the ways in which Tajima's "slack object" calls attention "to the 'surface,' 'structure,' and medium, refusing to be legible as representation." Huang explains, "an art object slacks…when it offers a screen when depth was desired" (2015, 171). Here screen and depth are counterposed. Televisual

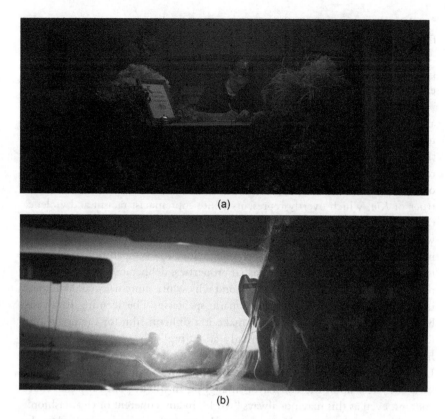

FIGURE 13.3 *Kin* experiments with sympathy through alluring cinematography.

slack, or Netflix ambience, offers the (mis)use of Netflix as background noise, an aural screen but which is nevertheless "narcotic and culinary" without depth (Stam 37). We are uncomfortable relinquishing the ostensible mastery we have over the basic, good-enough Netflix show, which we may watch in distraction and still feel we comprehend (well enough). Therefore, we desire the slack in our home spaces, since it offers a sense of control over our environment, a place of refuge from the chaos out there – a stark contrast to MacDonald's notion of slow cinema as a refuge for immersion in, and becoming with, nature/the out there. On the other hand, some challenging films are also "slack objects" in that they resist such legibility, offering a kind of transitional play that is aggressively destructive, but which is also a necessary aspect of comprehending aliveness. I caution that it is precisely these types of slack objects that are the first to be excised in festival programming, as I have witnessed during my time as a programmer, and particularly under the domestic-aesthetic constraints of the online fest, which will be even more risk averse than a traditional festival because of its aesthetic competition with televisual films and shows, which however complex, were designed with streamification in mind.

Coda: Streaming, Flowing, *Feng Shui?*

Vivian Sobchack remarks on the ways in which QuickTime movies are like memory boxes, in that through their distinct miniaturization and condensation they construct reliquaries that cherish ephemerality and provoke nostalgia. She regrets the streaming of desktop media, contending that QuickTime's "miniature spatial forms and temporal lacunae struggle against (as they struggle to become) cinema, [and that] they poetically dramatize and philosophically interrogate the nature of memory and temporality, the value of scale, and the meaning of animation" (2004, 307). Although QuickTime stutters, creating an enchantment of diminution and fragmentariness that evokes nostalgic loss, streaming media aestheticize the blur between life and (house)work. The blur is a logical extension of the flow and the stream. The blur is a smoothing of smoothness, recalling Han's notion of today's beauty as the smooth, and as that which "embodies a *society of positivity*. What is smooth does not *injure*. Nor does it offer any resistance. It is looking for *Like*" (2018, 1, italics in original). Smoothness abolishes critical distance and turns alterity into diversity—and in this way, the blur in fact reinforces boundaries, erupting, for example, in national xenophobia, racial violence, and in geoblocking. For Han, "In this *digital inwardness* there can be no sense of wonder. The only thing human beings still like are themselves" (2018, 26). Like, as a diluted feeling, suggests our digital compliance and soft complicity. We like the basic, we don't love it. We seek Facebook likes, in a world that filmmaker Andrey Zvyagintsev has otherwise defined as "loveless" (2017).

But if flow is about a certain in-home experience, then we can also think about ways in which blur, flow, and streams have been mobilized in other domiciliary ways. Take, for instance, the ancient metaphysical practices of geomancy, or what I would term the "abject epistemology" of *feng shui* (which translates to "wind water," and implicitly to their flow in-between). If we are to connect to an ecocinematic way of knowing, we might shift our epistemological orientations toward occulted, other non-Western knowledge, or what Walter D. Mignolo refers to as "border gnosis, [which is] knowledge conceived from the exterior borders of the modern/colonial world system" (2012, 11). For practitioners of *feng shui*, humans live in concert with the elements; we cannot overpower them but we can draw upon them to welcome auspiciousness. Analogously, mid-twentieth century American design also emphasized aesthetic seamlessness, the illusion of continuity between indoors and outdoors, most notably via picture windows and sliding glass doors. Spigel connects this to television by arguing that TV "was often figured as the ultimate expression of progress in Utopian statements concerning 'man's' ability to conquer and to domesticate space" (1992, 102). In contrast to the illusion that we dominate nature through the picture window or televisual appliance, however, *feng shui* practitioners advocate harmonious living with the environment to seek a flow and balance of *qi* (the life force) throughout one's living space. Accordingly, the television set and the computer are high emitting, or hot energy sources. *Feng shui* practitioners, therefore, warn against having such appliances in the bedroom because of their emission of electromagnetic, yang energy. *Feng shui* is thus in agreement with Beller's caution of digital devices' neurological takeover. What is in part contributing to Jonathan Crary's renowned "ends of sleep" in late capitalism is not just the encroachment of work into our 24/7 digital devices, but also the encroachments of "basic (premediocre) pleasures" through such media (2013).

In this chapter, I have discussed the online pandemic film festival and reflected on the effects of the online film festival, its aesthetic consequences, as well as their entangled ecocinematic impacts through an analytic of blur. I contended that risk-averse, unchallenging ambiences would become privileged and celebrated within the domain of online-only film festivals, due to the further domestication of cinema and to the detriment of creative destruction. Offerings from online festival films may become nearly indistinguishable from mainstream or ambient streamers. In addition to its outsized carbon footprint, home viewing prefers genteel aesthetic objects, and Netflix offers few objects for transitional play. However, cinema, like the coyote, ought to remain feral, unknowable, and dangerous. For the sake of our inner and outer worlds, let us bring cinema and festivals back into the dark, undomestic, and mystical spaces of the theater where we can be *near*, even if not *with*, such works.

Notes

1 John T. Caldwell and Henry Jenkins have observed, for example, that the film and television industry has adapted to this attention deficiency by drawing upon convergence and "second-shift media aesthetics" to prolong interactive transmedial engagement (Caldwell 2003; Jenkins 2006). Meanwhile blockbuster franchises and companies like Marvel Studios provide seamless transitions between films and television shows operating within the same "cinematic universes," thereby extending viewers' interest in their conglomerated objects indefinitely.

2 Nevertheless, it is important to keep in mind the class divide for such an allowance; the Pew Research Center finds that 62% of workers with a bachelor's degree or higher work from home, while only 23% of those without a four-year degree do (Parker et al. 2020).

3 Marks's Small File Media Film Festival was founded in 2020 and features small file-size films under 5 MB, countering the fetishization of the high-emitting, high-resolution 4K moving image by embracing the blur.

4 When *Kin* was selected for its premiere at the Portland International Film Festival, the overall experience felt underwhelming, with no filmmaker Q&A or interaction with audiences. *Kin* then played at the hybrid (in-person and streaming) Brooklyn Film Festival, for which there was a Zoom filmmaker Q&A moderated by shorts film director Natalie Gee, before it went to a hybrid Local Sightings Film Festival based at the Northwest Film Forum. It also screened at the hybrid HollyShorts Film Festival in Los Angeles, before it won an award at the George Lindsey UNA Film Festival, nominally in Alabama, but which in 2021 only took place online.

5 It is worth noting that others prefer the bombastic aural wallpaper of 24/7 cable news, such as Fox News.
6 Ambient television arose in the early days of television via soap operas, carried over from radio, as a way to partially engage housewives who used the appliance while they tended to the home.

Works Cited

Beller, Jonathan. 2018. *The Message Is Murder: Substrates of Computational Capital.* London: Pluto Press.

Berlant, Lauren. 2011. *Cruel Optimism.* Durham: Duke University Press.

Boddy, William. 1993. *Fifties Television: The Industry and Its Critics.* Urbana: University of Illinois Press.

Brown, William. 2021. "Making Kin, Making Children, and Making Coyote under Lockdown." *The Projector: Journal of Film, Media, and Culture* 22. https://www. theprojectorjournal.com/making-coyote-under-lockdown?fbclid=IwAR3r9Nrch 6qS6qiWbbBUV95E54WZwJwOpFQcoa5IUh_phAxOaXzbDjdwxeo

Caldwell, John. 2003. "Second-Shift Media Aesthetics: Programming, Interactivity, and User Flows." In *New Media: Theories of Practices of Digitextuality*, edited by Anna Everettand John T. Caldwell, 127–144. New York: Routledge.

Chayka, Kyle. 2020. "'Emily in Paris' and the Rise of Ambient TV." *The New Yorker.* November 16, 2020. https://www.newyorker.com/culture/cultural-comment/ emily-in-paris-and-the-rise-of-ambient-tv

Chu, Jon M., dir. *Crazy Rich Asians.* 2018; Warner Bros. Pictures, 2018. https://www. netflix.com/be-en/title/80239019.

Cinema-19: Filmmakers Respond to Covid-19. 2020. Facebook, August 13, 2020. https://www.facebook.com/filmgroupcinema19/

Comolli, Jean-Luc and Paul Narboni. 1971. "Cinema/Ideology/Criticism." *Screen* 12.1: 27–38.

Crary, Jonathan. 2013. *24/7: Late Capitalism and the Ends of Sleep.* Brooklyn: Verso.

Ellis, John. 1982. *Visible Fictions: Cinema, Television, Video.* London: Routledge.

Feuer, Jane. 1983. "The Concept of Live Television: Ontology as Ideology." In *Regarding Television: Critical Approaches*, edited by E. Ann Kaplan, 12–22. Frederick: University Publications of America.

Gaskell, Adi. 2020. "Is a Blurred Work-Life Balance the New Normal?" *Forbes.* May 11, 2020. https://www.forbes.com/sites/adigaskell/2020/05/11/is-a-blurred-work-life-balance-the-new-normal/?sh=3d1964021813

Han, Byung-Chul. 2018. *Saving Beauty.* Translated by Daniel Steuer. Cambridge: Polity Press.

Hanzlík, Jan and Ewa Mazierska. 2021. "Eastern European Film Festivals: Streaming through the Covid-19 Pandemic." *Studies in European Cinema.* August 14. https:// doi.org/10.1080/2040350X.2021.1964218

Huang, Vivian L. 2015. "Modern, Modular, Model: Mika Tajima and the Racial Good-Enough Environment." *Journal of Asian American Studies* 18.2: 165–192.

Hwang Dong-hyuk, dir. *Squid Game.* 2021; Siren Pictures, 2021. https://www.netflix. com/ca/title/81040344

Jenkins, Henry. 2006. *Convergence Culture: Where Old and New Media Collide.* New York: New York City.

Le Page, Michael. 2019. "Streaming Online Pornography Produces as much CO_2 as Belgium." *New Scientist*. July 11, 2019. https://www.newscientist.com/article/2209569-streaming-online-pornography-produces-as-much-co2-as-belgium/

Lorde, Audre. 2018. *The Master's Tools Will Never Dismantle the Master's House*. London: Penguin.

Macaulay, Scott. 2020. "Watch: Experimental Filmmakers Imaginatively Respond to the Pandemic in Cinema-19." *Filmmaker*. August 25, 2020. https://filmmakermagazine.com/110178-watch-experimental-filmmakers-imaginatively-respond-to-the-pandemic-in-cinema-19/#.YZMMGL3MLUK

MacDonald, Scott. 2012. "The Ecocinema Experience." In *Ecocinema Theory and Practice*, edited by Stephen Rust, Salma Monani, and Sean Cubitt, 17–42. New York: Routledge.

Marks, Laura U., Joseph Clark, Jason Livingston, Denise Oleksijczuk, and Lucas Hilderbrand. 2020. "Streaming Media's Environmental Impact." *States of Media+Environment* 2.1. https://mediaenviron.org/article/17242-streaming-media-s-environmental-impact.

McLuhan, Marshall [1964] (2001). *Understanding Media: The Extensions of Man*. Cambridge: MIT Press.

Mignolo, Walter. 2012. *Local Histories/Global Designs: Coloniality, Subaltern Knowledges, and Border Thinking*. Princeton: Princeton University Press.

Mittell, Jason. 2015. *Complex TV: The Poetics of Contemporary Television Storytelling*. New York: New York University Press.

Morton, Timothy. 2013. *Hyperobjects: Philosophy and Ecology after the End of the World*. Minneapolis: University of Minnesota Press.

Nichols, Bill. 1994. "Discovering Form, Inferring Meaning: New Cinemas and the Film Festival Circuit." *Film Quarterly* 47.3: 16–30.

Parker, Kim, Juliana Menasce Horowitz, and Rachel Minkin. 2020. "How the Coronavirus Outbreak Has – and Hasn't – Changed the Way Americans Work." *Pew Research Center*. December 9, 2020. https://www.pewresearch.org/social-trends/2020/12/09/how-the-coronavirus-outbreak-has-and-hasnt-changed-the-way-americans-work/

Phruksachart, Melissa. 2020. "The Bourgeois Cinema of Boba Liberalism." *Film Quarterly* 73.3: 59–65.

Rao, Venkatesh. 2017. "The Premium Mediocre Life of Maya Millennial." *RibbonFarm: Constructions in Magical Thinking*. August 17, 2017. https://www.ribbonfarm.com/2017/08/17/the-premium-mediocre-life-of-maya-millennial/

Richards, Rashna Wadia. 2021. *Cinematic TV: Serial Drama Goes to the Movies*. Oxford: Oxford University Press.

Rustad, Guy. 2018. "Skam (NRK, 2015–17) and the Rhythms of Reception of Digital Television." *Critical Studies in Television: The International Journal of Television Studies* 13.4: 505–509.

Scott, A.O. 2021. "Is Moviegoing Undemocratic?" *New York Times*. October 6, 2021. https://www.nytimes.com/2021/10/06/movies/memoria-release-moviegoing.html

Sobchack, Vivian. 2004. "Nostalgia for a Digital Object: Regrets on the Quickening of QuickTime." In *Memory Bytes: History, Technology, and Digital Culture*, edited by Lauren Rabinovitz and Abraham Geil, 305–329. Durham: Duke University Press.

Spigel, Lynn. 1992. *Make Room for TV: Television and the Family Ideal in Postwar America*. Chicago: The University of Chicago Press.

Stam, Robert. 1983. "Television News and Its Spectator." In *Regarding Television: Critical Approaches*, edited by E. Ann Kaplan. 23–43. Frederick: University Publications of America.

Strong, Hannah. 2021. "How Film Festivals Have Managed the Shift to Virtual." *Hyperallergic*. March 9, 2021. https://hyperallergic.com/626125/virtual-festivals-covid-19/

Watson, R.T. 2021. "World-Wide Streaming Subscriptions Pass One Billion During Pandemic." *The Wall Street Journal*. May 18, 2021. https://www.wsj.com/articles/worldwide-streaming-subscriptions-pass-one-billion-during-pandemic-11616079600

You, Isa. 2021. "ACAM Dialogues Mini-Episode: An Interview with Mila Zuo." *Asian Canadian and Asian Migration (ACAM) Dialogues*. October 29, 2021. https://acamdialogues.arts.ubc.ca/mini-episode-dr-mila-zuo-transcript/.

Zvyagintsev, Andrey, dir. 2017. *Loveless*. Arte France Cinéma and Why Not Productions.

14

SEEING LOCALLY, EXPRESSING GLOBALLY

Participatory Filmmaking and Aesthetics

Mariam Abazeri

A group of rural female filmmakers from the Takab district in South-Central Iran sit in the bed of a moving truck as it drives off-road past their village and into the desert. The air is dry but light with excitement as Zahra, one of the filmmakers, addresses the camera:

> Friends, I'm so happy, I wish all of you could be here sharing this incredible moment with us! As you can see, the truck behind us has the dredging equipment we bought for the water channels. We're no longer the ones pursuing it, our dreams are pursuing us! Wow, what a great feeling! I wish all of you could be here sharing this wonderful moment with us!

The truck reaches a clearing where a few men stand around an opening in the ground that accesses a sloping subterranean water channel. The women have just bought a winch that will replace the manual dredging system villagers use to clear the channel, lessening the physical labor and financial cost needed to maintain this historic method of water extraction. Intensified cyclical effects of drought and heat waves have exacerbated the impacts of modern industrialization on rural livelihoods, lifestyles, and ecologies throughout the Iranian central plateau (Madani 2014; Mirzaei et al. 2019; Maghrebi et al. 2020). These pressures challenge communities like the one in Takab to reevaluate the means through which they cope and adapt to changing climatic conditions.

For the past six years, Zahra and five other women have been collectively filming how they address these concerns through multiple social interventions they have implemented in their district. These interventions include the revival of traditional textile arts, the development of an artisan cooperative, the creation of a communal fund, and the restoration of several water channels,

DOI: 10.4324/9781003246602-18

all of which have been carried out as part of a participatory video (PV) project colleagues and I in Tehran helped produce. The project, which we first envisioned as a workshop in filmmaking in Takab, gradually evolved into the facilitated production of several social interventions filmed through collective filmmaking practices. This footage was edited into multiple videos and a feature film that highlights how, as feminist scholar Andrea Nightingale (2016) notes, relationships between subjectivities, (re)productive work, and environmental outcomes, while imbued with power, are mutually constituted. As an intervention, the filmmaking process became a way to understand these social and ecological entanglements, giving a richer sense of how the visual and its production permeate, pattern, and embody culturally inflected ways of seeing and being in the world.

This chapter examines how participatory videomaking shapes and represents a self-conscious expression of culture, enacting and communicating a social system of values and behaviors referred to here as *adab* that helps determine individual and collective socialities of ethics and aesthetics. I begin by first exploring how PV methods differ from conventional ethnographic filmmaking practices and suggest how this intervention works to realign production power dynamics. I then introduce how adab communicates attitudes and sensibilities on Persianate ethics and aesthetics and apply it as a lens for reading the participatory film and its production process. By considering how residents in Takab communicate and reproduce the cultural system of adab through filmmaking, I argue for a hybridized logic and analytical framework for reading film processes and products to better understand how film and aesthetic expression are deeply embedded within cultural systems that connect social structures, knowledge, cosmology, belief, and action. During the project, conventional structures of social organization around economic labor, natural resource management, and political participation were revived and revised through the filmmaking process to create a more inclusive, cooperative, and resilient space for residents. Such hybridity helps engender a new understanding of cultural identity while challenging globalizing forces and gender norms.

Participatory Video as Ontological Communication

Canonical ethnographic films have typically centered the Euro-American gaze of filmmakers portraying subjects almost always from a class or culture different from their own (MacDougall 1997). In these films, the moving image is typically perceived as representing what it appears to capture, with the filmmaker persuading the viewer that what appears to be, *is* (Vaughan 1999, 59). This tradition, which emphasizes the impression of objectivity and of well-substantiated judgment, tends to evoke a colonial legacy of displaying, fetishizing, and otherwise controlling images of the Other (Fusco 2003, 210). It accepts the filmmaker's way of seeing and interacting through their cinematic arrangement of expressions, relations, and values as a universalized perspective on the nature of being. In this way, the filmmaker's ontology (as philosophies of being) is made visible and shared as objective truth, raising ethical issues of voice as the filmmaker and text speak for or on behalf of a mediated subject to an audience whose agreement is sought (Nichols 1991). Representation in conventional ethnographic films is therefore often limited to the filmmaker's ontological understanding of a subject as it is constructed and reproduced through their own ethics and ideology, and points to the agentic limits of such mediation. These limits may be summed up in the sardonic statement by feminist performing arts scholar Peggy Phelan who points out that "if representational visibility equals power, then almost-naked young white women should be running Western culture" (2003, 112). In contrast to this practice, a shift toward autoethnographic filmmaking presents a case of ethnographic media as an evolving cultural form that reclaims conscious self-determination of political and cultural identity, countering in part representations by others while making visible and sharing multiple understandings of the world and the interactions that enact it (MacDougall 1997, 284).

PV is a way by which media makers and practitioners are engaging more reflexively with the ontological politics that define and communicate the world and its relationships. PV does not follow conventional ethnographic production processes; instead, it calls upon various production methods, styles, and formats that facilitate groups or communities to create films on their own subjects. While there is a diversity of methods used in its practice, common threads point to an emphasis on participant control of production and a focus on process over product, maintaining an approach centered on participants' own objectives (White 2003; Lunch and Lunch 2006; Jewitt 2012). The agency to choose what is (in)visibilized, in what manner, and for what end enables PV as a practice in communicative authority. This agency matters because visual media can structure expectations about the nature of relating in and organizing society, which in turn, as environmental anthropologist Sian Sullivan (2017) points out, can influence human action in the world and thus have effects of social and ecological consequences.

In the following sections, using my production experiences working alongside the Takab PV group in the film *Women of the Sun: A Chronology of Seeing* (2020), I examine how participatory filmmaking communicates culturally inflected understandings of nature and sociality through aesthetic expression and discuss the ethical implications of collaborative representation. I was drawn to participate in and study this project to learn what it could teach me about ethnography, video production, and the politics of representation as someone working both in socioecological research and documentary filmmaking in Iran. I wondered as I learned about PV methods through the project if filmmaking practices could subvert the dominant Eurocentric worldmaking so commonly presented throughout conventional ethnographic films. Could participatory media resist the accelerating homogenization of cultural perspectives of being in the world and how could it communicate and bridge some of these ontological differences? Most importantly, as a young woman interested in gender justice and far removed from rural women's experiences, I wanted to understand what these women expressed about themselves, their positions, demands, and feelings as embedded within the (re)production of material and symbolic social realities and inequalities and I sought to explore the contexts within which gender and other social relations were performed, challenged, and recreated.

Aesthetic Expressions, Hybridity, and *Adab*

Aesthetics is the discipline conventionally concerned with the nature and value of symbolic expression (Leuthold 2011). Aesthetic expression is an important aspect of manifesting group identity through symbols, activities, and relational behaviors between people and their environments that are either explicitly or implicitly pronounced. In this way, aesthetics are expressed performatively as much as they are semiotically,

> Via the mediation of the *ethos*, the internalization of objective and common regularities, the group places this practice under its collective rule, so that the most trivial [image] expresses, apart from the explicit intentions of the photographer, the system of schemes of perception, thought, and appreciation common to a whole group.
>
> *(Bourdieu 1965, 6)*

Art and symbolic expression thus serve social and ethical functions as they enact and make meaning of the world and help establish and maintain social order. In intercultural terms, studying aesthetic expressions of other cultures does not mean investigating a style or code that depicts a certain cultural approach but rather examining whether styles or codes express alternative perspectives of knowing and structuring the world. These differences can allow for an expansion of understanding of one's own culture and worldview and potentially yield new ways of seeing, being, and creating for the viewer. As documentary film editor and scholar Dai Vaughan puts it, "That which is an inflection of our experience is inevitably also an interpretation of it. Parallels do not have to be spelled out. They are spelled in" (1999, 116).

Cultural distinctions that create Otherness, however, are increasingly blurred in a homogenizing mediascape that centralizes and blends diverse traditions into more unified expressions (Leuthold 2011, 17). This hybridity can result in "cultural incorporation," in which non-native technology and culture are absorbed to conform to an existing cultural system; "cultural integration," in which a fusion of cultural systems leads to distinguished practices from the existing culture because of the encounters; and/or "homogenization," in which the diffusion of mass culture's expressive forms replace existing ones to assimilate the Other into dominant cultural systems (20). Due to the political and economic forces of cultural diffusion, the direction of influence between cultures has not been equal. Much of this diffusion relies on economies of scale, with cultures that produce and distribute more products holding greater influence over others. For example, as early as 1912, policymakers in the United States became aware that wherever Hollywood films traveled, demand was generated for American products and lifestyles; by the 1920s, Commerce Secretary Herbert Hoover praised the film industry for pushing "intellectual ideas and national ideals...and as a powerful influence on behalf of American goods" (quoted in Miller and Maxwell 2011, 25).

This unequal diffusion can work to realign and reproduce social and ecological value systems worldwide through the internalization of hegemonic cultural processes. For example, Chinese filmmaker Jia Zhangke, whose films contrast "the enveloping monopoly of the Hollywood-style commercial blockbuster," (Zhang 2011, 143) often critiques the spread of neoliberal ethics and socialities within Chinese politics and society by exploring the loss of "some beautiful things [that] are quickly disappearing from our lives" (Zhangke 2009, 25): mutual dependence, family ties, entire communities and cities (the "work unit" compounds in 24 City; the city of Fengjie in Still Life), and myths (Three Gorges as a cultural reference point), and entire subcultures and species (Zhang 2011). Additionally, the disparity in influence between cultures can externally dictate the aesthetics and rendering of others through the politics of accessibility to global platforms. Mexican/Chicano performance artist Guillermo Gomez-Peña laments:

> The cost of visibility, unfortunately, is good behavior. If Latin American artists wish to be included in the club, we must be willing to paraphrase, represent, mimic, and echo the stylistic trends set by the North...we are allowed to perform our stylized 'difference' with an obvious understanding of Northern 'sophistication' and current art trends.
>
> *(Gomez-Peña and Levin 2011, 6)*

Despite a global progression from cultural incorporation to homogenization, several Indigenous and Global South artists have responded through a reassertion of non-hegemonic cultural identities and aesthetic expressions, negotiating between distinct cultural systems through a process of "cultural reintegration." Guillermo Gomez-Peña and Iranian visual artist Shirin Neshat, both naturalized to the US, explore an expanded notion of homeland that is both political and personal, with many of their works rooted in experiences connecting cultures between their places of origin and their current residences. In this way, the lines between the local and global blur as encounters between cultures hybridize the way identity and sociality are defined and experienced, shaping the way these values are politically and aesthetically expressed: "The intercultural is the culture of our time" (Leuthold 2011, 23).

In thinking of homeland and subjectivities, Mana Kia rejects a geographically essentialist notion of origin and identity, proposing instead an understanding of place and selves through a symbolic system of behavior and suitability, which in Persian is understood as social *adab*. Adab reflects and transmits cultural attitudes and sensibilities through "proper aesthetic and ethical forms, of thinking, acting and speaking, and thus of perceiving, desiring, and experiencing" (2020, 5). As a proper form, the way language, concepts, and traditions are used and accumulated is necessarily central to the notion of adab as its aporetic and relational character allows for multiplicities of meaning-making and interpreting sociality and place. Adab thus depends on how the self identifies relative to the perceiver and the multiple relations they may have to people and place. In both these contexts, neither are defined in absolute or exclusive categories such that the subjectivities, modes of expressions, specifics of language, articulation of ideas, and proper form of relating may be multiple and shifting. In other words, adab instructs how people are situated, how origins and relations to geographies and ecologies are conceived, and how those relationships are expressed to others, realizing ethics through a mastery of aesthetics. On the rules of generosity, for example, the *Shahnameh,* an epic poem (c. 977–1010 CE) written by the Persian poet Ferdowsi, instructs the giver of gifts on the proper conduct and expression for giving that avoids humiliating or hurting the receiver. It explains giving as an act in which the giver must be grateful to the recipient, not vice versa, as the offering enables the giver to secure their own inner peace. In this context, the giver is universalized as part of an established order in which generosity is presented as a common practice of social exchange, regardless of the giver's own subjectivity. In such a performance, adab also acknowledges a set of subtle rules of conduct for giving, e.g., offering according to age within a group of receivers, that maintains a hierarchy and logic of social order within the exchange.

Adab can be reflected in the ways people see and film themselves and others in their social roles and interactions carried out in the filmmaking process and its text. As a Persian notion of an aesthetic system, I apply adab here as a framework through which I analyze the PV project's production process and footage featured in the documentary film: *Women of the Sun: A Chronology of Seeing.* By examining how the PV group produced their interventions that address gender roles and drought and paying particular attention to how participants negotiate social and environmental relations and values, I theorize the production of this participatory film through a lens of adab to advocate for more culturally attuned forms of filmmaking practice and analysis that encourage better visibility and reception of socioecological ontologies and aesthetics.

Stylistic Decisions of *Women of the Sun* Production: Gender and the Eco-Collective

Women of the Sun: A Chronology of Seeing is an 86-minute participatory film produced by the Takab PV team, which consists of six young rural women from this desert region along with our group of five filmmakers and facilitators from Tehran. The film, developed for audiences in Takab and abroad, documents how the team collaborates to learn and revive textile arts and traditions and mobilize other female artisans into a regional cooperative to address some of the women's livelihood concerns. Through the cooperative, the women work to not only improve handcraft wages but also become an agentic body through which they can participate more freely in public life and communal decision-making. By establishing a public works fund financed through a percentage of their needlework sales, the cooperative decides to address limitations on water access and lead rehabilitation efforts of traditional water infrastructure and cooperative water governance.

In one of the opening sequences of the film, the women are sitting in a PV workshop in a participant's living room learning about videomaking and the PV process. Through their formal body language, intonation, and speech, they show their reservations with the new experience and their discomfort with each other and the camera through a stiffness they maintain throughout the workshop. While this can be expected of any group in front of a camera convening for the first time, the formality displayed is also partially a presentation of social order and adab to each other and onlookers, legitimizing the activity on record through the presentation of socially proper behavior and control. Their conduct is stylized and gendered in the way it upholds regional expectations of suitable female demeanor, making the space in front of the camera a "front region" for gendered performance (Goffman 1959, 107). Their solemn attire, deferent gaze, and formal syntax contrast subsequent footage they include as "bloopers" where they are more relaxed and carefree with their manner, revealing the borderlines between the front and back regions of the camera and the public and private spheres of gendered sociality. Despite a progressive opacity between these regions further along in the project, the group never fully erases these barriers, manifesting how these contexts exist alongside each other through a system of adab.

Gendered behavior and expressions in many ways function through the aporia of adab, aporia not as a paradox but as fluidity between states of being and affiliating. For example, a sequence in the film shows members of the PV team interviewing a farmer by his field on the role of the water channels on his livelihood and well-being. On one side of a clearing, we see the elderly man sitting under a tree waiting to be interviewed. On the other side, Fariba, Asma, and Zahra, three of the PV participants, exhaustively debate how best to structure their interview. Frustrated, each one opines on the appropriate manner for questioning, switching between formal and informal vocabulary and conjugation and between a stiff and relaxed demeanor. At one point, Fariba asks the facilitators on-site how they think the question should be posed, "since I'm his daughter and this affects me too" (Figure 14.1). In a similar sequence, the elderly farmer and his wife are seated in their home introducing themselves and their work to the team in front of the camera. Their rigid introductions are punctuated by bursts of laughter from members of the team/family and the couple themselves and the scene is reshot several times, a progression that viewers see in the final cut. The formality they adhere to under the public gaze created by the camera feels out of place for the intimacy between the PV group and the couple, who are the parents and grandparents of two of the group members. In these exchanges, viewers see the subjects and PV participants struggling with the ambiguity of presenting and relating through multiple social roles to identify the terms of appropriate visualized expression and conduct.

Along with the articulation of behavior, certain aesthetic activities and expressions are also delimited and dictated by gender. Gendered norms and regulations can call for differences in the use and specialization of materials, media, and subjects based on access and exposure to certain gendered knowledge sets, opportunities, and spaces. Throughout Iran and certainly in Takab, activities associated with fiber media (weaving, stitching, sewing, etc.) are primarily mastered by women, though generally appraised and sold by men. This often results in a marginal portion of the profits returning to the female artisans and a larger share returning to the male brokers. The first part of the PV team's social activism, therefore, involved reviving needlework practices among a younger generation of women who aspired to collectively manage the sale and production of pieces and improve their profits through the development of an artisan cooperative. These trainings and working sessions gave women a rare opportunity to convene and communicate in an intimate yet public environment (Figure 14.2).

FIGURE 14.1 Takab PV members interviewing other residents about water channels.

FIGURE 14.2　Takab PV members discussing artisan working conditions.

Homosocial spaces are still prevalent in Iran and engender distinct modes of behaving and communicating from ways of being in heterosocial spaces (Najmabadi 1993). For women, homosocial settings, which tend to invite more informal and intimate social expression, are typically guarded from the camera, which is seen as a tool conveying public heterosocial space. This explains why certain performances of adab, from choices in attire to particular mannerisms and gestures between people of the opposite gender, are adopted in the camera's presence. Indeed, the borders between these two worlds can be sensed, if not always seen, throughout the film. For example, when the cooperative visits their new workshop in a renovated historic building, Mina films a solemn group of her colleagues gathering in front of their new headquarters. As they step inside a dark room, their laughter and jovial conversations are recorded while their image remains out of view. In the next scene, viewers see a few women exchanging furtive smiles as they readjust their cloaks and scarves and readopt a formal affect and tone once again in the line of sight of her camera. The intimacy conveyed in the transition from one space to the next raises an interesting question on how these front and back spaces are defined among women and how that difference shapes the performance and presentation of adab.

While the Islamic Republic normalized desubjectivizing and decorporealizing women onscreen after the revolution due to conservative readings of Islamic adab (Naficy 2012, 118), their footage shows the women challenging some of these state-sanctioned aesthetics. From sartorial choices that offset a gendered monochromatic visual culture to the central leadership roles they assume, the women contest and subvert expressions of the proper that challenge positions and expectations for women onscreen. These subversions heighten attention to the semiotic significance of visual aesthetics on gender norms and point to the opportunities their filming activities create in transforming these standards. For example, with the purchase of the winch for water channel restoration, the women film a luncheon they host in the ceremonial hall where residents gather to celebrate the event. At the front of the large room, members of the PV group address the audience on the importance of cooperation and women's participation in public decision-making. This moment is significant not only as a culmination of the group's efforts in addressing the impacts of drought but also as a practice of communicative agency within their community through the enactment of adab, encouraging a proper social culture of collective action through a revised understanding of collectivity that includes women's participation. The PV process, which encourages the women to express themselves semiotically and relationally, helps build their confidence to challenge the way these expressions are mediated and transform them into new collective forms of conduct and aesthetics.

Along with *how* they show themselves and their work, *what* they show informs the ways members engage adab in the film's production. The group's personal lives, independent of the PV activities, remain largely hidden from their footage. Instead, there is a focus on the collective's work over the individual's more personal narratives, highlighting their emphasis on shared modes of identification and representation as an enactment of adab. Adab, as a value system of appropriate behavior and expression, is shown throughout the film's footage as an ethical act of sociality that underpins a broader and common cultural sense within Iranian society of collectivity over individualism. An emphasis on the multiple and shared forms of meaning-making and relating are presented throughout their footage in the ways they frame their shots (mostly medium long or full shots of multiple people and places), the events they record (Fariba avoids presenting herself during her pregnancy, the fact that there is very little footage of the women recording themselves alone or in intimate settings), and even the way they engage with the character and significance of the world around them (the natural environment is introduced alongside the built one in an introduction of their village and lifestyle) (Figures 14.3).

According to Kathryn Babayan, a notable reference within Persian literary aesthetics is a sense of cyclical being and time in which different figures face similar ethical qualms in different political realities and domains (2002, 29). Poems and literary texts like the *Shahnameh* circulate widely among contemporary Iranians as a history of geocultural landscapes. Some of these works are understood as myth and some as history, both as integral to a traditional sense of being and meaning-making of place. Poor physical and mental health reflects the menace of ecological crises, such as drought and floods, signaling a relationship of discord between people and place. This notion draws on cultural understandings that circulate in Persian mythology and aesthetics, relating the "humorial theory of health to a justly ruled realm, which shared a notion of individual and collective bodies in harmony with their environment" (Kia 2020, 63). Elements like air and water affect the humor of a body nested within its habitat, requiring an oversight that keeps both balanced and healthy (Alavi 2008, 27–33). Through common social understandings of adab, ethical governance works to keep these relationships in harmony, protecting against

FIGURE 14.3 Zahra taking a walk through the village.

FIGURE 14.4 Residents discuss restoring water channels in a subterranean atrium.

disruption and calamity in and between the social and ecological worlds. The PV group frames their connection with water and its governance as a cyclical and sustainable relationship, or a hydrosocial cycle (Linton and Budds 2014), that emphasizes the dialectic and relational processes through which water and society interrelate and are continuously shaped by each other. The group presents this human ecosystem through activities, language, institutions, and infrastructures that show how water is highly valued and internalized within relationships and livelihoods among residents who live in a very arid and harsh climate. Fatemeh, for example, films children playing in the channels while she talks about the functionality of the waterways and laments their deteriorating state, presenting them as a place of work and leisure while evoking a shared memory of a thriving past. In another scene, a farmer talks about his livelihood and dependence on the channels as he digs out water trenches in his field, and in another, elder residents share memories of their youth in a carved subterranean atrium, admiring the water infrastructure as a site and symbol of their culture while they discuss hydrologic tools for improving water channel management with the women (Figure 14.4). Each perspective shows how these cultural elements embody socioecological narratives through which people know and inhabit the world. Moral valence and multiple associations characterize relationships between people and their environments, "creating a palimpsest of place unlike the singular, "natural" connection common to modern empiricism" (Kia 2020, 37). In this aporia, the health and balance of social ecologies are mutually constituted through the performance of adab.

Conclusion

In the case study presented in this chapter, I have considered filmmaking practices and theoretical frameworks that help enact and understand particular and multiple ways of seeing and being in the world. The reflexive, collective, and autoethnographic elements of participatory filmmaking foreground and make visible cultural interactions that yield hybrid creations of practice and sociality, which would otherwise be obscured or silenced via conventional ethnographic methods and analysis. To better understand this process, I have used a theoretical lens of adab, a Persianate understanding of proper conduct and aesthetics, to demonstrate how this logic informs the ways gendered norms, socioecological orders, and cultural values are represented, challenged, and reimagined in the filmmaking process of *Women of the Sun: A Chronology of Seeing*. Adab not only serves to structure what is shown by the PV members but also how and why these choices are made, decentering Western frames of interpreting the worlds the film presents. By applying diverse practical and theoretical methods to film production and analysis, cinema scholarship gains much by thinking through the dynamic ways films, while not necessarily bound by local cultures, are still rooted in local experiences, offering global viewers a way to see the world, others, and themselves through a local perspective.

Works Cited

Alavi, Seema. 2008. *Islam and Healing: Loss and Recovery of an Indo-Muslim Medical Tradition, 1600–1900*. New York: Palgrave Macmillan.

Babayan, Kathryn. 2002. *Mystics, Monarchs and Messiahs: Cultural Landscapes of Early Modern Iran*. Cambridge: Harvard University Press.

Bourdieu, Pierre. 1965. *Photography: A Middle-Brow Art*. Redwood City: Stanford University Press.

Ferdowsi, Abolqasem. 2007. *Shahnameh: The Persian Books of King*. Translated by Dick Davis. London: Penguin.

Fusco, Coco. 2003. "The Other History of Intercultural Performance." In *The Feminism and Visual Culture Reader*, edited by Amelia Jones, 205–217. New York: Routledge.

Goffman, Erving. 1959. *The Presentation of Self in Everyday Life*. New York: Anchor Books.

Gomez-Peña, Guillermo and Laura Levin. 2011. *Conversations across Borders: A Performance Artist Converses with Theorists, Curators, Activists, and Fellow Artists*. New York: Seagull Books.

Jewitt, Carey. 2012. "An Introduction to Using Video for Research." *National Centre for Research Methods*. London: Institute of Education.

Kia, Mana. 2020. *Persianate Selves: Memories of Place and Origin Before Nationalism*. Redwood City: Stanford University Press.

Leuthold, Steven M. 2011. *Cross-Cultural Issues in Art: Frames for Understanding*. New York: Routledge.

Linton, Jamie and Jessica Budds. 2014. "The Hydrosocial Cycle: Defining and Mobilizing a Relational Dialectical Approach to Water." *Geoforum* 57: 170–180.

Lunch, Nick and Chris Lunch. 2006. *Insights into Participatory Video: A Handbook for the Field*. Oxford: Insight.

MacDougall, David. 1997. "The Visual in Anthropology." In *Rethinking Visual Anthropology*, edited by Marcus Banks and Howard Morphy, 276–295. New Haven: Yale University Press.

Madani, Kaveh. 2014. "Water Management in Iran: What Is Causing the Looming Crisis?" *Journal of Environmental Studies Science* 4.4: 315–328.

Maghrebi, Mohsen, et al. 2020. "Iran's Agriculture in the Anthropocene." *Earth's Future* 8: 1–15.

Miller, Toby and Richard Maxwell. 2011. "'For a Better Deal, Harass Your Governor!': Neoliberalism and Hollywood." In *Neoliberalism and Global Cinema: Capital, Culture, and Marxist Critique*, edited by Jyotsna Kapur and Keith B. Wagner, 19–37. New York: Routledge.

Mirzaei, Atena, Bahram Saghafian, Ali Mirchi, and Kaveh Madani. 2019. "The Groundwater-Energy-Food Nexus in Iran's Agricultural Sector: Implications for Water Security." *Water* 11.1835: 1–15.

Naficy, Hamid. 2012. *A Social History of Iranian Cinema, Volume 4: The Globalizing Era, 1984–2010*. Durham: Duke University Press.

Najmabadi, Afsaneh. 1993. "Veiled Discourse—Unveiled Bodies." *Feminist Studies* 19.3: 487–518.

Nichols, Bill. 1991. *Representing Reality*. Bloomington: Indiana University Press.

Nightingale, Andrea. 2016. "The Nature of Gender: Work, Gender, and Environment." *Environment and Planning D: Society and Space* 24.2: 165–185.

Phelan, Peggy. 2003. "Broken Symmetries: Memory, Sight, Love." In *The Feminism and Visual Culture Reader*, edited by Amelia Jones, 105–114. New York: Routledge.

Shafiabad Participatory Video Group and Hamed Zolfaghari, directors. 2020. *Women of the Sun: A Chronology of Seeing*. Crazy Woodpecker Studio and Agat Films. 86 mins.

Sullivan, Sian. 2017. "What's Ontology Got to Do with It? On Nature and Knowledge in a Political Ecology of the 'Green Economy.'" *Journal of Political Ecology* 24.1: 217–242.

Vaughan, Dai. 1999. *For Documentary*. Berkeley: University of California Press.

White, Shirley A. 2003. *Participatory Video: Images that Transform and Empower*. Thousand Oaks: Sage Publications.

Zhang, Xudong. 2011. "Market Socialism and Its Discontent: Jia Zhangke's Cinematic Narrative of China's Transition in the Age of Global Capital." In *Neoliberalism and Global Cinema: Capital, Culture, and Marxist Critique*, edited by Jyotsna Kapur and Keith B. Wagner, 19–37. New York: Routledge.

Zhangke, Jia. 2009. *Jia Xiang (Jia's Reflections—Notes from a Filmmaker, 1996–2008)*. Beijing: Peking University Press.

AFTERWORD

The Sequel Effect

Jennifer Fay

"The desire for the sequel," writes Marjorie Garber, "is part of the impulse to hear stories and to tell them, the desire that they never come to a definitive end" (2016, 73–74). While there are commercial reasons to reboot a profitable franchise, the impulse to sequelization runs deeper and is bound to an optimism that some version of a storyworld will persist, adapt, become happier, or better attuned to its ever-changing contemporary moment. Extending backward and forward in time, re-centering on the original's peripheral characters or events, sequels help us to find new histories and novel imagined futures. And it is this expansive feature that makes the sequel a theoretically "more adventurous if not radical departure from the expectation of closure and the boundedness of the text" (76). The sequel does not endeavor to bring that story to a close by tying up loose narrative threads; instead, the story that follows takes the original, writes Garber quoting Gérard Genette, "beyond what was initially considered to be its ending" (74). The "sequel effect," as Garber calls it, prompts us to read in the first version the seeds of what has been written in the story's future or past (74). The relation of the New Testament to the Hebrew Bible may be the founding "sequelmania" of Christianity, whereby the New Testament "performs an act of theological and textual legerdemain, not only 'completing' the previous text but in doing so declaring the prior text to be 'incomplete,' in effect the 'prequel' to the revealed word" (78). This is all to say that a sequel is no mere continuation; it is a re-casting, sometimes a radical revising, of the first. It can also upend the very concept of an "original" or "origin" story.

My interest in writing an afterword for *Ecocinema Theory and Practice 2* (hereafter, *Ecocinema 2*) is to consider its "sequel effect" primarily on the first volume, which must now be considered *Ecocinema Theory and Practice 1* (*Ecocinema 1*), and also how these two collections, taken together, reflect on the

DOI: 10.4324/9781003246602-19

field of ecocinema and environmental media studies, areas of inquiry that have bloomed in the intervening decade between volumes. How does the second volume expand and extend the story, the world, and the past of ecocinema? It does not "improve" or provide a happy or redemptive ending to the first (if anything the topics of *Ecocinema 1* are now generally regarded in the context of environmental *crisis* and non-redeeming catastrophe). But by expanding the field of inquiry and finding new genealogies of thought and traditions of critique, *Ecocinema 2* opens in time, space, and method what ecocinema studies is and was. We can say that the urgencies of the first volume may now, in retrospect, be understood as among the founding problems of ecological thought and activism in the face of environmental damage—namely, the problem of perception.

Ecocinema 1 set a critical agenda that has shaped the multiple fields in which it intervenes. Editors Stephen Rust, Salma Monani, and Seán Cubitt published their first volume in 2012, three years after the interdisciplinary Anthropocene Working Group was created to investigate the proposal to change the name of our current geological epoch and four years before the Paris Climate Agreement was signed. This collection set out to define ecocinema as both a property of some films that explicitly thematize the webbed relations between people, things, and the more-than-human world, as well as a critical practice whereby any film could be read for its eco-logics, -poetics, and/or -political (mis)directions. The justified presumption of the first volume was that many people have a relationship to nature and ecology primarily, which is to say, first, through cinema (Disney, for many) and that this artform harbors within it the possibility of teaching viewers how to see our entanglements with the nature-cultures all around us in ways that elude what we might call ordinary perception. Indeed, this pedagogy of seeing was the guiding force of many of the essays, which take their inspiration from Scott's MacDonald *Garden in the Machine* and from a longer tradition of film theory that understands the potential of the medium to retrain, restore, or productively disrupt modes of seeing and acts of perceiving and that may challenge anthropocentrism and human exceptionalism. If mainstream cinema keeps the world hidden from view, or subsumes the non-human world into narratives that re-center the human subject, that cinema can, at the very least, explain how habits of misperception and cultures of ecological abuse develop. Alternative cinemas, documentaries, and experimental forms represent ways of seeing differently. This recognition— that cinema both conditions perception and could be a tool for a better way of seeing the complexities of ecology—may be the first step in any ecocritical project, certainly any involving cinema.

It merits emphasizing both how true and how utterly strange it is that this technology, a product of the industrial revolution that is mechanical, synthetic, wholly unnatural, and devoid of so many of the other sensory outputs, can teach us to perceive something like "nature," or our kinship with "animals" as these phenomena recede from everyday experience. The urgency of the first volume was really a call to investigate the ways that cinema, in general, teaches us to think ecologically and to reflect on how we viewers inhabit the world. The arguments in that book pushed film theory intriguingly toward what I'm inclined to call a kind of environmental anthropology of and on film. All films provide some reflection of and instruction on how we live and also provide an archive of our changing networks and entanglements. Climate change is part of this story in *Ecocinema 1* (for example, two essays—Rust's and Cubitt's—take up Al Gore's 2006 activist documentary *An Inconvenient Truth* and consider its efficacy for environmentally-minded reform), but I take the point of the collection to be rather diagnostic and anticipatory more than raising the alarm. Yet we learn that so-called "first" cinema and mainstream wildlife/nature documentaries index mostly Global North and privileged ways of seeing that may be inadequate to the political and environmental realities of our epoch. How can we perceive the effects of climate *change*, process the big data evidence, and act meaningfully to mitigate its uneven effects and violences, if we do not perceive the environment and our place in it, to begin with? And, of course, the question here is always "who" is the "we" of spectatorship? The point of the first volume was not to declare good and bad objects or even actors, but, in thinking with films, to work out methodologies of ecocritical spectatorship and filmmaking practices that may exceed or surprise our expectations of what counts as ecological critique.

But the time of the Paris Agreement is now past (along with the acceptable thresholds of atmospheric CO2), political will is divided, the Sixth Extinction is well documented, and the racialized, gendered, geographically uneven, and deeply classed violence of climate change are at the forefront of analysis and activism. Thus, *Ecocinema 2* continues the story by foregrounding different archives and genealogies, many of which the Introduction to the first volume highlighted for further research. The films under analysis here are not ethnographies imposed from without but studies collaboratively composed from within to provide a glimpse of otherwise "silenced ways of seeing and being in place" (Abazeri). We find here films not about the global south, but *from* it, including Aarón Lacayo's analysis of Julio Hernández Cordón's *Polvo* (2012), Elio Garcia's engagement with Lav Diaz's *Storm Children* (2014), and Cajetan Iheka's discussion of Safi Faye's drought cinema. We know what mainstream cli-fi has to offer by way of frightening with the apocalypse to come, but we find new dimensions of ideology critique (Hageman and Wang) when the American blockbuster *Interstellar* (2014) is compared with one of China's highest grossing films of all times, *The Wandering Earth* (2019), a film whose sequel is in already in the making. What kind of futures do these two high-budget odysseys offer to the millions of people who have absorbed their messages, mesmerized by the star power of actors and the thrill of special effects? Mainstream science fiction (whatever its ecological message) is often complicit with

nationalist ideologies which provincialize the climate and our sense of the planetary. Turning to the fan cultures and sequelmania of the Marvel Universe,
Anthony Lioi explores how media ecologies envelop audiences in "different
modes of environmentalities." The study of media ecology can model a study of
environmental thinking. It is fitting that the authoritarian agents in the Marvel
off-shoot television series *Loki* are named the "Time Variance Authority," or
TVA. Readers may be reminded of the environmentally coercive practices of
the Tennessee Valley Authority (also the TVA). This is the U.S. government
agency that dammed rivers and disappeared towns in the US South creating its
own world and temporal order. Buster Keaton's Appalachian cinema, as Christian Quendler argues, is a cinematic reordering and reassemblage of southern terrain that may be read as a critique of Hollywood's appropriation of the
South, and proleptically, we may add, of the U.S. government's environmental
interventions.

Indigenous Futurism and its mythic storytelling offer an alternative politics of resistance to petroleum capitalism as a strategy of survival (Roehl). As
Angelica Lawson explains with reference to the collaborative work of Jonathan Thunder and Missy Whiteman, Indigenous cosmologies not only model
non-linear temporalities that are more attuned to planetary rhythms and climate cycles, the vocabularies and grammars of Indigenous languages structure
different orders of perceiving, knowing the world, and taking stock of the slow
extinction of a people and their culture. In this respect, and as understood by
some Indigenous communities, the Anthropocene is not a new emergency, but
a continuation of settler colonial genocidal violence and its assaults on linguistic diversity, as well as biodiversity. Creating new grammars of digital media,
Thunder and Whiteman explore Indigenous epistemologies and visions for
environmental responsibilities that also look back to far older traditions.

Finally, there is no denying that in all of its manifestations, cinema is fully
imbricated within the extractive economies and environmental ruin that film
often helps us to see in the first place. Cinema is not only an image of ecology but also an image and product of energy that registers natural and human
exhaustion, as Debashree Mukherjee explains in her analysis of the high-budget
Hindi coal mining melodrama *Kaala Patthar* (1979). The labor of extraction
touchingly told in the film is mirrored in the extraction of labor to make
the film. The audience is hardly left out of this energy economy. Melodrama
extracts feeling from its viewers (very often in this period of post colonial
celebration, it is warm and happy feelings about resource extraction and the
prospect of energy independence). Rather than produce more power, however,
melodrama is a genre of exhaustion, generating a kind of emotional pollution or
"residue that accrues in the shadows" (Mukherjee). Spectators are emotionally
mined and perhaps through this feeling of exhaustion come to some sense of
being themselves part of the coal economy that the film both foregrounds and
aestheticizes. It is not only that all films are energy films (some more explicitly

than others) but that all spectators are also, to borrow Mukherjee's phrasing from Kathryn Yusoff "geologic bodies." Those who watch are another resource for use and part of the planetary history and multi-scalar sense of the present as constituted through deep time.

While green cinema and more sustainable modes of filmmaking (see Lopera-Mármol & Jiménes-Morales on Green Shooting in Catalonia) and exhibition (see the marvelous scenario of "pedal cinema" in Mexico in Carolyn Fornoff's essay) make it possible to redeem this artform, *Ecocinema 2* is not a Good News sequel. We must attend to the costs of this artform and the price we pay to view the world through its optics. We have become isolated from the world and one another through cultures of lonely streaming (see Mila Zuo's chapter), and, as Seán Cubitt provocatively argues, cinema in its variety of forms separates us from the outside world as much as it draws us into its fictions while also "screening off the privileged site of viewing." Put differently, ecocinema is a sign and symptom of sense-making in a period shaped profoundly by changing climates, global pandemics, stalled economies and supply chains, and extreme politics, racial violence, and radically undistributed wealth. Cinema today is both a consolation and the most poignant sign of our extreme alienation. Yet, as Cubitt's essay intimates, breaking points may bring about ends, but they also mark beginnings. These studies of our media, our environments, and our entanglements with each other and with what's left of a natural world will hopefully be continued—which is to say that *Ecocinema 2* will surely need its sequels. These are stories and critical practices that will not/cannot come to a definitive end.

Works Cited

Garber, Marjorie. 2016. *Quotation Marks*. New York: Routledge.

INDEX